# Baseball's Great Moments

# Baseball's Great Moments

by Joseph Reichler

A Rutledge Book
BONANZA BOOKS
New York

**Photography Credits**

Daniel S. Baliotti—90
Melchior DiGiacomo—2-3
Hall of Fame, Cooperstown, New York—67
Fred Kaplan—197
Richard Raphael—193, 227
Ken Regan—127, 138
Joseph Reichler—23, 25, 135, 141, 155, 159, 161, 163, 172, 178-179, 182, 185, 199, 201, 205, 206, 212, 214, 217
United Press International—11, 14-15, 15, 16, 18-19, 21, 22, 26, 33, 35, 38, 39, 41, 42, 43, 49, 51, 53, 59, 61, 64, 66, 70, 79, 81, 85, 88-89, 89, 93, 94, 96-97, 98-99, 109, 111, 113, 124, 131, 137, 142, 151, 153, 171 bottom, 166, 167, 168, 169, 175, 181, 187, 189, 202, 204-205, 208-209, 211, 215, 221, 223, 228, 229, 230, 234, 236, 238, 239, 241, 242, 244, 245, 246, 247, 248, 249, 251, 253, 254, 255, 256-257, 258, 260-261, 262, 263, 264, 265, 268-269, 270, 273, 274, 282, 283, 287
UPI/Bettmann Newsphotos—289, 290, 291, 292, 295
Wide World Photos—11, 12, 28, 20-31, 37, 41 top, 45, 54, 56-60, 69, 74, 84-85, 102-103, 103, 105, 111, 115, 117, 119, 120-121, 143, 145, 148, 149, 157 top, 159 bottom, 173, 213, 218, 224-225

This 1986 updated edition
prepared and produced by Rutledge Books
Published by Bonanza Books,
distributed by Crown Publishers, Inc.


Library of Congress Cataloging in Publication Data

Reichler, Joseph L., 1915-
    Baseball's great moments.

    "A Rutledge book."
    1. Baseball—United States—History—Miscellanea.
I. Title.
GV863.A1R45   1986      796.357″0973      84-28581
ISBN 0-517-61087-6

h g f e d c b a

# Contents

Foreword **7**
Introduction **9**
Ted Williams: All-Star **10**
Floyd Bevens: The Lost No-hitter **13**
Al Gionfriddo: The Impossible Catch **17**
Satchel Paige: His Greatest Games **20**
Bob Feller: The Pick-off **24**
Joe DiMaggio: The Comeback **27**
Robin Roberts: The Pennant-winning Twentieth **32**
Allie Reynolds: The Pennant-clinching No-hitter **36**
Jackie Robinson: A Pennant Saved **40**
Bobby Thomson's Homer **44**
Bobo Holloman: The Most Unlikely No-hitter **47**
Seventeen Runs in One Inning **49**
Joe Adcock: 18 Total Bases **52**
Willie Mays: The Greatest Catch **55**
The Dodgers Finally Win the World Series **58**
Dale Long: Eight Games, Eight Home Runs **62**
Mickey Mantle: The Home Run that Just Missed **65**
Don Larsen: The Perfect World Series Game **68**
Eleven Runs on One Hit **72**
Harvey Haddix:The Imperfect Masterpiece **75**
Warren Spahn: No-hitters at 39 and 40 **79**
Ted Williams: Last Time at Bat **82**
Mazeroski's Series-winning Home Run **86**
Willie Mays: Four Home Runs **90**
Warren Spahn: The Three-Hundredth Victory **92**
The Phil's Longest Month **95**
Roger Maris: The Record **100**
Bo Belinsky: A Flash of Greatness **104**
Sandy Koufax: Four No-hitters **107**
Maury Wills: 100 Steals **110**
Giants-Dodgers: The Second Play-off **114**
The Longest World Series **118**
Early Wynn:The Three-Hundredth Victory **123**
Mickey Mantle: Comeback **126**
Stan Musial: The Last Game **129**
Moe Drabowsky to the Rescue **132**
Carl Yastrzemski: The Year **134**
Don Drysdale: 58⅔ Consecutive Scoreless Innings **138**
Ron Hansen: Unassisted Triple Play **140**
Denny McLain: 30 Victories **144**
Gaylord Perry, Ray Washburn: Back-to-Back No-hitters **147**
Pete Rose: A Batting Crown on the Final Day **150**

Bob Gibson: 17 World Series Strikeouts **152**
Mickey Lolich: Three World Series Victories **154**
Rod Carew: Seven Steals of Home **158**
Don Wilson: Vengeance Victory **160**
Steve Carlton: A Strikeout Record **163**
The Miracle Mets **165**
Tom Seaver: 19 Strikeouts **171**
Hoyt Wilhelm: The Thousandth Appearance **174**
Ernie Banks: Number 500 **177**
Hank Aaron: 3,000 Hits **180**
Cesar Gutierrez: Seven for Seven **184**
Willie Stargell: Five Extra-base Hits **186**
Roberto Clemente: 10 Hits in Two Games **188**
Vida Blue: Double Gem **192**
Billy Williams: 1,117 Consecutive Games **196**
Brooks Robinson: One-Man Show **200**
Frank Robinson: Back-to-Back Slams **203**
Pittsburgh versus San Diego: A Seesaw Battle **207**
Amos Otis: It Takes a Thief **210**
Ron Hunt: HBP **213**
Willie Mays: The Triumphant Return **216**
Nate Colbert: Five Home Runs **220**
Roberto Clemente: The Last Hit **222**
The Magnificent Deception: Johnny Bench Strikes Out **226**
Nolan Ryan: 383 Strikeouts **228**
Hank Aaron: Touches the Untouchable **233**
The Finest World Series Game Ever Played **237**
Tom Seaver's First Game Against the Mets **240**
The Dodgers Accomplish the Impossible **243**
Reggie Jackson: Three Swings in a Row **246**
Pete Rose: 44-Game Hitting Streak **248**
Pops Did It! **251**
A 30-Year Wait **254**
Nolan Ryan's Record Fifth **259**
Dodgers Win in Final Inning of Final Game **263**
Gaylord Perry's 300th **267**
Darrell Porter's Greatest Battle **271**
Pine Tar Episode **275**
Steve Carlton Strikes Again **278**
Dwight Gooden: A Record Breaking Rookie **281**
Sparky Anderson: A Winner in Both Leagues **284**
They Climbed Mt. Everest **289**
Backs to the Wall **294**

# Foreword

Roger Angell said it best when he wrote, "Baseball in the mind . . . is a game of recapturings and visions; figures and occasions return, sounds rise and swell in our remembrance and the interior stadium fills with light and yields up the sight of some young ballplayer . . . perfectly memorized."

It always has seemed to me that of all our sports, baseball is the one most distinguished by the number of its remarkable incidents that our memories preserve. These memories accumulate over the years, yielding a full feast of recollection for the baseball follower's pleasure.

I've known the author of this volume some 30 years or more, and can't imagine a man better suited for the purpose of selecting the more remarkable baseball moments. Joe Reichler was with the Associated Press as baseball editor for some twenty years and since 1966 has worked in the baseball commissioner's office.

Joe's close-up view of baseball hasn't diminished his enthusiasm one whit. He brings to his job the unfettered enthusiasm of an undergraduate, but he writes with a sports editor's wry observation.

The great moments Joe has selected and recalled in the pages of this book make a rich mosaic of the game of baseball. For my money it's a fitting tribute to our national pastime.

*Stan Musial*

# Introduction

Not long after renegade owner Bill Veeck began building exploding scoreboards and sending up dwarfs to pinch-hit for incompetent batters, with which his St. Louis Browns were abundantly equipped, baseball critics concluded that such promotional antics signaled baseball's demise. In the fifties football had begun its meteoric rise. In the sixties hockey and basketball would capture a national audience. Baseball, said its critics, was in decline—a quaint but doomed remnant of a more leisurely and innocent era.

At first baseball's aristocracy resisted the bleak predictions and frowned on Veeck's whimsical gimmicks. But before long, apparently disconcerted by sluggish attendance figures, major league baseball launched its PR blitz. Today, in new, multi-colored, multi-tiered stadiums, ballplayers ply their craft wearing flashy colored double knit uniforms. The majestic electronic scoreboards that loom over the outfield entertain the crowds with cartoons, sing-alongs, and unsubtle editorial comment, as well as with triumphant fireworks. In Atlanta, Braves homers dislodge Chief Nokahoma in bounding celebration from his tepee. In Houston facsimile astronauts clean the infield. In Baltimore, as women's liberationists grit their teeth, blonde-haired beauties in hot pants subserviently dust the shoes of Orioles infielders. In Kansas City a majestic fountain dispenses colored water by the ton-load. With free autographed pictures, caps, bats, and balls for the kids, owners persuade Dad to bring the whole family to the ball park. Ballplayers studiously lose Family Day games to their infant sons and encourage their wives in pregame softball exhibitions.

Now baseball is flourishing as never before, but amidst the tinsel of promotional spectacles, it is too easy to forget that the game itself is as colorful as it once was. Its stars are as prodigious, its eccentricities are as pronounced, and its championships are as exciting as their forerunners. Baseball's great stories are not, as it sometimes seems, limited to old-time legends. This volume, therefore, narrowed its scope to stories from 1946 and after, not to denigrate the tales of Ruth, Gehrig and company but only to better reveal postwar baseball's fine history.

There are 85 stories here, far more than one ought to attempt to ingest at one sitting. The reader is advised to savor his reminiscences a few at a time and not to confront too vigorously the traditionalist who prefers his baseball nostalgia aged a bit longer.

*The Editors*

July 9, 1946

# Ted Williams: All-Star

You can rack your brain, read record books, or listen to Howard Cosell, but you won't find a player with an All-Star feat that surpasses the incredible display of batting power exhibited by Ted Williams in the 1946 midsummer classic at Fenway Park in Boston. Nothing like it has been seen before or after.

Ted came into the game on July 9, 1946, armed with two new bats made especially for his use in the All-Star Game. When he picked up one of the bats before the game, he smiled, looked at the grain carefully, and said, "This bat really has some wood in it. They ought to ride off this today."

His spectacular hitting exhibition that July day included two home runs and two singles. He drove in five runs, scored four, and drew a walk in five trips to the plate. The walk was issued in the first inning by Claude Passeau, the same pitcher who was the victim of Williams's dramatic three-run homer with two out in the ninth inning of the 1941 All-Star Game. That blow had given the American League a spectacular 9–7 triumph over the National League. Passeau obviously remembered that other game.

Williams followed the walk with a home run and single against Kirby Higbe in his next two times at bat, then singled off Ewell Blackwell, and climaxed the day with a home run against Truett ("Rip") Sewell with two on in the eighth inning. Only two other

Below: *Ted Williams crosses the plate after fourth-inning home run in the 1946 All-Star game. Opposite: left to right, Mickey Vernon of the Senators, Williams, Johnny Hopp of the Braves, and Dixie Walker of the Dodgers.*

players in the history of the All-Star Game have made four hits in one contest. Joe Medwick walloped two doubles and two singles in 1937, and Carl Yastrzemski had three singles and a double in 1970. Only one other player, Al Rosen in 1954, drove in five runs in an All-Star Game.

"That was one of the greatest one-man batting shows I've ever seen," recalls Charlie Grimm, who managed the losing National Leaguers. "It figures, he's the greatest hitter I've ever seen."

The game was no contest: Americans 12, Nationals 0, the soundest thrashing ever administered to either team in the history of the All-Star Game. The Americans had fourteen hits, five for extra bases. The Nationals accomplished three singles, two of them scratches, and did not get a man to third base after they stranded Stan Musial there in the first inning. Bob Feller, Hal Newhouser, and Jack Kramer worked three innings each for the American Leaguers, and they were superlative. The trio struck out 10.

Williams's second homer came off Sewell's celebrated blooper pitch. The pitch was nothing more than a soft lob that came to the plate in a high arc. If Sewell intended to inject comic relief, he succeeded. The first blooper that Sewell tossed was out of the strike zone. Ted strained to hit it and missed. When the Pittsburgh right-hander came back with another, Williams actually ran

11

Williams's heroics continued after the All-Star game. Here he scores the pennant-winning run against the Cleveland Indians.

toward the pitch, walloped it into the right field bullpen, and laughed all the way around the bases.

"That was the first homer ever hit off that pitch," Sewell said later, "and I still don't believe it."

Williams still grins when he remembers the occasion. "I got a charge out of that one," he says. "The ball came up to the plate like a pop fly. It had a twenty-foot arc. I remember watching him warm up. I was standing in the dugout with Bill Dickey and saying to Dickey, 'Gee, I don't think you could generate enough power to hit that pitch out of the park.' Nobody ever had, but Dickey said the way to do it was to advance a step or two as it came toward you. That's about what I did, and I hit it into the bullpen in right field. You should have seen Sewell's face. I had to laugh. I couldn't help it."

October 3, 1947

# Floyd Bevens: The Lost No-hitter

It has been more than 25 years, but almost every time Dodgers baseball fans get together to talk about "those good old days," they ask whether Bucky Harris should have walked Pete Reiser in the ninth inning of the fourth game of the 1947 World Series between Brooklyn and the New York Yankees. Most fans, it is true, talk of the generally shoddy pitching in that Series, the amazing relief jobs of Hugh Casey and Joe Page, Bobby Brown's remarkably perfect four pinch-hitting appearances (two doubles, a single, and a walk), Johnny Lindell's .500 batting average, and Al Gionfriddo's acrobatic catch of Joe DiMaggio's bid for a home run. But the conversation seems always to return to Cookie Lavagetto's hit after Harris ordered an intentional walk to Reiser.

It was October 3, 1947, and the Dodgers and Yankees were playing the kind of game that gives the World Series its hold on the American public. For eight innings Yankees right-hander Floyd ("Bill") Bevens, a second-flight starter who had won only seven games while losing thirteen during the regular season, had crazily been setting a new record for wildness while putting together the longest stretch of no-hit pitching the Series had ever known.

Going into the ninth, Bevens and the Yankees were enjoying a 2–1 lead, the Dodgers having gotten a run without a hit in the fifth on two passes, a sacrifice bunt, and an infield out. The Yankees had several opportunities to salt away the game for Bevens but wasted them. They muffed a glorious opportunity in the first when Dodgers manager Burt Shotton took an almost fatal gamble by starting Harry Taylor, a nondescript pitcher. After two singles and Pee Wee Reese's error had filled the bases, Taylor walked Joe DiMaggio, forcing in a run, but Hal Gregg replaced Taylor and retired the side without further scoring.

The Yankees scored again in the fourth on a triple by Bill Johnson and a double by Johnny Lindell. In the ninth it looked as if the Yankees would finally give Bevens a real lead. With one out they filled the bases on singles by Lindell and George Stirnweiss and on Bruce Edwards' wild throw on Bevens's sacrifice bunt. But Hugh Casey came on to pitch for the third time in the Series and retired the side on exactly one pitch, a sinker that Tommy Henrich hit back to the box. Casey fielded the ball and started an inning-ending double play by way of the plate.

It was still Bevens's game. The only question seemed to be whether the big right-hander would get his no-hitter. Bruce Edwards, the first batter to face Bevens in the home ninth, drove Lindell back to the left field fence for a spectacular put-out. Carl Furillo drew Bevens's ninth pass. Spider Jorgensen fouled to George McQuinn for the sec-

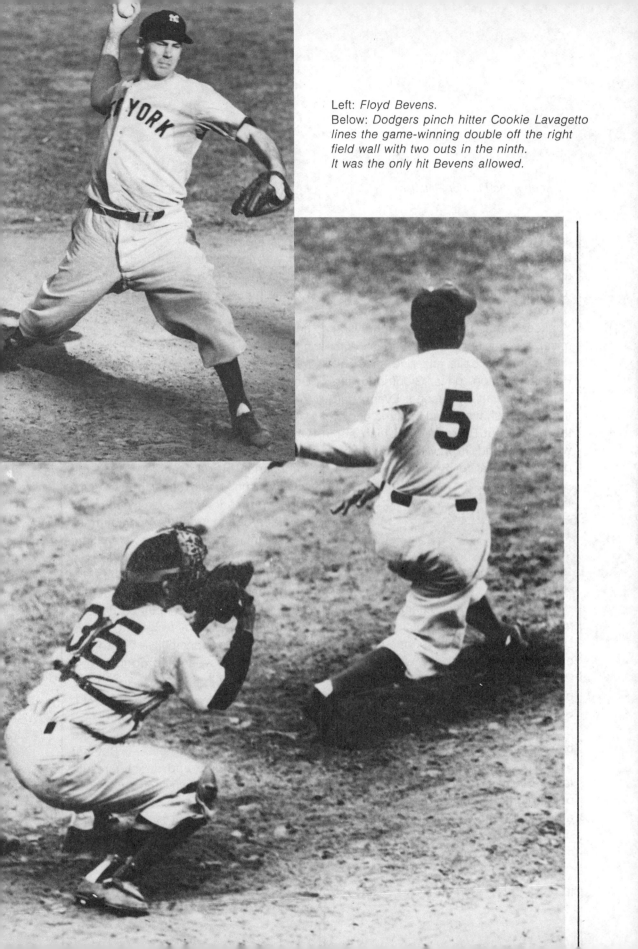

Left: *Floyd Bevens.*
Below: *Dodgers pinch hitter Cookie Lavagetto lines the game-winning double off the right field wall with two outs in the ninth. It was the only hit Bevens allowed.*

ond out. Playing out the string, Shotton sent Pete Reiser, barely able to run because of a leg injury, to bat for Casey and Al Gionfriddo, a reserve outfielder, to run for Furillo.

Yogi Berra, in his first season as Yankees catcher, had been throwing miserably throughout the Series. With the count two balls and one strike on Reiser, Shotton gave Gionfriddo the signal to break for second. Even a fair throw would have nailed him and ended the game, but Berra pegged high and wide of second. It proved to be a most opportune steal for Brooklyn.

The pitch on which Gionfriddo stole made the count three balls and one strike and left first base open. Harris ordered the intentionally wide pitch—the controversial walk—to put Reiser on base. The next batter was Eddie Stanky, but instead Shotton sent up pinch hitter Cookie Lavagetto, who, having failed earlier in the Series, was almost as surprised as Harris and the fans at the assignment. On the second pitch, high and outside, Lavagetto lined a double off the right field wall. The ball caromed past the startled Henrich and not only Gionfriddo but Eddie Miksis,

Reiser's pinch runner, came dashing across the plate.

It was Lavagetto's only hit in seven at bats in the Series and the only ball Cookie hit to right all season. The joyous Brooklyn fans knocked down ushers and special policemen to mob him. Meanwhile, Bevens stood on the mound in a daze as the hysterical Dodgers fans carried their hero off on their shoulders.

Hardly had the run crossed the plate when criticism of Harris began. One of baseball's unwritten laws makes it a managerial misdemeanor to put the winning run on base. Harris's supporters argued that Bevens could not have afforded to groove one on a three-one count, as Reiser was expecting. The critics responded that Reiser was so badly hobbled that even had he hit the ball it would have been doubtful that he could have reached base.

Never one to alibi in defeat, Harris took the full responsibility. "I ordered him put on—yes—and I'd do the same thing tomorrow."

As if to prove he meant what he said, he did do the same thing "tomorrow." That was the fifth game, in which the Yankees beat the Dodgers 2–1. But that was another game and another result. As far as the Brooklyn fans were concerned, it was "today" that counted, when the Dodgers won 3–2 on just one hit, a two-out double by Cookie Lavagetto, the last man to bat.

October 5, 1947

# Al Gionfriddo:
# The Impossible Catch

### Brooklyn (NL)

| | AB | R | H |
|---|---|---|---|
| Stanky, 2b | 5 | 2 | 2 |
| Reese, ss | 4 | 2 | 3 |
| J. Robinson, 1b | 5 | 1 | 2 |
| Walker, rf | 5 | 0 | 1 |
| Hermanski, lf | 1 | 0 | 0 |
| b Miksis, lf | 1 | 0 | 0 |
| Gionfriddo, lf | 2 | 0 | 0 |
| Edwards, c | 4 | 1 | 1 |
| Furillo, cf | 4 | 1 | 2 |
| Jorgensen, 3b | 2 | 0 | 0 |
| c Lavagetto, 3b | 2 | 0 | 0 |
| Lombardi, p | 1 | 0 | 0 |
| Branca, p | 1 | 0 | 0 |
| d Bragan | 1 | 0 | 1 |
| e Bankhead | 0 | 1 | 0 |
| Hatten, p | 1 | 0 | 0 |
| Casey, p | 0 | 0 | 0 |
| Total | 39 | 9 | 12 |

### New York (AL)

| | AB | R | H |
|---|---|---|---|
| Stirnweiss, 2b | 5 | 0 | 0 |
| Henrich, rf-lf | 5 | 1 | 2 |
| Lindell, lf | 2 | 1 | 2 |
| Berra, rf | 3 | 0 | 2 |
| DiMaggio, cf | 5 | 1 | 1 |
| Johnson, 3b | 5 | 1 | 2 |
| Phillips, 1b | 1 | 0 | 0 |
| a Brown | 1 | 0 | 1 |
| McQuinn, 1b | 1 | 0 | 0 |
| Rizzuto, ss | 4 | 0 | 1 |
| Lollar, c | 1 | 1 | 1 |
| A. Robinson, c | 4 | 1 | 2 |
| Reynolds, p | 0 | 0 | 0 |
| Drews, p | 2 | 0 | 0 |
| Page, p | 0 | 0 | 0 |
| Newsom, p | 0 | 0 | 0 |
| f Clark | 1 | 0 | 0 |
| Raschi, p | 0 | 0 | 0 |
| g Houk | 1 | 0 | 1 |
| Wensloff, p | 0 | 0 | 0 |
| h Frey | 1 | 0 | 0 |
| Total | 42 | 6 | 15 |

a—Singled for Phillips in third.
b—Popped out for Hermanski in fifth.
c—Flied out for Jorgensen in sixth.
d—Doubled for Branca in sixth.
e—Ran for Bragan in sixth.
f—Lined out for Newsom in sixth.
g—Singled for Raschi in seventh.
h—Forced A. Robinson for Wensloff in ninth.

| | | |
|---|---|---|
| **Brooklyn** | 2 0 2 0 0 4 0 0 0—8 | |
| **New York** | 0 0 4 1 0 0 0 0 1—6 | |

Errors—Jorgensen, McQuinn, A. Robinson. Runs batted in— J. Robinson, Walker, Stirnweiss, Lindell, Johnson, Brown, Berra, Lavagetto, Reese 2, Frey, Bragan. Two-base hits—Reese, J. Robinson, Walker, Lollar, Furillo, Bragan. Double play—New York 1. Left on base—Brooklyn 6, New York 13. Bases on balls—Reynolds 1, Drews 1, Hatten 4. Struck out—Lombardi 2, Branca 2, Page 1, Raschi 1. Hits off—Reynolds, 6 in 2 1/3; Drews, 1 in 2; Page, 4 in 1; Newsom, 1 in 2/3; Raschi, 0 in 1; Wensloff, 0 in 2; Lombardi, 5 in 2 2/3; Branca, 6 in 2 1/3; Hatten, 3 in 3 (pitched to two batters in ninth); Casey, 1 in 1. Wild pitch—Casey. Passed ball—Lollar. Winner—Branca. Loser—Page. Umpires—Pinelli (NL), Rommel (AL), Goetz (NL), McGowan (AL), Boyer (AL), and Magerkurth (NL). Time—3:19. Attendance—74,065.

"Swung on," cried Red Barber, "and belted. It's a long one, deep to left field. Back goes Gionfriddo. Back . . . back . . . back. It may be out of here. No! Gionfriddo makes a one-handed catch against the bullpen fence. Ohhhhhh doctor!"

A quarter century since Al Gionfriddo made the spectacular catch for Brooklyn in the 1947 World Series baseball fans still talk about it.

"I think it's fantastic that people still remember," says the man who raced to the bullpen fence at Yankee Stadium to rob Joe DiMaggio of a three-run homer. "I don't believe it." Just as no one believed the catch itself.

Al Gionfriddo will never forget his moment of glory. The catch was not merely the highlight of Gionfriddo's major league career. It *was* his career. He did not know it at the time, but that game was his last in the majors.

"Red Barber told me after the game," Gionfriddo explains, "that he witnessed a lot of great catches but mine was an impossible catch."

It is ironic that this catch, which may be the greatest in all World Series history, was made by an obscure player at the expense of one of the most brilliant of all diamond stars.

It happened in the sixth game of the Series, on October 5, 1947. The Yankees needed only one more victory to claim the world championship. The Dodgers, trailing 5–4 after five innings,

17

*Al Gionfriddo, Dodgers utility outfielder, after his historic, one-handed catch of Joe DiMaggio's long drive. The catch saved the game for the Dodgers and forced the Series into a seventh and deciding game.*

had taken an 8–5 lead in the sixth, routing relief pitcher Joe Page with a four-run outburst. Lefty Joe Hatten was on the mound when the Yankees came to bat in the bottom of the sixth. Dodgers manager Burt Shotton, moving to protect his team's three-run lead, installed Gionfriddo in left field as defensive insurance. The strategy paid off

run. Gionfriddo turned and raced back to deepest left. His efforts seemed little more than the old college try, but then, literally outrunning the ball, he turned a moment before he reached the 415-foot mark, leaped high, and gloved the ball just over the bullpen fence. The crowd rocked the stadium with thunderous applause. DiMaggio, who was roaring into second, couldn't believe it. He stopped, shook his head, and disconsolately kicked the infield dirt.

The catch saved the Dodgers for one day, at least. The Dodgers won 8–6, but the Yankees captured the Series the next day. Gionfriddo, hero of the sixth game, was back at his accustomed spot on the bench. He never appeared in another major league box score. The Dodgers sent him to their Montreal farm club the following season, never to recall him.

While "the Catch" did not keep him in the big leagues, it has made Gionfriddo's life more memorable. Today, on the wall of his modest little cafe on a side street of Coletta, California, one of the most prominently displayed photographs is one of a hatless Gionfriddo, leaning precariously against the fence in front of the 415-foot sign with the white of the ball showing in his glove. To this day Al gets letters asking him to autograph pictures cut out of magazines. Customers at "Al's Dugout" look at the little guy and say, "Are you *the* Al Gionfriddo?"

immediately. The Yankees got a pair of runners on base on a pass to George Stirnweiss and a two-out single by Yogi Berra. The next batter was Joe DiMaggio.

Joe didn't waste any time. He swung at Hatten's first pitch and sent a screaming drive to left field. It was headed for the bullpen, a sure home

19

# Satchel Paige: His Greatest Games

Leroy ("Satchel") Paige was a legend before he entered the major leagues. The greatest pitcher in the history of the Negro Leagues was rated one of the wonders of all ages, including his own. No one has ever found out how old he is.

Paige toiled 20 years in the Negro Leagues before he got a chance to pitch in a major league game. By then he was 42 years old (estimated). The night he made his first start, 51,013 fans, the most ever to see a night game at Comiskey Park, jammed the stadium. They were curious to see whether the ageless one had anything left.

Many others attended free. Thousands surrounded the park and threatened to tear down the gates. People came around the gates, over them, under them, bursting through the police line, swamping the turnstiles, and jamming together underneath the stands.

Bill Veeck had signed Paige a month earlier and was immediately accused of making a travesty of the game. "It's a cheap publicity stunt," read an editorial. "Paige was a great pitcher in his day," wrote a veteran columnist, "but the guy must be approaching fifty. What can he do now?"

Paige had joined the Indians on July 7, 1948. Two days later, he had made his big league debut, relieving Bob Lemon in the top of the fifth. He pitched two scoreless innings against the St. Louis Browns. He won his first

Baseball's "Ageless Wonder," Satchel Paige, in the year he helped Cleveland to capture the American League flag.

big league game six days later, hurling 3⅓ scoreless innings against the Philadelphia Athletics.

Veeck's vindication was complete after the first full game Paige pitched, on August 13, when it seemed all Chicago turned out to see what he could do against the White Sox. From the start Satch did all that anyone could have expected. With an assortment of fastballs, hesitation pitches, and "bat dodgers," he was in constant control. He threw overhand and three-quarters and kept the Sox popping up. He didn't walk a man all night. The Sox could muster only five hits, all singles, and Paige beat them, 5–0.

A week later, on August 20, Paige beat the White Sox again, this time 1–0. The game was played in Cleveland before a standing-room-only assemblage of 78,382, at that time the largest crowd ever to see a night game. Old Satch twirled a teasing three-hitter for his second straight shutout. He walked only one and struck out five. No Chicago player advanced beyond second and only two passed first. The Indians reached Paige's opponent Bill Wight, a left-hander, for the only run of the game in the fourth when Lou Boudreau, Ken Keltner, and Larry Doby singled.

Paige was an important factor in the Indians' pennant drive that season. He finished with a 6–1 won-lost record and a better-than-commendable 2.48 earned run average over 72⅔ innings. The Indians won the American League championship in a play-off. They couldn't have done it without the contributions of Satchel Paige.

Opposite: *Before beating Chicago 5–0, Paige takes time out to chat with Joe Louis.*
Below: *Pitching in Cleveland before a crowd of 78,382, Paige beats the White Sox again, 1–0, allowing only three hits.*

October 6, 1948

# Bob Feller: The Pick-off

The tall figure on the mound shifted into his stretch position. Runners danced off first and second. Suddenly the pitcher whirled. He fired the ball to second. The shortstop darted to the bag, caught the ball, and tagged the runner in one swift motion. To most of those present, it appeared that the pick-off play had worked perfectly. Not to the umpire, however. He signaled the runner safe. The shortstop protested vehemently, but the umpire was implacable.

Instead of the inning being over, there still were only two out in the last of the eighth. The score stood Cleveland 0, Boston 0. The next batter lashed a single down the third base line, and the runner on second streaked around third and crossed the plate for the only run of the game.

Thus did Bob Feller, one of baseball's all-time great pitchers, go down to defeat in the opening game of the 1948 World Series. It was the closest Feller came to winning a World Series game.

It happened at Braves Field in Boston, where 40,135 fans had turned out for what promised to be a pitcher's duel between Feller and Johnny Sain, the Braves' right-handed ace. The promise held true as the two craftsmen worked carefully on each batter: Feller hurled hitless ball for four innings. Sain gave up only one hit, a single by Ken Keltner in the second. Boston got its

*Bob Feller, who threw the fastest fastball of his time, prepares to deliver his blazer.*

first hit in the fifth when Marv Rickert opened with a single to center, but Feller disposed of the next three batters easily. No other Boston player reached base until the eighth, when Bill Salkeld opened with a walk and Phil Masi, sent in to run for him, was sacrificed to second by Mike McCormick.

Eddie Stanky was the next batter. As he stepped to the plate, manager Lou Boudreau called time and came in from his shortstop position for a conference with his pitcher. "Walk Stanky," Boudreau ordered.

Feller shook his head. "I'd rather pitch to him," he said.

"If anybody's going to break up this game," the manager replied, "I don't want Stanky to do it."

Feller reminded Boudreau that Stanky had a bad leg and that he hadn't hit the ball hard the previous two times up. Bob also mentioned that the next two hitters were Sain and Tommy Holmes. Sain wasn't a bad hitter, and Holmes, a left-hander, led the National League in hitting.

"I know," Boudreau said, "but if we put Stanky on, maybe Sain will hit into a double play."

"You can say," Feller recalls now, "that we had a firm discussion out there on the mound. But he was the manager."

Stanky was walked intentionally, and Sibby Sisti ran for the scrappy second baseman. Feller couldn't induce Sain to hit the ball on the ground, but he got the pitcher to lift a fly to right field for the second out.

With Holmes at bat, Boudreau hovered at second to keep Masi close. Masi refused to stay put, however, and edged off the bag. On signal Feller wheeled and let fly directly to second. Boudreau, who had timed the play perfectly, was there. He speared the ball and slapped it on Masi diving desperately back to the base. Umpire Bill Stewart made his decision without hesitation, spreading his arms in the "safe" motion. Boudreau's protestations did no good. Feller resumed pitching to Holmes. With the count one ball and one strike, Tommy singled to left, scoring Masi. Alvin Dark grounded out, but the damage was done. The Indians failed to score in the ninth.

"I knew Boudreau was going to call for the play," Feller says. "It was a perfect pick-off. Everybody in the park saw it except the umpire. Sure I was disappointed, but I wasn't bitter against Stewart. You can't win if you don't get any runs."

# Joe DiMaggio: The Comeback

Anyone who ever saw Joe DiMaggio perform remembers the slim, graceful slugger. The second of three playing brothers was the greatest of his day, but he would have been a stickout at any time. He had the talent to rank with the immortals. He was an inspirational leader, admired by older players, adored by younger ones. He was a complete ballplayer.

Joe has made the record books, of course—for hitting safely in the most consecutive games, for being named the league's Most Valuable Player three times, for leading the league in home runs and batting, and for being selected on the All-Star team for 13 successive seasons, his tenure in the majors. But these figures only begin to tell his story. They cannot, for example, show the superb team man he was. When DiMaggio joined the Yankees in 1936, they had won four pennants in 11 years. In the 13 years he spent with them, the Yankees won ten pennants and nine world championships.

DiMaggio's only weakness was physical. He was prone to injuries, and he was a slow healer. Because of those physical deficiencies, he missed an average of 20 games a season. His worst year from a physical standpoint was 1949, when he missed spring training and half the season. He had played most of the previous campaign with excruciating pain in his right heel as a result of a calcium deposit.

"There were days," DiMag recalls, "when every step on the field was like someone driving an ice pick into my heel. I tried various cushions and padding devices, but none helped. I tried running and walking on my toes, but this only strained the leg muscles and sometimes gave me a Charley horse in the thighs. I think I overworked every nerve in my body making it to that last game."

The bone spur was removed in November, 1948, but the cast was not removed until New Year's Day. DiMaggio reported to spring training, but he suffered a recurrence of the severe pain and had to be flown to Johns Hopkins Hospital, where he learned that the spur was growing back. As time went on, the foot got worse, and when the season opened, DiMaggio was virtually crippled. The fear that he was through

*Surrounded by sportswriters at*
*the Yanks' hotel in St. Petersburg, Florida,*
*Joe DiMaggio describes the condition of his right heel.*

remained with the Yankee Clipper for nearly half the season. He brooded whether he had hit his last home run. He ate and slept little.

Then a miracle. DiMag got out of bed one morning, put his foot on the floor, and stood up without pain. He pressed his weight down again—no pain. Joe reported to Yankee Stadium and told manager Casey Stengel he would like to take batting practice. He needed the work to toughen his hands. A week later, he played in an exhibition game against the Giants. A crowd of 37,537 came to Yankee Stadium and gave DiMaggio a tumultuous welcome as he trotted out to reclaim his center field position. The Jolter was supposed to try it for four innings, but he went nine. He didn't get a hit, but he handled several chances flawlessly. More importantly, the foot no longer caused him any trouble.

The Yankees went to Boston for a crucial three-game series. The Red Sox were hot—they had won 10 of their last 11 and were in first place. DiMaggio didn't leave with the team. It wasn't until midday that he decided to make the trip. He had to be fitted for a special high, orthopedic shoe, built up at the heel and without spikes. He arrived in Boston at five o'clock, was in uniform at six, and was in the starting lineup two hours later. The date was June 28, 1949. A crowd of 36,228 was waiting expectantly at Fenway Park.

It was in this series that DiMaggio, who hadn't seen really competitive pitching in more than eight months, proved that he was a superman in a baseball suit, a man who could defy all laws of logic. In his first time at bat, after missing all 66 games the Yankees had played that year, he lashed a single off lefty Maury McDermott in the second inning. In his next time at bat, in the third inning with two outs and Phil Rizzuto on base, Joe blasted a home run over the left field wall. As DiMaggio circled the bases, the Yankees' bench erupted in ecstasy. The blow proved to be the pivotal hit in the Yankees' 5–4 triumph and one of the greatest thrills of all time to Yankees fans.

Joe wasn't through at Fenway. The next night, the Yankees were trailing by six runs, 7–1, when the Clipper came up with two men on and homered. Later in the game, with the score tied 7–7, he hit another off Earl Johnson, this time with one mate aboard. The Yankees won 9–7.

The third day, Mel Parnell, southpaw ace of the Red Sox, and Vic Raschi hooked up in a tight pitching duel. The Yankees held a precarious 3–2 lead in the seventh. Two were out when DiMag caught a three-one pitch and sent the ball screaming over the left field wall for a three-run homer. The Yankees swept the series.

The Yankee Clipper lashes a base hit during his record-breaking 56-game hitting streak.

"Those three days in Boston were the most satisfying of my life," says DiMaggio.

DiMaggio emerged from his first series of the year with nine runs batted in, four homers, a single, and a .455 batting average. It was a fusilade of base hits. The slugging provided the Yankees with the inspiration they needed. They held first place until the Red Sox closed with a rush in the final week, and then they prevailed in a neck-and-neck battle.

The Red Sox had forged ahead of the Yankees by one game when the challengers met in a final two-game showdown series at Yankee Stadium. The Yankees needed to win both games to capture the pennant. DiMaggio had caught viral pneumonia. He was desperately ill with a high temperature, and it looked as if his season had come to an end. But Joe insisted on playing. He singled and doubled in the first game as the Yankees won 5–4 and caught the league-leading Red Sox in the standings. And the Bombers beat the Red Sox again in the final game, 5–3, for the pennant.

DiMaggio finished his 76-game season with a .346 batting average, 14 home runs, and 67 runs batted in. Led by DiMaggio, the Yankees went on to win five straight pennants and world championships under Casey Stengel.

October 1, 1950

# Robin Roberts: The Pennant-winning Twentieth

### Philadelphia

| | AB | R | H | PO | A |
|---|---|---|---|---|---|
| Waitkus, 1b | 5 | 1 | 1 | 18 | 0 |
| Ashburn, cf | 5 | 1 | 0 | 2 | 1 |
| Sisler, lf | 5 | 2 | 4 | 0 | 0 |
| Mayo, lf | 0 | 0 | 0 | 1 | 0 |
| Ennis, rf | 5 | 0 | 2 | 2 | 0 |
| Jones, 3b | 5 | 0 | 1 | 0 | 3 |
| Hamner, ss | 4 | 0 | 0 | 1 | 2 |
| Seminick, c | 3 | 0 | 1 | 3 | 1 |
| a Caballero | 0 | 0 | 0 | 0 | 0 |
| Lopata, c | 0 | 0 | 0 | 1 | 0 |
| Goliat, 2b | 4 | 0 | 1 | 1 | 3 |
| Roberts, p | 2 | 0 | 1 | 1 | 6 |
| Total | 38 | 4 | 11 | 30 | 16 |

### Brooklyn

| | AB | R | H | PO | A |
|---|---|---|---|---|---|
| Abrams, lf | 2 | 0 | 0 | 2 | 0 |
| Reese, ss | 4 | 1 | 3 | 3 | 3 |
| Snider, cf | 4 | 0 | 1 | 3 | 0 |
| Robinson, 2b | 3 | 0 | 0 | 4 | 3 |
| Furillo, rf | 4 | 0 | 0 | 3 | 0 |
| Hodges, 1b | 4 | 0 | 0 | 9 | 3 |
| Campanella, c | 4 | 0 | 0 | 2 | 4 |
| Cox, 3b | 3 | 0 | 0 | 1 | 2 |
| b Russell | 1 | 0 | 0 | 0 | 0 |
| Newcombe, p | 3 | 0 | 0 | 3 | 2 |
| c Brown | 1 | 0 | 0 | 0 | 0 |
| Total | 33 | 1 | 5 | 30 | 17 |

a—Ran for Seminick in ninth.
b—Struck out for Cox in tenth.
c—Fouled out for Newcombe in tenth.

| | | |
|---|---|---|
| **Philadelphia** | 0 0 0 0 0 1 0 0 0 3 | —4 |
| **Brooklyn** | 0 0 0 0 0 1 0 0 0 0 | —1 |

Errors—none. Runs batted in—Jones, Reese, Sisler 3. Two-base hit—Reese. Home runs—Reese, Sisler. Sacrifice —Roberts. Double plays—Reese, Robinson, and Hodges; Roberts and Waitkus. Left on base—Philadelphia 7, Brooklyn 5. Bases on balls—Roberts 3, Newcombe 2. Struck out—Roberts 2, Newcombe 3. Umpires—Goetz, Dascoli, Jorda, and Donatelli. Time—2:35. Attendance— 35,073.

Few pitchers went so far so fast. Robin Roberts graduated from Michigan State University in 1948 and came to the Philadelphia Phillies after only two months of minor league seasoning. He qualified immediately as a starting pitcher. By 1950, he was a 20-game winner.

The 1950 Phillies should not be mistaken for the Phillies of the 1930s or the 1970s. Only the name is the same. By 1950 owner Bob Carpenter had spent an estimated two million dollars to rebuild the club. More than half a million dollars had gone in bonuses to young prospects. The club even adopted a new uniform, a handsome red-and-white peppermint-striped suit that had a championship look about it. It seemed to symbolize the new order.

No one expected the Phillies to win the pennant that year, though they had finished strong in 1949. No one had reason to suspect that Jim Konstanty, an obscure relief pitcher, would appear in 74 games and compile a 16–7 record. Nor did anyone guess that Robin Roberts, a young bonus pitcher, would win 20 games in only his second full season in the big leagues. Or that Curt Simmons, another bonus hurler, would win 17 before being inducted into the army in September.

The biggest threat in the Phillies' batting order was Del Ennis, who hit .311 and smashed 31 home runs. Richie Ashburn was the only other regular to hit over .300.

*Robin Roberts shows the graceful form that enabled him to become one of the winningest pitchers in Philadelphia history.*

The club reached first place on July 25 and extended its lead to 7 games in mid-August, winning 12 of 16 at home. It looked as though the Phils would breeze in. On September 19, they were 7½ lengths in front of Boston and 9 ahead of Brooklyn. The whole country had been stirred by the "Whiz Kids," as they were popularly called. Not since 1915 had the Phillies won a pennant.

Eddie Sawyer's youngsters didn't breeze in. They stumbled badly, dropping eight of ten while the Dodgers took seven in a row. On September 27 and 28, they lost doubleheaders to the Giants. When they entered Brooklyn for the last two games of the season, they had a slim two-game lead.

The Dodgers took the Saturday game 7–3 and moved within a game of a tie. It was up to the Phillies to take the last one or be forced into a postseason play-off. Philadelphia fans were nearly frantic. Most experts and fans were sure the Whiz Kids had choked.

The rubber arm of Robin Roberts was stretched to the full in the homestretch, yet for a while it appeared that even Roberts couldn't check the collapse. He had tried for his twentieth victory and had failed four times. When he faced the Dodgers on the season's final day, October 1, it was his third start in five days, his fourth in eight. He was opposed by Don Newcombe before 35,073 at Ebbets Field. Each

pitcher sought his twentieth victory. The tension, palpable when the game began, only increased as the teams completed the first five innings with no score. Each pitch was made in silence, each crack of the bat let loose a roar from the crowd.

The Phillies were the first to break through, picking up a run in the top of the sixth. The Dodgers got it back quickly when Pee Wee Reese hit a freak homer. The ball lodged on a ledge at the base of the screen in right field, instead of falling back on the field. With the score tied at 1–1, Cal Abrams opened the bottom of the ninth for Brooklyn with a walk, and Reese singled him to second. Duke Snider drilled a single to center. Abrams rounded third and was waved home. Anticipating a sacrifice bunt, center fielder Ashburn had been playing shallow. Now he streaked in, grabbed the ball on one bounce, and rifled a perfect strike to catcher Stan Lopata, nipping Abrams at the plate. It was a vital play, but Roberts was not yet out of the inning. Still having to contend with runners on first and third and only one out, Robbie intentionally walked Jackie Robinson to fill the bases. Then the iron-nerved right-hander got Carl Furillo and Gil Hodges on easy pop flies.

Roberts opened the tenth with a single, and Eddie Waitkus followed suit, but Roberts was forced sliding into third on Ashburn's bunt. He trotted to the

*The Phillies mob
Roberts after he pitched a
five-hitter and beat Brooklyn 4–1. It
was Roberts's twentieth victory and the Phils'
first pennant in 35 years.*

dugout rubbing his eyes in irritation.

"You all right?" asked Sawyer. The pitcher nodded without blinking, though the lime from the foul line had burned his eyes. While the rest of the team stood in excitement, he slumped in his seat, his head in his hands. The sharp crack of Dick Sisler's bat startled him. He looked up to see Waitkus and Ashburn trotting home ahead of Sisler, who had dented the left field stands for a three-run homer and a 4–1 lead.

Roberts was ready for the bottom of the tenth. He set down Roy Campa-nella and pinch hitters Jimmy Russell and Tommy Brown in order, and the game was over. The Phillies had won their first flag in 35 years, and Roberts had become their first 20-game winner since Grover Cleveland Alexander turned in his third straight 30-game season in 1917.

Lopata grabbed Roberts. "You did it," he shouted. "You got your twenty and we got the pennant." Roberts looked at his catcher with red-rimmed eyes.

"I couldn't have gone much further."

September 28, 1951

# Allie Reynolds: The Pennant-clinching No-hitter

| Boston | | | | |
|---|---|---|---|---|
| | AB | R | H | PO | A |
| D. DiMaggio, cf | 2 | 0 | 0 | 2 | 0 |
| Pesky, 2b | 4 | 0 | 0 | 1 | 2 |
| Williams, lf | 3 | 0 | 0 | 3 | 0 |
| Vollmer, rf | 2 | 0 | 0 | 0 | 0 |
| Goodman, 1b | 3 | 0 | 0 | 12 | 0 |
| Boudreau, ss | 3 | 0 | 0 | 0 | 1 |
| Hatfield, 3b | 3 | 0 | 0 | 3 | 2 |
| Robinson, c | 3 | 0 | 0 | 3 | 0 |
| Parnell, p | 1 | 0 | 0 | 0 | 2 |
| Scarborough, p | 1 | 0 | 0 | 0 | 1 |
| Taylor, p | 0 | 0 | 0 | 0 | 2 |
| a Maxwell | 1 | 0 | 0 | 0 | 0 |
| Total | 26 | 0 | 0 | 24 | 10 |

| New York | | | | |
|---|---|---|---|---|
| | AB | R | H | PO | A |
| Rizzuto, ss | 5 | 1 | 1 | 1 | 2 |
| Coleman, 2b | 3 | 2 | 1 | 2 | 3 |
| Bauer, rf | 4 | 0 | 1 | 5 | 0 |
| J. DiMaggio, cf | 4 | 0 | 1 | 0 | 0 |
| McDougald, 3b | 3 | 1 | 1 | 0 | 1 |
| Berra, c | 4 | 0 | 1 | 9 | 1 |
| Woodling, lf | 4 | 2 | 2 | 2 | 0 |
| Collins, 1b | 4 | 2 | 2 | 8 | 0 |
| Reynolds, p | 3 | 0 | 0 | 0 | 1 |
| Total | 34 | 8 | 10 | 27 | 8 |

a—Grounded out for Taylor in ninth.

| Boston | 0 0 0 0 0 0 0 0 0—0 |
|---|---|
| New York | 2 0 2 1 0 2 0 1 x—8 |

Errors—D. DiMaggio, Vollmer, Hatfield, Berra. Runs batted in—Bauer, Berra, McDougald, Coleman, Collins 2, Woodling. Two-base hit—Coleman. Home runs—Collins, Woodling. Stolen base—Coleman. Sacrifice—Reynolds. Double plays—Hatfield and Goodman; Rizzuto and Collins. Left on base—Boston 3, New York 5. Bases on balls—Parnell 2, Reynolds 4. Struck out—Parnell 2, Reynolds 9. Hits off—Parnell, 5 in 3; Scarborough, 3 in 3; Taylor, 2 in 2. Loser—Parnell. Umpires—Hubbard, McGowan, Berry, and Hurley. Time—2:12. Attendance—39,038.

It was said of Allie Reynolds that for one game you would have to pick him over any other pitcher. Take 1951, for example, when Reynolds pitched two no-hitters for the New York Yankees, each at a crucial moment in the pennant race.

The Yankees needed a victory badly on July 12, 1951. Having dropped three in a row in Boston and two of three in Washington, they had fallen to third place. Vic Raschi had lost two in a row, and the Senators had blasted Eddie Lopat off the mound. The red-hot Cleveland Indians were coming to town with Bobby Feller fresh from pitching the third no-hitter of his career. Casey Stengel needed help.

Stengel chose Reynolds to oppose Feller. It was a dogfight from the start. Neither team got a hit until Mickey Mantle doubled in the sixth. It was still 0–0 in the seventh when the Yankees' Gene Woodling belted a home run over the right field fence for the first and only run of the game. Reynolds cut down the Indians like wheat and closed out the game by whiffing Bobby Avila. The Yankees had their win. Reynolds had his victory and the first of his two no-hitters.

On September 28, with four games left in the season, the Yankees needed two victories to clinch their third straight pennant. The Red Sox were the opposition at Yankee Stadium. It was a typical Red Sox team, loaded with power. But

*"The Chief," Allie Reynolds of the New York Yankees, tied an American League record by pitching two no-hitters in a single season.*

Allie was killing them; he was even stronger than he'd been against Cleveland. Nobody had reached second. Except for a walk or two, nobody had even reached first. What the Red Sox managed to hit was handled easily in the field.

By the seventh inning, it had become clear to the 39,038 spectators that the Chief was advancing on an American League record—two no-hitters in one season.

The Yankees made it as easy as pos-sible for Reynolds by sewing up the ball game early. With typical muscle-flexing, they tagged Mel Parnell for two runs in the first and polished him off with two more in the third. They rapped Ray Scarborough for three runs in the next three innings. Then a Gene Woodling homer made it 8–0 in the eighth.

Reynolds took his position on the mound to start the ninth, the crowd shouting in anticipation. Charley Maxwell fouled out. Dom DiMaggio waited out a walk. Johnny Pesky fanned for the second out. It was Reynolds' ninth strikeout. Ted Williams ambled up to the plate.

Yogi Berra tiptoed to the mound. "Take it easy, Chief," he said. "What do you want to throw?"

"Anything," said Allie, and Yogi returned to the plate.

There were howls from the stands to walk Williams. It would have made sense—avoid the big man; pass him to get to a right-handed hitter. Anything to preserve the record. Allie said later it never occurred to him. A no-hitter means nobody hits, including the guys most likely to hit. Passing Williams would have been percentage, but it wouldn't have been Reynolds.

Allie poured a fast one in for a called strike. Williams swung at the second and fouled it straight up behind the plate. Berra sprang from under his mask and positioned himself for the

Below: *Yankees catcher Yogi Berra and*
*Reynolds surround Ted Williams's*
*foul pop that should have been the final out.*
Opposite: *Yankees congratulate Reynolds*
*after his first no-hitter against Cleveland.*

routine catch. The game appeared over.

Suddenly Berra began to circle as a capricious breeze played tricks with the ball. Yogi made a desperate, diving stab at the last moment. The ball hit his glove and bounded away.

Reynolds had rushed from the mound as if to help Yogi make the catch, and his momentum carried him into and over the stocky receiver. A lesser man might have blown up. Instead, Allie bent over to help Yogi to his feet. "Are you all right?" he asked.

"Gee, Chief, I'm sorry," muttered the crestfallen Berra.

"Don't worry Yog," said Reynolds. "We'll get him again."

They were brave words. The most dangerous batter in the game had a second chance. Reynolds walked purposefully back to the mound and confronted the hitter. Yogi retrieved his mask and squatted behind the plate. He signaled and rose in a half crouch. Umpire Cal Hubbard bent to watch the pitch. Williams poised. Reynolds wound up and threw.

It was another fastball—sheer madness, of course. You didn't slip three in a row past Williams. But Reynolds did. Ted popped it up in front of the Yankees' dugout, Yogi ran for it, and Reynolds ran to back him up. "Lots of room," Tommy Henrich called, preparing to catch Berra in his arms if he fell. Three feet from the dugout steps, Yogi grabbed the ball in his big mitt.

The Yankees had clinched at least a tie for the pennant, and the Chief had his second no-hitter of the season. In the clubhouse Casey shook Reynolds's hand. "You can have the rest of the season off," the manager said.

September 30, 1951

# Jackie Robinson:
# A Pennant Saved

### Brooklyn

|  | AB | R | H | PO | A |
|---|---|---|---|---|---|
| Furillo, rf | 7 | 1 | 2 | 2 | 0 |
| Reese, ss | 6 | 0 | 3 | 3 | 3 |
| Snider, cf | 7 | 1 | 3 | 3 | 0 |
| Robinson, 2b | 6 | 2 | 2 | 6 | 5 |
| Campanella, c | 7 | 1 | 2 | 8 | 0 |
| Pafko, lf | 7 | 0 | 1 | 7 | 2 |
| Hodges, 1b | 5 | 1 | 2 | 10 | 5 |
| Cox, 3b | 6 | 1 | 1 | 2 | 3 |
| Roe, p | 0 | 0 | 0 | 0 | 0 |
| Branca, p | 0 | 1 | 0 | 0 | 0 |
| a Russell | 1 | 0 | 0 | 0 | 0 |
| King, p | 0 | 0 | 0 | 0 | 0 |
| Labine, p | 0 | 0 | 0 | 0 | 0 |
| b Belardi | 1 | 0 | 0 | 0 | 0 |
| Erskine, p | 0 | 0 | 0 | 0 | 0 |
| c Walker | 1 | 0 | 1 | 0 | 0 |
| d Thompson | 0 | 1 | 0 | 0 | 0 |
| Newcombe, p | 2 | 0 | 0 | 1 | 0 |
| Podbielan, p | 0 | 0 | 0 | 0 | 0 |
| Total | 56 | 9 | 17 | 42 | 18 |

### Philadelphia

|  | AB | R | H | PO | A |
|---|---|---|---|---|---|
| Pellagrini, 2b | 6 | 1 | 2 | 5 | 6 |
| Ashburn, cf | 8 | 0 | 4 | 2 | 0 |
| Jones, 3b | 4 | 0 | 1 | 3 | 3 |
| Ennis, lf | 8 | 0 | 1 | 6 | 1 |
| Brown, 1b | 2 | 1 | 1 | 7 | 2 |
| Waitkus, 1b | 6 | 0 | 0 | 10 | 1 |
| Clark, rf | 1 | 0 | 0 | 1 | 0 |
| Nicholson, rf | 6 | 2 | 2 | 2 | 0 |
| Hamner, ss | 5 | 3 | 2 | 2 | 6 |
| Seminick, c | 2 | 1 | 0 | 7 | 1 |
| Church, p | 2 | 0 | 1 | 1 | 0 |
| Drews, p | 2 | 0 | 1 | 0 | 1 |
| Roberts, p | 1 | 0 | 0 | 0 | 1 |
| Total | 53 | 8 | 15 | 42 | 21 |

a—Struck out for Branca in fourth.
b—Struck out for Labine in sixth.
c—Doubled for Erskine in eighth.
d—Ran for Walker in eighth.

**Brooklyn**    0 0 1 1 3 0 0 3 0 0 0 0 0 1—9
**Philadelphia**   0 4 2 0 2 0 0 0 0 0 0 0 0 0—8

Errors—Jones, Robinson. Runs batted in—Brown, Pellagrini 2, Ashburn 2, Church 2, Hamner, Reese, Pafko 2, Snider, Robinson 2, Walker 2, Furillo. Two-base hits—Jones, Hamner, Pellagrini, Snider, Walker, Campanella. Three-base hits—Reese, Campanella, Robinson. Sacrifices—Jones 2, Robinson, Pellagrini. Double plays—Hamner, Pellagrini, and Brown; Ennis, Pellagrini, and Waitkus; Seminick, Hamner, and Pellagrini. Left on base—Brooklyn 9, Philadelphia 18. Bases on balls—Church 3, Roe 1, Branca 2, Labine 1, Newcombe 6. Struck out—Church 3, Drews 2, Roberts 1, Roe 1, Branca 1, Labine 2, Newcombe 3. Hits off—Roe, 5 in 1 2/3; Branca, 2 in 1 1/3; King, 3 in 1; Labine, 1 in 1; Church, 6 in 4 1/3; Drews, 5 in 3; Roberts, 6 in 6 2/3; Erskine, 2 in 2; Newcombe, 1 in 5 2/3; Podbielan, 1 in 1 1/3. Hit by pitch—by King (Jones), by Newcombe (Pellegrini). Wild pitch—Branca. Winner—Podbielan. Loser—Roberts. Umpires—Jorda, Gore, Warneke, and Goetz. Time—4:30. Attendance—31,755.

He created havoc on the base paths. He carried a flaming spirit into every contest. He took risks that other performers shunned, and he actually stole runs for the Dodgers. His mere presence on the base lines was enough to upset the opposing pitcher. He was a tiger in the field and a lion at the plate. He was at his best when it counted the most. All those things made Jackie Robinson, the man who broke the color line in baseball, the most dynamic figure, the most exciting player, the fiercest competitor, and perhaps the greatest all-around ballplayer that Brooklyn ever had.

The 10 years that Jackie Robinson played at Ebbets Field were the 10 most exciting years in the 68-year history of the Dodgers in Brooklyn. During those hectic 10 years, the team won six pennants and a world championship. It is ironic, however, that Robinson achieved his greatest moment of personal glory when the Dodgers failed to win the pennant, when the Dodgers fell apart and lost a championship they had all but wrapped up.

Robinson's heroics came in a suspense-packed game—the final game of the regular 1951 campaign. Because of him, the dying Dodgers stayed alive for a few days longer before succumbing to the Giants in the three-game playoff that was climaxed by Bobby Thomson's storied home run.

The beginning of the end for the

Left: *Robinson in Yankee Stadium.* Below: *Scoring after game-winning homer.*

Dodgers was August 12, when the Giants, 13½ games back, began their amazing surge. For seven weeks the baseball world looked on in disbelief as the Giants inched nearer and the Dodgers grew more jittery each day. Finally, there was no longer any need for them to look back. On Friday, September 28, two days before the end of the season, the Giants pulled abreast when the Dodgers lost to the Phillies.

The Dodgers finally won on Saturday night as Don Newcombe beat Robin Roberts in shutting out the Phillies 5–0. But the Giants also won, and the teams remained deadlocked.

On Sunday, September 30, 1951, the final day of the regular season, Brooklyn battled the Phillies in Philadelphia while the Giants played in Boston. A crowd of 31,755 came to Shibe Park to attend the Dodgers' final rites. Death seemed imminent as the Dodgers quickly fell behind 6–1. Then, in the top of the fifth with the Dodgers trailing 6–2, Jackie Robinson came to bat with a runner on base. He hammered a triple to deep center, scoring the runner, and later scored himself as the Dodgers scraped together three runs to make it 6–5.

The Phillies bounced back and increased their lead to 8–5. At the start of the sixth, a roar went up from the stands when the scoreboard reported that the Giants had won their game in Boston. A Brooklyn loss to Philadelphia would mean the pennant for the Giants.

In the eighth the Dodgers stormed back for three runs to tie the game. Then it was Saturday night again: Newcombe and Roberts came in as relievers and continued their grueling battle. The two magnificent right-handers mowed down batters until the bottom of the twelfth, when Newcombe tired. With two out the Phillies loaded the bases. Darkness made it difficult to follow the flight of the ball. Eddie Waitkus strode to the plate. He swung at a fastball and whacked a low line drive up the middle. As the game, the season, and the Dodgers' dreams hung in suspense Robinson sped to his right and flung himself in desperation full length at the ball. Somehow he caught it. As he fell to the earth, his right elbow crashed into his stomach, but by instinct he held onto the ball for the final game-saving out of the inning.

Bud Podbielan replaced Newcombe in the thirteenth. In the fourteenth, when Roberts easily retired the first two batters, it looked as though the tie might never be broken. The inning's third hitter was Robinson. With the count one-one, Roberts offered a curve. Jackie swung and hammered it into the left field stands for a home run. Brooklyn held the Phillies in the last of the fourteenth, and the Dodgers were saved, at least for the moment, although the Giants were not to be staved off much longer.

October 3, 1951

# Bobby Thomson's Homer

**Brooklyn**

| | AB | R | H | PO | A |
|---|---|---|---|---|---|
| Furillo, rf | 5 | 0 | 0 | 0 | 0 |
| Reese, ss | 4 | 2 | 1 | 2 | 5 |
| Snider, cf | 3 | 1 | 2 | 1 | 0 |
| Robinson, 2b | 2 | 1 | 1 | 3 | 2 |
| Pafko, lf | 4 | 0 | 1 | 4 | 1 |
| Hodges, 1b | 4 | 0 | 0 | 11 | 1 |
| Cox, 3b | 4 | 0 | 2 | 1 | 3 |
| Walker, c | 4 | 0 | 1 | 2 | 0 |
| Newcombe, p | 4 | 0 | 0 | 1 | 1 |
| Branca, p | 0 | 0 | 0 | 0 | 0 |
| Total | 34 | 4 | 8 | x25 | 13 |

**New York**

| | AB | R | H | PO | A |
|---|---|---|---|---|---|
| Stanky, 2b | 4 | 0 | 0 | 0 | 4 |
| Dark, ss | 4 | 1 | 1 | 2 | 2 |
| Mueller, rf | 4 | 0 | 1 | 0 | 0 |
| c Hartung | 0 | 1 | 0 | 0 | 0 |
| Irvin, lf | 4 | 1 | 1 | 1 | 0 |
| Lockman, 1b | 3 | 1 | 2 | 11 | 1 |
| Thomson, 3b | 4 | 1 | 3 | 4 | 1 |
| Mays, cf | 3 | 0 | 0 | 1 | 0 |
| Westrum, c | 0 | 0 | 0 | 7 | 1 |
| a Rigney | 1 | 0 | 0 | 0 | 0 |
| Noble, c | 0 | 0 | 0 | 0 | 0 |
| Maglie, p | 2 | 0 | 0 | 1 | 2 |
| b Thompson | 1 | 0 | 0 | 0 | 0 |
| Jansen, p | 0 | 0 | 0 | 0 | 0 |
| Total | 30 | 5 | 8 | 27 | 11 |

a—Struck out for Westrum in eighth.
b—Grounded out for Maglie in eighth.
c—Ran for Mueller in ninth.
x—One out when winning run scored.

| | | |
|---|---|---|
| **Brooklyn** | 1 0 0 0 0 0 0 3 0—4 | |
| **New York** | 0 0 0 0 0 0 1 0 4—5 | |

Errors—None. Runs batted in—Robinson, Thomson 4, Pafko, Cox. Lockman. Two-base hits—Thomson, Irvin, Lockman. Home run—Thomson. Sacrifice—Lockman. Double plays—Cox, Robinson, and Hodges; Reese, Robinson, and Hodges. Left on base—Brooklyn 7, New York 3. Bases on balls—Maglie 4, Newcombe 2. Struck out—Maglie 6, Newcombe 2. Hits off—Maglie, 8 in 8; Jansen, 0 in 1; Newcombe, 7 in 8 1/3; Branca, 1 in 0. Wild pitch—Maglie. Winner—Jansen. Loser—Branca. Umpires—Jorda, Conlan, Stewart, and Goetz. Time—2:28. Attendance—34,320.

Babe Ruth, Henry Aaron, Willie Mays, Ted Williams, and Joe DiMaggio will be remembered for hundreds of home runs. Bobby Thomson will be remembered for one—the home run that gave the New York Giants the pennant in the ninth inning of the final game of the 1951 play-off. Hard to believe, it was a homer impossible to forget. Fewer than 35,000 spectators actually saw it, yet tens of thousands who heard the radio broadcast consider themselves bona fide witnesses to the miracle of Coogan's Bluff.

The saga of the Giants' 1951 pennant began in mid-August, when the Giants trailed the league-leading Dodgers by 13½ games. By the end of the regular season, they trailed no longer, having won 37 of their final 44 games. Only the Dodgers' thrilling, come-from-behind victory over the Phils on the last day of the season had kept the race deadlocked.

A lot of people have forgotten that Bobby Thomson's two-run homer off Ralph Branca won the first game of the best-of-three play-off for the pennant. Nor do they recall Thomson's blundering baserunning and two errors at third in the second game, won by Brooklyn 10–0 behind Clem Labine. Bobby's dazzling heroics of the final game left prior feats and boners obscured. That final game, after all, was the pennant winner.

In the finale, the Dodgers sent 20-

The "shot heard 'round the world"—Giants'
Bobby Thomson hits his famous home run,
capping the miracle of Coogan's Bluff.

game winner Don Newcombe against the Giants' 23-game winner, Sal Maglie. With a run in the first and three more in the eighth, the Dodgers took a 4–1 lead to the ninth.

Newcombe struck out the side in the eighth but confided to manager Charlie Dressen after the inning, "It looks like I don't have it any more. . . . Better take me out." Having seen no evidence to support Newcombe's modest self-assessment, Dressen demurred, and Jackie Robinson talked Newcombe into pitching the ninth. It proved to be an unfortunate bit of persuasion.

Alvin Dark led off the Giants' ninth with a single, and Don Mueller followed with another. Monte Irvin fouled out, but Whitey Lockman sliced a double to left, scoring Dark. With the tying runs on base and only one out, Newcombe was through.

In the bullpen Dressen had Clem Labine, but he had pitched the day before. Preacher Roe was throwing too, but Clyde Sukeforth, the pitching coach, recommended Ralph Branca. Once again, Dressen was ill-advised.

Branca threw two pitches to Bobby Thomson, the only batter he faced. The first was a fastball over the inside corner for a strike. The second was a fastball not quite in far enough.

Thomson connected solidly and sent the ball on a line to left field. A picture taken moments later shows Dodgers left fielder Andy Pafko waiting futilely at the base of the left field wall as the ball enters the stands just above.

Hardly a titanic drive, the homer nonetheless unleashed a tidal wave of emotion. Thomson led a delirious throng as he happily circled the bases and arrived at home plate to be welcomed by even greater hysteria.

While every member of the Giants and half the spectators in the Polo Grounds tried to embrace Thomson at one time, the Dodgers stood stolidly unbelieving at their positions. Later, while the Giants exulted in their dressing room, Branca lay on the clubhouse steps, crying.

Baseball miracles are cruelly double-edged; for some they are disasters. After throwing that gopher ball to Thomson, Branca would never regain his domineering relief pitching form. Neither are baseball miracles as bountiful as they sometimes seem; though the Giants won the pennant, they lost the World Series to the Yankees in six games. Nonetheless, divine good fortune strikes too rarely to be slighted for its cruelties and limitations. As the symbol of hope for ninth inning diehards everywhere, Bobby Thomson's shot heard 'round the world still echoes.

May 6, 1953

# Bobo Holloman: The Most Unlikely No-hitter

```
                    Philadelphia
                                AB  R  H  PO  A
Joost, ss ...................... 3  0  0   3  3
Philley, cf ................... 4  0  0   0  0
Babe, 3b ...................... 3  0  0   1  0
Robinson, 1b .................. 4  0  0   8  0
Clark, rf ..................... 3  0  0   2  0
Zernial, lf .................. 3  0  0   1  0
Michaels, 2b .................. 3  0  0   5  3
Astroth, c ................... 1  0  0   4  2
Martin, p .................... 1  0  0   0  0
a Hamilton ................... 1  0  0   0  0
Scheib, p .................... 0  0  0   0  1
b Valo ....................... 0  0  0   0  0
c DeMaestri .................. 0  0  0   0  0
            Total ........... 26  0  0  24 15

                    St. Louis
                                AB  R  H  PO  A
Groth, cf .................... 5  0  2   4  0
Hunter, ss ................... 5  1  2   1  4
Dyck, lf ..................... 3  1  1   1  0
Elliott, 3b .................. 4  0  2   1  0
Wertz, rf .................... 3  0  1   3  0
Moss, c ...................... 5  2  2   3  0
Sievers, 1b .................. 3  1  1  12  0
Young, 2b .................... 2  1  0   1  7
Holloman, p .................. 3  0  2   1  1
            Total ........... 33  6 13  27 12
```

a—Struck out for Martin in third.
b—Walked for Scheib in ninth.
c—Ran for Valo in ninth.

**Philadelphia**    0 0 0 0 0 0 0 0 0—0
**St. Louis**       0 1 1 1 1 2 0 0 x—6

Errors—Michaels, Holloman. Runs batted in—Holloman 3, Dyck, Wertz, Groth. Two-base hits—Moss 2, Hunter, Elliott, Wertz. Sacrifice—Holloman. Double plays—Philadelphia 2, St. Louis 2. Left on base—Philadelphia 4, St. Louis 12. Bases on balls—Holloman 5, Martin 4, Scheib 3. Struck out—Holloman 3, Martin 2, Scheib 1. Hits off—Martin, 7 in 5; Scheib, 6 in 3; Holloman, 0 in 9. Hit by pitch—by Scheib (Young). Loser—Martin. Umpires—Duffy, Grieve, Passarella, and Napp. Time—2:09. Attendance—2,413.

The entire major league career of Alva ("Bobo") Holloman was wrapped up in one night. He lasted less than one season in the majors. In all he appeared in 22 games, 10 as a starter, and only once did he finish a game he started. That took place at Busch Stadium, in St. Louis, on May 6, 1953. That night Holloman pitched a no-hit game against the Philadelphia Athletics. It was the most bizarre no-hit game, by the most ordinary no-hit pitcher.

Holloman, a strapping right-hander from Thomaston, Georgia, was no callow rookie. Twenty-nine at the time, he had bounced around in the minors for a decade. He had a good fastball, but wildness had kept him from the big leagues. Bill Veeck, owner of the Browns, had purchased his contract from Syracuse after Holloman won 18 games in the International League in 1952.

Holloman worked without distinction for the Browns, mostly in the bullpen. He had started two games, both of which had been postponed by rain before they had gone five innings. So this was his first official start.

The evening of Wednesday, May 6, was not a pleasant one for baseball. It had rained off and on throughout the day, and it was still humid at game time. Only 2,413 fans showed up, Veeck among them. In the fourth inning, he passed a note around the press box. "Anybody who shows up on a night like this," the note read, "is a loyal fan. Please inform the fans that their rain checks will be honored at any future game the rest of the season."

Only a few availed themselves of the privilege. Most preferred to keep the rain checks as souvenirs and as proof that they were there the night Bobo Holloman pitched the no-hitter.

The rookie was far from sensational, but no matter what the A's did, they couldn't get a base hit off him. Even a rain delay didn't dampen Holloman's good fortune. The A's hit the ball solidly in all directions but the acrobatics of shortstop Billy Hunter, left fielder Jim Dyck, and first baseman Roy Sievers, stymied them.

Holloman fanned three and walked five—three in the ninth inning. The Browns made one error—by Holloman himself. In the fifth inning, Gus Zernial bounced one to the left of the mound. Holloman speared the ball but could not get it out of his glove until he dropped it for an error. He had another scare in the sixth inning, when Joe Astroth topped a trickler along the third base line. Unable to make a play on Astroth, third baseman Bob Elliott let the ball roll, and it finally trickled foul.

Holloman's biggest ordeal came in the ninth. The Browns had the game well in hand, but the rookie right-hander, sweating and tiring in the sultry weather, was staggering. Pinch hitter Elmer Valo coaxed a walk, opening the inning, and Eddie Joost followed with another pass. Dave Philley then grounded viciously to second, where Bobby Young began a double play that momentarily eased the pressure. Joe DeMaestri, running for Valo, reached third on the play, the only one of the A's six baserunners who advanced past first.

Still unsteady, Holloman walked Loren Babe and then served a one-one offering to A's clean-up hitter Eddie Robinson that Robinson sent sizzling down the first base line—foul by inches. Then Robinson laced Holloman's next pitch toward Vic Wertz in deep right field. Wertz started back, then came in, stumbled slightly, and caught the ball.

Shaky throughout, Bobo Holloman had nonetheless become the only pitcher in modern times to pitch a no-hitter in his first start in the major leagues. Though he won two more games, Bobo never pitched another complete game in the majors. He had a 3–7 record when the Browns sold his contract to Toronto, just 10 weeks later. He never again pitched in the majors.

Six nights after his no-hitter, Holloman again started against the A's. This time he lasted only 1⅓ innings. Three hits and a walk dispatched him in a hurry. But he didn't lose the game. Another pitcher arrived in relief. He shut out the A's the rest of the way and won 6–3. His name? Don Larsen.

June 18, 1953

# Seventeen Runs in One Inning

*Seventeen runs go up
on the scoreboard for Boston.*

It was like a bad dream. Steve Gromek sat in the bullpen in Boston's Fenway Park watching in stunned silence as the Red Sox mauled a quartet of Tigers pitchers for 20 hits. The date was June 17, 1953, Gromek's first day in a Detroit uniform. He'd joined the Tigers after a trade with the Cleveland Indians —he, pitchers Al Aber and Dick Weik, and shortstop Ray Boone for pitchers Art Houtteman and Bill Wight, catcher Joe Ginsberg, and infielder Owen Friend. He knew he had joined the most inept club in the American League, winner of only 14 of 57 games and hopelessly mired in the basement, but he had no idea the club was this bad.

It wasn't a defeat; it was a massacre. Gromek felt sorry for the four Detroit pitchers. He vowed a similar fate would never befall him. He'd quit first.

The Tigers, by edict of the American League, were forced to show up in Fenway the next day. It was Ned Garver's turn on the chopping block. He pitched surprisingly well until the sixth, when Boston broke a 3–3 tie. Gromek, summoned to the rescue, managed to retire the side but not before two runs had scored to give the Red Sox a 5–3 lead.

On his own in the seventh, Gromek never got out of the inning. Before the avalanche had ended, the Red Sox had scored 17 runs, a modern record for one inning, an incredible, illogical, impossible inning. Twenty-three men

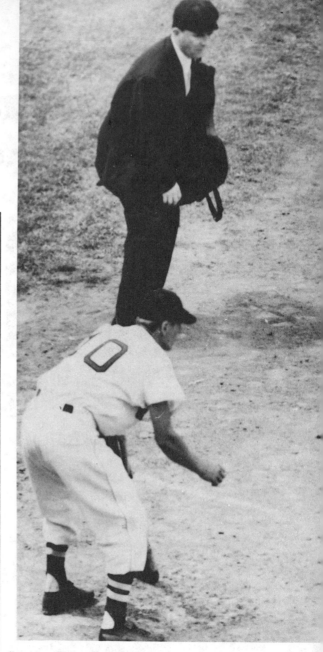

came to bat, collecting a total of 11 singles, two doubles, a home run (by Dick Gernert), and six bases on balls. Gromek, a 12-year veteran who several years ago had registered 19 victories for the Indians, was shelled for six hits and three walks in two-thirds of an inning. He allowed 9 runs, all earned.

Gromek remembers it vividly. "I never saw anything like it," he recalls. "They got some clean hits, but most of them were flukes. The ball kept bouncing just out of reach of our infielders or falling in front of our outfielders."

One clean hit was Gernert's homer, which fell just out of reach of a fan sitting on the roof in back of the left field wall. "Yes," admitted Gromek. "I set a long distance record that day."

After being lifted by Fred Hutchinson, the Tigers' compassionate manager, Gromek trudged to the clubhouse and sat in front of his locker in a state of shock. "I was wondering if that was the end," he says, "if I was going to keep right on going to the minors. I was feeling pretty sick."

The Red Sox broke or tied 16 major league records in that inning as they continued to shell Dick Weik and Earl Harrist en route to a 23–3 rout. Outfielder Gene Stephens cracked three hits in that inning—a double and two singles. Sammy White and Tom Umphlett also reached base three times. The Red Sox had twenty-seven hits in the game,

five by Billy Goodman, four by White, and three each by Stephens and Umphlett. The seventh inning lasted 48 minutes. The Tigers' only consolation was that only 3,198 witnessed the carnage.

Gromek would have preferred to go into hiding for the rest of the week, but he came to the park each day and faced his new teammates. He tried to read his manager, but the stone-faced Hutchinson gave no indication of his sentiment. Not until five days later did

Hutch speak his first word to Gromek. "You pitch today," he said gruffly. The date was June 23, 1953.

"I was flabbergasted," says Gromek. "I thought I would never pitch again, at least not for Detroit."

Against the Philadelphia Athletics, Gromek appropriated the businesslike demeanor of his manager and shut out the A's 5–0, limiting them to only four hits. He didn't walk a batter, and no Philadelphian reached third.

*Gene Stephens scores the eleventh run of the inning as Tigers catcher Matt Batts receives late throw. Billy Goodman, the on-deck hitter, assists Stephens on the play. Weary umpire is Jim Hurley.*

July 31, 1954

# Joe Adcock: 18 Total Bases

## Milwaukee

| | AB | R | H |
|---|---|---|---|
| Bruton, cf | 6 | 0 | 4 |
| O'Connell, 2b | 5 | 0 | 0 |
| Mathews, 3b | 4 | 3 | 2 |
| Aaron, lf | 5 | 2 | 2 |
| Adcock, 1b | 5 | 5 | 5 |
| Pafko, rf | 4 | 2 | 3 |
| Pendleton, rf | 1 | 1 | 0 |
| Logan, ss | 2 | 1 | 1 |
| Smalley, ss | 2 | 1 | 1 |
| Crandall, c | 4 | 0 | 0 |
| Calderone, c | 1 | 0 | 1 |
| Wilson, p | 1 | 0 | 0 |
| Burdette, p | 4 | 0 | 0 |
| Buhl, p | 0 | 0 | 0 |
| Jolly, p | 0 | 0 | 0 |
| Total | 44 | 15 | 19 |

## Brooklyn

| | AB | R | H |
|---|---|---|---|
| Gilliam, 2b | 4 | 1 | 4 |
| Reese, ss | 3 | 0 | 2 |
| Zimmer, ss | 1 | 0 | 0 |
| Snider, cf | 4 | 0 | 1 |
| Shuba, lf | 1 | 0 | 0 |
| Hodges, 1b | 5 | 1 | 1 |
| Amoros, lf-cf | 5 | 2 | 3 |
| Robinson, 3b | 0 | 0 | 0 |
| Hoak, 3b | 2 | 1 | 1 |
| Furillo, rf | 5 | 1 | 1 |
| Walker, c | 5 | 1 | 1 |
| Newcombe, p | 0 | 0 | 0 |
| Labine, p | 0 | 0 | 0 |
| a Moryn | 1 | 0 | 0 |
| Palica, p | 0 | 0 | 0 |
| Wojey, p | 1 | 0 | 0 |
| b Podres, p | 2 | 0 | 2 |
| Total | 39 | 7 | 16 |

a—Hit into double play for Labine in second.
b—Singled for Wojay in seventh.

| | | |
|---|---|---|
| Milwaukee | 1 3 2 0 3 0 3 0 3—15 | |
| Brooklyn | 1 0 0 0 0 0 0 4 1— 7 | |

Error—Hoak. Runs batted in—Bruton, Mathews 2, Adcock 7, Pafko 2, Logan, Snider, Hodges, Hoak 2, Furillo, Walker 2. Two-base hits—Gilliam, Pafko, Bruton 3, Amoros, Adcock, Aaron. Three-base hit—Amoros. Home runs—Mathews 2, Adcock 4, Hoak, Pafko, Hodges, Walker. Sacrifice—O'Connell. Sacrifice fly—Hoak. Double plays—Milwaukee 2, Brooklyn 1. Left on base—Milwaukee 6, Brooklyn 10. Bases on balls—Burdette 2, Jolly 1, Palica 2. Struck out—Burdette 3, Jolly 1, Palica 1, Wojey 3, Podres 1. Hits off—Wilson, 5 in 1; Burdette, 8 in 6 1/3; Buhl, 2 in 0; Jolly, 1 in 1 2/3; Newcombe, 4 in 1; Labine, 1 in 1; Palica, 5 in 2 1/3; Wojey, 4 in 2 2/3; Podres, 5 in 2. Wild pitch—Podres. Hit by pitch—by Wilson (Robinson). Winner—Burdette. Loser—Newcombe. Umpires—Boggess, Engel, Stewart, and Pinelli. Time—2:53. Attendance—12,263.

Joe Adcock did not play his first game of baseball until he was an 18-year-old freshman at Louisiana State University. Nine years later, he established a record for power hitting that has yet to be equaled.

As a youngster, Joe Adcock had no time for baseball. He was too busy working on his father's farm. At Coushatta High School, he was good enough to win a basketball scholarship to LSU, where in his freshman year he was the varsity center. It happened that Red Swanson, the basketball coach, also handled the baseball squad. In the spring of Adcock's freshman year, Swanson approached him and asked if he wanted to play baseball.

"No," replied Adcock. "I don't know how."

Swanson urged him to take a crack at it and asked him to come out for practice the next day with his spikes and glove. Joe told him he had neither. Swanson stared at him unbelievingly and told him to come anyway.

That was in 1945. Five years later, Adcock was in the big leagues with the Cincinnati Reds. In 1953, with the Milwaukee Braves, he became the first player ever to hit a ball into the center field bleachers at the Polo Grounds in a regular league game. Three years after that, he became the only player ever to hit a ball over the left field grandstand at Ebbets Field. In between he became the only player to hit four

home runs and a double in one game.

They had been playing ball at the Polo Grounds for more than three decades. It was in 1923 that the distant center field bleachers were erected, giving the park the deepest center field point in baseball, 483 feet from home plate. In those 30 years, the greatest hitters of the National League failed to reach the bleachers, which used to jut out around the flag pole at the most distant center field point. But on April 29, 1953, Joe Adcock did it.

He was hitting against Jim Hearn, the right-hander of the New York Giants, with two out in the third inning. Andy Pafko, who had singled, was on first, and the count was two balls and

*Braves' Joe Adcock crosses the plate on the day he wore out Dodger pitchers by blasting four home runs in one game.*

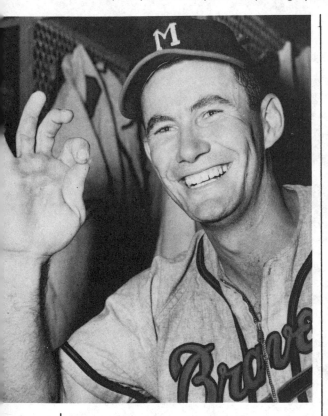

*In the dressing room after his four homers, Adcock seems quite pleased to pose for photographers.*

one strike when Hearn came in with a fastball that Adcock caught on the meat part of his bat.

As the ball started to rise, center fielder Bobby Thomson drifted back. When he reached the four-foot wall in front of the bleachers to the left of the clubhouse exit stairs, he watched the ball sail over his head. It cleared the wall and the five-foot wire fence atop the wall with something to spare and landed 10 rows up in the stands. Observers in the press box estimated that the drive had traveled close to 500 feet.

Warren Spahn beat the Giants 3–2 that day. Joe Adcock's homer proved to be the difference.

It was a year, two months, and two days later that Adcock staged another awesome one-man display of hitting power, in Brooklyn this time. He went to the plate five times, slammed four home runs and a double for 18 total bases, a new major league record for a single game. Eight others have hit four home runs in one game, but none have added a fifth extra-base hit, as Adcock did that day, and none have hit four homers off four different pitchers, as Adcock did.

Don Newcombe, Erv Palica, Pete Wojey, and Johnny Podres were the victims. Two of Adcock's homers and the double were hit on first pitches; the other two homers came on second pitches. The second homer bounced off the facade between the upper and lower stands. The others went into the lower stands in left center field.

Adcock drove in seven runs. He walloped his second homer in the fifth inning with two aboard, his third in the seventh with one on. Joe's final homer, and third in a row, came in the ninth.

The Braves collected 19 hits, and beat the Dodgers 15–7. The following day, the Braves again routed the Dodgers, 14–6. They walloped three home runs and again amassed 19 hits. To this second outpouring Adcock's contribution was miserly—a double.

September 29, 1954

# Willie Mays: The Greatest Catch

*Running at top speed, Willie Mays hauls in Wertz's drive.*

Willie Mays has made so many spectacular catches in so many ball parks that he cannot pick the one he considers his greatest. "You know something? I've got to think about it," he says. "Think about it a lot. I hope it doesn't sound like a boast when I say I have made a lot of good plays in the field."

Mays has stopped counting the number of times he has been asked to select his greatest defensive play. "I don't want to compare 'em," is his stock answer. "I just want to catch 'em."

The catch people remember most was the one he made off Vic Wertz in the 1954 World Series between the New York Giants and the Cleveland Indians. It was a catch that helped win the Series, but the one that he made off Bobby Morgan of the Brooklyn Dodgers at Ebbets Field in 1952 gave him even more satisfaction, he says.

Willie remembers the Giants were leading by a run in the eighth inning, and Morgan, a pinch hitter, sent a screamer down the alley in left center close to the wall to the right of the 351-foot sign. Willie ran as hard as he could and at the last instant, threw himself, glove outstretched, into a headfirst dive. He hit the wall hard and knocked himself unconscious.

"The next thing I knew," Mays says, "Leo Durocher was bending over me and asking if I was all right.

" 'Where's the ball?' I asked. 'Did I catch it?'

" 'You caught it all right, kid,' Durocher said. 'The umpire ran out, rolled you over and took the ball out of your glove.' "

When Mays jogged back to the bench, he passed Jackie Robinson. "Willie," said Jackie, "that was the most amazing catch I ever saw."

Mays's catch of Wertz's drive in the 1954 Series brought him the greatest publicity. The score was tied at 2–2 in the eighth inning. Sal Maglie was locked in a pitching duel with Cleveland's Bob Lemon. Larry Doby led off with a walk, and Al Rosen beat out an infield hit. With runners on first and second and nobody out, Wertz stepped to the plate, having tripled in the first, singled in the fourth, and singled again in the sixth.

The Indians had been hitting Maglie pretty well throughout the game but had had trouble scoring. Leo Durocher figured Sal's luck might have run out, so he sent to the bullpen for Don Liddle, a left-hander.

Wertz, a left-handed hitter, swung at Liddle's first pitch. The instant Mays saw Wertz's bat swing around, he was running. Willie sped toward the bleachers with his back to the plate. He caught up to the ball about 10 feet from the wall in front of the bleachers in right center. With his back to the plate and his arms outstretched, he

*Mays unleashes strong throw as the runner tags up.*

gloved the ball on the dead run 460 feet from the plate.

Perhaps even more amazing than the catch itself was the ensuing throw. Mays still had to turn around and get the ball away, which he somehow did before he went sprawling. Davey Williams took the throw in back of second and held Doby to one base after the catch, permitting the Giants to escape the inning without a Cleveland score.

Mays made another defensive gem two innings later that hardly anybody noticed. Oddly enough, it too was against Wertz. The score was still tied at 2–2 when the Indians came up in the tenth. By this time Marv Grissom, a right-hander, was pitching for the Giants. Wertz slammed a screwball, Grissom's best pitch, up the left center slot. Mays claims it was a tougher chance than the previous Wertz drive. The vicious line drive bounced and headed between the outfielders toward the bleacher wall, but Mays, running at full speed, managed to spear it backhanded and held Wertz to a double. Had it gone through, it would have been an inside-the-park home run.

Wertz advanced to third on a sacrifice. Grissom walked Dave Pope, struck out Bill Glynn, a pinch hitter, and retired Bob Lemon for the final out on a hot liner to Whitey Lockman at first. In the Giants' tenth after Mays had walked and stolen second, Bob Lemon issued an intentional pass to Hank Thompson in the hope of setting up a double play. But pinch hitter Dusty Rhodes foiled the strategy and won the game with a homer.

October 4, 1955

# The Dodgers Finally Win the World Series

### Brooklyn (NL)

| | AB | R | H | PO | A |
|---|---|---|---|---|---|
| Gilliam, lf-2b | 4 | 0 | 1 | 2 | 0 |
| Reese, ss | 4 | 1 | 1 | 2 | 6 |
| Snider, cf | 3 | 0 | 0 | 2 | 0 |
| Campanella, c | 3 | 1 | 1 | 5 | 0 |
| Furillo, rf | 3 | 0 | 0 | 3 | 0 |
| Hodges, 1b | 2 | 0 | 1 | 10 | 0 |
| Hoak, 3b | 3 | 0 | 1 | 1 | 1 |
| Zimmer, 2b | 2 | 0 | 0 | 0 | 2 |
| a Shuba | 1 | 0 | 0 | 0 | 0 |
| Amoros, lf | 0 | 0 | 0 | 2 | 1 |
| Podres, p | 4 | 0 | 0 | 0 | 1 |
| Total | 29 | 2 | 5 | 27 | 11 |

### New York (AL)

| | AB | R | H | PO | A |
|---|---|---|---|---|---|
| Rizzuto, ss | 3 | 0 | 1 | 1 | 3 |
| Martin, 2b | 3 | 0 | 1 | 1 | 6 |
| McDougald, ss | 4 | 0 | 3 | 1 | 1 |
| Berra, c | 4 | 0 | 1 | 4 | 1 |
| Bauer, rf | 4 | 0 | 1 | 1 | 0 |
| Skowron, 1b | 4 | 0 | 1 | 11 | 1 |
| Cerv, cf | 4 | 0 | 0 | 5 | 0 |
| Howard, lf | 4 | 0 | 1 | 2 | 0 |
| Byrne, p | 2 | 0 | 0 | 0 | 2 |
| Grim, p | 0 | 0 | 0 | 1 | 0 |
| b Mantle | 1 | 0 | 0 | 0 | 0 |
| Turley, p | 0 | 0 | 0 | 0 | 0 |
| Total | 33 | 0 | 8 | 27 | 14 |

a—Grounded out for Zimmer in sixth.
b—Popped out for Grim in seventh.

| | | |
|---|---|---|
| **Brooklyn** | 0 0 0 1 0 1 0 0 0 | —2 |
| **New York** | 0 0 0 0 0 0 0 0 0 | —0 |

Error—Skowron. Runs batted in—Hodges 2. Two-base hits—Skowron, Campanella, Berra. Sacrifices—Snider, Campanella. Sacrifice fly—Hodges. Double play—Amoros, Reese, and Hodges. Left on base—Brooklyn 8, New York 8. Bases on balls—Byrne 3, Grim 1, Turley 1, Podres 2. Struck out—Byrne 2, Grim 1, Turley 1, Podres 4. Hits off—Byrne, 3 in 5 1/3; Grim, 1 in 1 2/3; Turley, 1 in 2. Wild pitch—Grim. Loser—Byrne. Umpires—Honochick (AL), Dascoli (NL), Sommers (AL), Ballanfant (NL), Flaherty (AL), and Donatelli (NL). Time—2:44. Attendance—62,465.

They moved the Dodgers. There's talk of dismantling the bridge. Even Coney Island isn't what it used to be. Things have changed in big and boisterous Brooklyn. But there's one day no one can take away from those who lived and died with their dear old Brooklyn Dodgers.

For these fans nothing will ever match the red-letter day of October 4, 1955, when the Dodgers beat the New York Yankees 2–0 in the seventh and deciding game of the World Series. In one blazing afternoon, the Dodgers wiped out long years of frustration and defeat.

At precisely 3:43 P.M. in Yankee Stadium, a new champion was born. From Greenpoint to Red Hook, from Sea Gate to Bushwick, from Coney Island to Flatbush, in every street and corner of Brooklyn, joy was unconfined. For the first time, a Brooklyn team had become the undisputed ruler of baseball. At the finish, when Pee Wee Reese threw out Elston Howard for the twenty-seventh out, the capacity-filled stadium exploded with emotion as the entire Dodgers team raced to maul their pitcher, a young, broad-shouldered, blue-eyed, straw-thatched southpaw named Johnny Podres. Nor did they forget a short, stocky, sawed-off gnome of an outfielder named Sandy Amoros, whose amazing catch had preserved Podres's shutout and prevented a certain tie.

*Sandy Amoros's great catch came as quite a surprise to Yankee base runners. Here Gil McDougald is doubled off first after the catch.*

All eyes are on Amoros as he makes his spectacular running catch of Yogi Berra's line drive. Opposite: A closer look at the magical catch that ensured Brooklyn its first and only world championship.

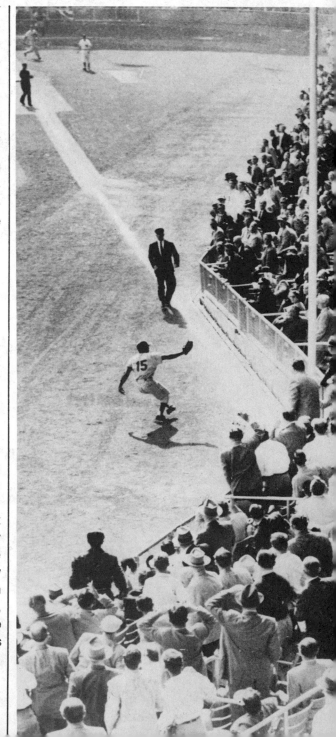

It was no longer a dream. After seven fruitless tries, the Dodgers were world champions. They had overcome baseball's most formidable barrier, the 21-time American League champion Yankees, on the magnificent pitching of Podres, a 23-year-old kid from Witherbee, New York, who had had only a 9–10 record during the regular season. It was Podres who set the dispirited Dodgers back on the right road, defeating the Yankees in Ebbets Field after the Bronx Bombers had taken the first two games of the Series and appeared headed for their sixth straight World Series triumph over the Dodgers. That first victory over the Yankees was the thrill of Podres's life—it had come on his twenty-third birthday.

Four days later, young Johnny Podres became the most talked about pitcher in baseball. His opponent on October 4 was 35-year-old Tommy Byrne, who had pitched a strong five-hitter against the Dodgers in the second game of the Series.

Byrne pitched well but Podres pitched even better, especially in the clutch. Five times Podres found himself in a jam as the Yankees fought bitterly to maintain their supremacy over the Dodgers. Each time he came through brilliantly. The Dodgers drew first blood, scoring a run in the fourth and another in the sixth. Gil Hodges, the big, amiable first baseman, who had gone 0 for 21 in the 1952 Series

his gloved hand to snare the ball before he collided with the barrier.

Martin and McDougald, not believing the catch possible, had been moving. Suddenly they had to reverse themselves, but McDougald had passed second and was doubled up as Reese took Amoros's accurate throw and relayed perfectly to Hodges at first. Reese then threw out the next batter, Hank Bauer, to end the inning.

Podres had to pitch out of still another jam in the eighth when Phil Rizzuto led off with a single and McDougald also singled after Martin had flied out. But Podres got Berra on a pop-up and threw a third strike past Bauer.

The Dodgers still led 2–0 as the Yankees came up in the ninth. Bill Skowron hit back to the box. Bob Cerv lifted a high fly to Amoros. Now only Elston Howard loomed between Podres and victory. The count on the Yankee hitter went to two and two. Podres shook off two signs from Roy Campanella and came in with a tantalizing change-up. Howard stepped forward, hesitated, then slapped a gentle ground ball to Reese, and there it was. Reese's strong throw to Hodges ended the game.

The bartenders in Brooklyn were pouring free drinks, women with babies in their arms were dancing in the streets. There would be no more "wait 'til next year."

and had been frustrated again in this one, finally had a good day. He drove in both runs.

Fortified with these two runs, Podres and the tenacious, inspired Dodgers fought to hold their advantage to the end.

In the sixth inning, a walk to Billy Martin and Gil McDougald's surprise bunt put two Yankees on base with nobody out. Then came the key play, the one that meant the championship. Yogi Berra came to the plate and left fielder Sandy Amoros moved over to left center for Berra, normally a right field hitter. (At the start of the inning, Amoros had taken over in left field for Jim Gilliam, who moved to second base.)

Berra crossed up Amoros by stroking a long, high fly down the left field line, about a foot inside fair territory. Amoros had to run 100 feet even to get to the ball. He ran full tilt toward the stands, twisted his body, and extended

May 19–28, 1956

# Dale Long: Eight Games, Eight Home Runs

Once in a lifetime, a journeyman ball-player, forever concerned with keeping his job, suddenly gets his day in the sun. Journeyman Dale Long spent 12 years playing for 15 clubs in 12 leagues before he got his chance.

The Dale Long epic began on Saturday, May 19, 1956. Playing against the Chicago Cubs in Forbes Field, the Pirates' first baseman, then 30 years old, hit a home run off left-hander Jim Davis. The next day, in a doubleheader with the Braves, he hit one off right-hander Ray Crone in the first game and one off southpaw Warren Spahn in the second game. Then he connected off Herm Wehmeier and Lindy McDaniel of the Cardinals in the next two games; five games, five homers. The record for home runs in consecutive games was six, held jointly by five players.

"I had been feeling loose," Long recalls. "Now it was getting to me. The next day, against Curt Simmons [a left-hander] of the Phillies, I hit my sixth. It really began to bother me then."

Pressure has a mechanical way of building. At the park the next day, a gang of photographers had Dale pose during batting practice with seven bats. "But what if I don't hit my seventh today?" he asked them. They just smiled and mumbled that they had to be prepared in case he did.

The strain showed as Long went after number seven. Each time he came up he would hold his 33-ounce, 35-inch bat at the end and swing from the heels. Up for the last time in the eighth inning, Long slashed at a fastball thrown by Ben Flowers and missed. He swung at the Phillie right-hander's next pitch and missed again. But somehow he managed to catch the third pitch and drive it out of the park. After he crossed the plate, his teammates literally picked him up and carried him into the dugout to the cheers of the crowd.

It rained the next day, Sunday, a long day for Dale Long. An agent called and wanted him to make an appearance on the "Ed Sullivan Show." Joe Brown, the general manager, called and gave him a raise. A Pittsburgh bread company and a milk firm paid him to endorse their products. A Philadelphia brewery signed him to praise their brew. A cigarette company hired him to plug their brand. A Dale Long T-shirt was rushed onto the market.

On Monday night, May 28, against Brooklyn, Long was struck out by Carl Erskine in the first inning, but in the fourth he connected with a curve ball thrown by the right-hander and sent a screaming liner into the right field seats, his eighth homer in eight straight games. It won the ball game, 3–2.

"When I hit it, I didn't think it was going in," Long said. "The ball just did clear the right field wall in Forbes Field."

As he passed manager Bobby Bragan coaching at third base, Dale smiled weakly and shook his head. Bragan shook his head back at him. Neither could understand it. After he touched home, with the entire Pirates team there to pound him on the back, Long trotted into the dugout. The 32,221 fans who had come out to see him refused to allow the game to continue until Dale came out for a bow. Erskine tried to pitch to Frank Thomas, the next batter, but the fans kept screaming until Long popped his head out of the dugout, doffed his cap, and waved.

In the eight games, Long batted .538 with 15 hits and 20 runs batted in. He had the Pirates fighting for the pennant. Dale didn't go to bed until 2:30 in the morning after the eighth game. At 4:00 A.M. the telephone rang. It was a publicity man asking if he wanted to go on the "Today" show that morning. He said yes and went back to sleep. At 7:00 A.M. he got up, dressed, and drove out to the Pittsburgh television studio for the interview. Then he had breakfast and drove to the park. Several hours later, Don Newcombe of the Dodgers stopped his streak.

"The newspaper fellows wrote afterward that Newcombe overpowered me," said Long, "but the fact is I was tired. I was so beat I couldn't get my bat around. You can't do that and face Newcombe and expect to hit a homer."

The streak was over but things were still going well. Number eight had been Dale's fourteenth homer of the season and had put him six days ahead of Babe Ruth's pace when he hit his record 60 in 1927. Long was leading the league in RBIs, and he was hitting .420. For a while at least, Long stayed hot, and so did the Pirates. The dizzy pace lasted for almost a month. Then Long and the Pirates hit the skids.

"I felt it coming," Long said. "I was beginning to get weak. I couldn't get the bat around. I didn't feel comfortable."

The good feeling never came back. He could remember exactly what he had been doing with the bat before, but he could no longer do it. By August he was being rested for a day or two at a time. By September, he was benched in favor of young Bob Skinner. By the season's end, his batting average had plummeted to .263, although he led the club with 27 home runs and 91 runs batted in. While the bottom hadn't fallen out, his headline days were over

May 30, 1956

# Mickey Mantle: The Home Run that Just Missed

*Mickey Mantle receives handshakes from teammates after his prodigious blast.*

"On two legs Mickey Mantle would have been the greatest player who ever lived. The man hit five hundred thirty-six home runs and did everything else on one leg," says Elston Howard. "I played with him ten years, and I can't remember when he wasn't hurting, but he never mentioned it. He was the greatest competitor I've ever known and the most inspiring leader. If he had been physically sound for a full season he would have hit seventy homers."

Dr. Sydney Gaynor, the New York Yankees' team physician: "It was truly remarkable that Mickey Mantle could play as long as he did on those legs of his, and it took a remarkable amount of determination to do it. He had two operations on his right knee and finally developed arthritis in it. He had operations on his left knee, right hip, and shoulders. He had a broken foot and several broken fingers. He had at least six painfully pulled hamstring muscles in his career and numerous muscle tears in his thighs and groin. For more than ten years, he played with elastic bandages wrapped around his right leg from mid-calf to upper thigh."

Mantle's career stretched 18 major league seasons with the Yankees and established him as one of the great players of our time. His tremendous power, his determination to play despite terrible injuries, his speed, his switch-hitting prowess, and his mammoth home runs are his legacy to the game.

Mantle could hit a baseball as could few men. Babe Ruth, Jimmy Foxx, and Hank Greenberg all hit the ball for great distances, yet the era of the "tape-measure" homer didn't arrive until Mantle did. On April 17, 1953, in old Griffith Stadium in Washington, Mickey unloaded a drive that carried over the left field fence, over the bleachers, and halfway up the scoreboard in back of the bleachers. The ball ticked the side of the scoreboard and flew out of the park, landing across the street. The next day, the papers carried the news that Mantle had hit the ball 565 feet. The press agent of the Yankees, Red Patterson, had found a tape measure and measured the distance.

Then, in Chicago, Mantle hit one 550 feet. In an exhibition game at Forbes Field, Pittsburgh, he cleared the right field stands, which only Babe Ruth and one Ted Beard had done. In the 1960 World Series, batting right-handed, Mickey cleared the right center field wall at Forbes Field. No one had done that before.

Ever since Yankee Stadium was built in 1923, fans have been asking the same question: "Has anyone ever hit a fair ball out of Yankee Stadium?" No, but Mickey Mantle came close on Memorial Day, 1956.

Batting left-handed against Pedro Ramos of the Washington Senators with two men on base in the fifth inning of the first game, Mantle connected with a fastball with all his power. The ball soared majestically high and far toward the right field roof. For a couple of breathless seconds, it looked as if Mantle had done it.

He just missed. The ball struck near the top of the roof's facade, high above the third deck in right field. Nobody had ever come close to hitting that copper filagree. Mantle hit it. The ball struck high on the facade, barely a foot or two from the edge of the roof. The ball might have gone over had it had help from the wind, but Mickey had hit the drive *against* a quartering breeze. The point of contact on the facade was 370 feet from home plate, 118 feet above the field level.

Those who saw this majestic drive could hardly believe it. "I didn't believe it myself," says Mickey now. "Even when I saw it, I couldn't believe it."

To this day as people come into Yankee Stadium and find their seats, invariably their eyes wander to the spot. Arms point, and people stare in admiration and skepticism. "Did Mantle really hit it there? Did anybody?"

*Arrow shows path of long homer.*

October 8, 1956

# Don Larsen: The Perfect World Series Game

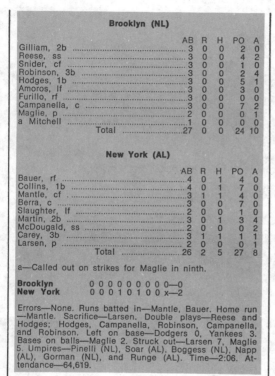

**Brooklyn (NL)**

| | AB | R | H | PO | A |
|---|---|---|---|---|---|
| Gilliam, 2b | 3 | 0 | 0 | 2 | 0 |
| Reese, ss | 3 | 0 | 0 | 4 | 2 |
| Snider, cf | 3 | 0 | 0 | 1 | 0 |
| Robinson, 3b | 3 | 0 | 0 | 2 | 4 |
| Hodges, 1b | 3 | 0 | 0 | 5 | 1 |
| Amoros, lf | 3 | 0 | 0 | 3 | 0 |
| Furillo, rf | 3 | 0 | 0 | 0 | 0 |
| Campanella, c | 3 | 0 | 0 | 7 | 2 |
| Maglie, p | 2 | 0 | 0 | 0 | 1 |
| a Mitchell | 1 | 0 | 0 | 0 | 0 |
| Total | 27 | 0 | 0 | 24 | 10 |

**New York (AL)**

| | AB | R | H | PO | A |
|---|---|---|---|---|---|
| Bauer, rf | 4 | 0 | 1 | 4 | 0 |
| Collins, 1b | 4 | 0 | 1 | 7 | 0 |
| Mantle, cf | 3 | 1 | 1 | 4 | 0 |
| Berra, c | 3 | 0 | 0 | 7 | 0 |
| Slaughter, lf | 2 | 0 | 0 | 1 | 0 |
| Martin, 2b | 3 | 0 | 1 | 3 | 4 |
| McDougald, ss | 2 | 0 | 0 | 0 | 2 |
| Carey, 3b | 3 | 1 | 1 | 1 | 1 |
| Larsen, p | 2 | 0 | 0 | 0 | 1 |
| Total | 26 | 2 | 5 | 27 | 8 |

a—Called out on strikes for Maglie in ninth.

| Brooklyn | 0 0 0 0 0 0 0 0 0—0 |
|---|---|
| New York | 0 0 0 1 0 1 0 0 x—2 |

Errors—None. Runs batted in—Mantle, Bauer. Home run —Mantle. Sacrifice—Larsen. Double plays—Reese and Hodges; Hodges, Campanella, Robinson, Campanella, and Robinson. Left on base—Dodgers 0, Yankees 3. Bases on balls—Maglie 2. Struck out—Larsen 7, Maglie 5. Umpires—Pinelli (NL), Soar (AL), Boggess (NL), Napp (AL), Gorman (NL), and Runge (AL). Time—2:06. Attendance—64,619.

A no-hitter perhaps, but a perfect game in World Series competition, and from this unheralded, undistinguished right-hander? It was hard to believe. Yet here was tall, 27-year-old Don Larsen standing on the mound and methodically setting down the Brooklyn Dodgers' power hitters almost as soon as they came to the plate. Pitching with no windup, the uninhibited right-hander was succeeding where the greatest pitchers in the game had failed. Yet only two years before, he had won 3 and lost 21, and only four days before, he had failed to last two innings against the Dodgers.

While 64,619 spectators in Yankee Stadium grew progressively more fidgety, Don Larsen calmly achieved the impossible. Seemingly unperturbed amidst the vast stadium's deceiving shadows and smoky haze, he would just shimmy his shoulders, shake his arm, peer at the squatting Yogi Berra, straighten up, and with a minimum of windup throw the ball as if he and Yogi were playing catch in a backyard.

For the fans his nonchalance made the performance even more difficult to believe. Whenever a Robinson, a Snider, a Campanella, or a Hodges would step in waving a bat menacingly, they suspected the magic couldn't continue. But it did.

By the eighth inning, every pitch brought an explosive gasp from the crowd, followed by a nervous, incom-

PINELLI   BERRA   MITCHELL   HERMAN   NAPP   CAREY   LARS

The final pitch of Yankee Don Larsen's perfect game: Brooklyn Dodgers pinch hitter Dale Mitchell is called out on strikes. Larsen's feat remains unequaled in World Series competition.

prehensible babbling that seemed to sweep through the stands in waves. Then the spectators would again edge forward in their seats, breathing softly as if any harshly spoken word or sudden movement might break the spell.

Larsen got through the eighth inning unscathed, and when he walked to the plate for his turn at bat to start the last of the eighth, the crowd gave him an ovation unequaled in Yankee Stadium history. Perhaps the cheers served as an outlet for the accumulated tension, or perhaps the fans just wanted to tell Larsen that even if the Dodgers finally opened up in the top of the ninth, they appreciated his effort.

That half inning—the toughest part of the job—lay just ahead. The veteran baseball writers, hardened over the years, looked at each other and shrugged or smiled wanly. They remembered Bill Bevens and his bid for a no-hitter in Brooklyn that was ruined by a double with two down in the ninth.

This was more than a no-hitter. Even a man reaching first by an error or a walk would tarnish Larsen's game. Twenty-four Dodgers had walked up to the plate, and all had been quickly, if not always easily, returned to the bench.

Larsen's perfect game had been in jeopardy five times. In the second inning, Jackie Robinson's line shot jumped out of Andy Carey's glove, but shortstop Gil McDougald fielded it in time. In the fifth Mickey Mantle, whose home run off Sal Maglie the inning before had given the Yankees a 1–0 lead, made a spectacular backhand catch of Gil Hodges's long drive to left center. Also in the fifth, Sandy Amoros's liner abruptly turned foul just as it reached the seats for what would have been a homer. McDougald made a fine play on Junior Gilliam in the seventh, and in the eighth Hodges hit a tricky low liner to the left of third base that Carey caught inches off the ground. True, Larsen had help from his teammates, but what pitcher doesn't?

Three outs to go. Carl Furillo, first up, flied out. Roy Campanella bounced out to McDougald. Dale Mitchell, a pinch hitter, came out of the Dodgers' dugout. Don Larsen was no longer nonchalant. The burden of baseball history was on his big-boned, slouching shoulders. He turned his back to the batter who stood between him and baseball's first perfect game in the World Series.

"I was so weak in the knees out there in the ninth inning," Larsen recalls,"I thought I was going to faint. Before I got Campanella to bounce out, he hit a long drive that I was sure would be a home run. But it curved foul at the last second. I was so nervous, I almost fell down. My legs were rubbery, and my fingers didn't feel like they were on my hand. I said to myself, 'Please help me out, somebody.' "

The crowd sent up a groan as Larsen's first pitch to Mitchell went wide. Don came back with a slider for a called strike. His next pitch was a fastball that Mitchell swung on and missed. Don threw another fastball, and Mitchell fouled it into the stands. By now the crowd was screaming with every pitch. Peering through the haze, Larsen caught Berra's signal for yet another hard one. He mumbled a prayer to himself: "Please help me get out of this." Then he pitched. As the ball shaved the outside corner, Mitchell cocked his bat, then held up. Umpire Babe Pinelli thrust his arm through the air in the out motion that ended the game, and all hell broke loose.

Berra raced toward the mound and hurled his stubby body into Larsen's arms. The other Yankees poured from the dugout to bury their hero under an avalanche of hugs, slaps, and violent handshakes. Frenzied fans tumbled from the stands to get their licks at the beleaguered pitcher before he disappeared down the steps into the Yankees' dugout.

Yankee Stadium had witnessed something never seen before and quite likely never to be seen again. The nearly 65,000 spectators will recount the story with pride enough to make it seem that their presence made the historic feat possible.

April 22, 1959

# Eleven Runs on One Hit

Ever since 1906, when the White Sox won the American League pennant despite hitting only seven home runs and finishing dead last in the league in team batting, the sobriquet "Hitless Wonders" has haunted the Chicago team. More often than not through the seasons, the White Sox' attack has more or less justified the name. In 1908, they hit only three home runs. In 1918, they boosted that total to eight. In the spacious expanse of White Sox Stadium, power hitters have always been at a distinct disadvantage.

Only one Chicago player has ever led the American League in batting, Hall of Famer Luke Appling, who paced all hitters in 1936 and in 1943. Only one White Sox player, Nellie Fox, has ever led the junior circuit in hits, and it was not until 1971 that the White Sox were able to boast a home run king, Bill Melton. When Dick Allen equaled Melton's achievement in 1972, he also became the first White Sox player in history to lead the American League in runs batted in.

Chicago baseball writers have long described a typical White Sox rally as a base on balls, a stolen base, a wild pitch, and a passed ball. On the night of April 22, 1959, in Kansas City, the White Sox tested the descriptive powers of the most imaginative sports writers.

The Sox had been in a batting slump, even for them. Manager Al Lopez, exasperated by the lack of hitting, brought his players out for a 2½-hour batting drill on the morning of the game. The workout seemed less than beneficial when in the early stages of the game the Sox fell behind, 6–1. Still, they fought back, scoring in four successive innings to grab an 8–6 lead entering the seventh inning.

Then came 45 minutes of misadventure—one of the most bizarre innings ever played in a major league baseball game.

Tom Gorman, the A's third pitcher, began the inning for Kansas City. Ray Boone, the first batter to face him, reached base when Joe DeMaestri, the shortstop, threw Boone's grounder wide of first. Al Smith, intending to sacrifice Boone to second, was himself safe when Hal Smith, the third baseman, fumbled the bunt. Johnny Callison singled to right, scoring Boone, and when Roger Maris misplayed the ball, Smith scored and Callison wound up on third. Gorman must have been upset, as any pitcher has a right to be when his fielders commit errors on the first three batters he faces. Gorman walked Luis Aparicio, who promptly stole second. When Gorman walked pitcher Bob Shaw, filling the bases, manager Harry Craft of the A's decided he had seen enough of his pitcher. (Not incidentally perhaps, Gorman retired after the 1959 season.)

Craft summoned Mark Freeman, another right-hander, from the bullpen, but Freeman had caught the wildness bug. He walked both Earl Torgeson and Nellie Fox with the bases full, forcing in two more runs. Jim Landis bounced to the mound, and Freeman, with efficiency uncharacteristic of the A's fielders this night, forced Shaw at the plate for the first out. But Freeman returned to form with a walk to Sherman Lollar that sent Torgeson home and brought in George Brunet, the third pitcher in one-third of an inning.

Brunet too couldn't find the strike zone. His walk to Boone, batting for the second time in the inning, brought Fox home with the inning's sixth run, and a free pass to Smith pushed Landis across with another. Varying the monotony, Brunet hit Callison with a pitched ball, scoring Lollar, but then settled down to walk Aparicio, sending Boone home. Pitcher Shaw obligingly struck out, no doubt embarassed for his colleague. Free of such inhibitions, Bubba Church pinch walked for Torgeson, forcing in the tenth run, and Fox walked, accounting for the eleventh. Only Jim Landis retained a sense of propriety. For the second time in the inning, he tapped a bouncer back to the pitcher, Brunet this time, who threw to first for the third out and an end to the agony.

The total: 11 runs on exactly one hit, Callison's single. Three jittery Kansas City pitchers issued 10 bases on balls, one short of the record, and hit a batter.

Led by manager Al Lopez, front center, the
1959 "Go Sox" celebrate the first
Chicago White Sox pennant in 40 years.

The A's defense committed three errors. Only 2 of the 11 runs were earned.

The morning batting drill, however, had not been in vain. The White Sox, when they weren't reaching base on A's miscues, amassed sixteen hits in their 20–6 triumph. They even had six extra-base hits, including a home run by Aparicio, who banged three hits, scored four runs, and drove in four. Nellie Fox had three singles and a double besides his two walks.

The game may have been a portent. Al Lopez's rejuvenated "White Sockers" went on to capture the American League pennant, their first in 40 years.

May 26, 1959

# Harvey Haddix: The Imperfect Masterpiece

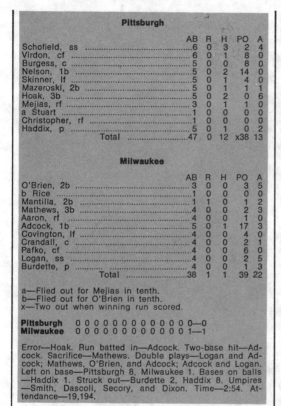

**Pittsburgh**

| | AB | R | H | PO | A |
|---|---|---|---|---|---|
| Schofield, ss | 6 | 0 | 3 | 2 | 4 |
| Virdon, cf | 6 | 0 | 1 | 8 | 0 |
| Burgess, c | 5 | 0 | 0 | 8 | 0 |
| Nelson, 1b | 5 | 0 | 2 | 14 | 0 |
| Skinner, lf | 5 | 0 | 1 | 4 | 0 |
| Mazeroski, 2b | 5 | 0 | 1 | 1 | 1 |
| Hoak, 3b | 5 | 0 | 2 | 0 | 6 |
| Mejias, rf | 3 | 0 | 1 | 1 | 0 |
| a Stuart | 1 | 0 | 0 | 0 | 0 |
| Christopher, rf | 1 | 0 | 0 | 0 | 0 |
| Haddix, p | 5 | 0 | 1 | 0 | 2 |
| Total | 47 | 0 | 12 | x38 | 13 |

**Milwaukee**

| | AB | R | H | PO | A |
|---|---|---|---|---|---|
| O'Brien, 2b | 3 | 0 | 0 | 3 | 5 |
| b Rice | 1 | 0 | 0 | 0 | 0 |
| Mantilla, 2b | 1 | 1 | 0 | 1 | 2 |
| Mathews, 3b | 4 | 0 | 0 | 2 | 3 |
| Aaron, rf | 4 | 0 | 0 | 1 | 0 |
| Adcock, 1b | 5 | 0 | 1 | 17 | 3 |
| Covington, lf | 4 | 0 | 0 | 4 | 0 |
| Crandall, c | 4 | 0 | 0 | 2 | 1 |
| Pafko, cf | 4 | 0 | 0 | 6 | 0 |
| Logan, ss | 4 | 0 | 0 | 2 | 5 |
| Burdette, p | 4 | 0 | 0 | 1 | 3 |
| Total | 38 | 1 | 1 | 39 | 22 |

a—Flied out for Mejias in tenth.
b—Flied out for O'Brien in tenth.
x—Two out when winning run scored.

| | | | |
|---|---|---|---|
| **Pittsburgh** | 0 0 0 0 0 0 0 0 0 0 0 0 0 | 0—0 |
| **Milwaukee** | 0 0 0 0 0 0 0 0 0 0 0 0 1 | 1—1 |

Error—Hoak. Run batted in—Adcock. Two-base hit—Adcock. Sacrifice—Mathews. Double plays—Logan and Adcock; Mathews, O'Brien, and Adcock; Adcock and Logan. Left on base—Pittsburgh 8, Milwaukee 1. Bases on balls —Haddix 1. Struck out—Burdette 2, Haddix 8. Umpires —Smith, Dascoli, Secory, and Dixon. Time—2:54. Attendance—19,194.

"A pitcher does this once in a lifetime —once in baseball history—and we can't win the game for him!"

Bill Virdon, the bespectacled Pittsburgh outfielder, made this most fitting comment in the visitors' dressing room of Milwaukee's County Stadium. It was shortly after the Braves had inflicted a 1–0 defeat in 13 grueling innings on Harvey Haddix and the Pirates.

"It still hurts," says Haddix today, nearly 15 years later. "It was a damn silly one to lose."

On a cold and threatening evening on May 26, 1959, Harvey Haddix, nursing a cold, had gone out in quest of his fourth win of the season. The little left-hander faced a team that had won two consecutive pennants and would lose out only in a play-off this year. The Braves had such hitters as Henry Aaron, Joe Adcock, Eddie Mathews, Wes Covington, Del Crandall, Andy Pafko, and Johnny Logan. Even Lew Burdette, the opposing pitcher, was no automatic out.

There was little reason to suspect that Haddix would turn in one of the greatest pitching performances in the long history of the game. A small, boyish-looking left-hander, Haddix hadn't accomplished much since winning 20 games for the St. Louis Cardinals in 1953. Since then, he had toiled without distinction for Cincinnati and Philadelphia before the Pirates acquired him in the winter of 1958.

*Pirates southpaw Harvey Haddix had masterful form as he retired every Milwaukee Braves batter to face him in 12 straight innings.*

Now 33 years old, Haddix was taking on the league-leading Braves. Milwaukee manager Fred Haney had stacked his lineup with seven right-handed batters. The only lefties were Mathews and Covington.

After Burdette had set down the Pirates in order in the first inning, Haddix returned the compliment by retiring Johnny O'Brien, Mathews, and Aaron. In the third inning, Logan drilled a hard liner that shortstop Dick Schofield caught with a short leap. In the sixth Logan again hit one between short and third, and Schofield again came to the rescue, this time with a deft scoop of the grounder and a long throw.

"I threw good right from the start," recalls Haddix. "I used two pitches mainly—fastball and slider. I was hardly behind on anybody, and I only went three-and-two on one man."

The crowd of 19,194 encouraged Haddix with standing ovations after each inning. It had started to rain in the seventh, but nothing seemed to bother Haddix. By the end of the eighth, he had retired 24 batters in a row. Only seven major league pitchers had hurled and won perfect games. But the Pirates weren't winning.

"We had a couple of threats," Haddix says. "A base-running blunder by Roman Mejias cost us a chance." The Pirates had put together three hits in the third, but Mejias was cut down trying to go from first to third on an infield single. They got two hits in the ninth but again failed to push across a run when Bob Skinner lined out to first baseman Joe Adcock with men on first and third. The Braves also turned in three double plays to erase three other hits by the Pirates.

In the last of the ninth, Pafko struck out, and Logan flied to Skinner in left. Haddix worked carefully to Burdette and sent him down swinging. He had pitched a perfect game for nine innings, but obviously, he would have to continue to pitch.

Haddix got through the tenth, eleventh, and twelfth without trouble. The standing ovations after each inning grew more fervent. Although the score was still 0–0, Haddix had already made baseball history. No one had ever pitched a no-hit game for more than eleven innings, much less a perfect game for more than nine.

Still, the Pirates couldn't reach Burdette. He gave up his twelfth hit in the Pittsburgh thirteenth, but Pittsburgh couldn't score. And then, disaster. Felix Mantilla, who had replaced O'Brien, led off the Braves' thirteenth with a routine ground ball to Don Hoak at third base. Hoak fielded the ball easily but threw it into the dirt. The ball bounced off first baseman Rocky Nelson's knee. Milwaukee had its first base runner, and Haddix had lost his perfect game.

"I thought I had Mantilla struck out on the pitch before," Haddix remembers. "If the umpire had called it a strike, Mantilla would have been out of there. I'll never forget that play. Hoak had all night after picking up the ball. He looked at the seams . . . then threw it away."

Mathews sacrificed Mantilla to second, and Haddix purposely passed Henry Aaron, hoping to set up a double play for Joe Adcock. "Maybe I should have walked Adcock, too," muses Haddix now. But pitching to the ponderous first baseman seemed like good strategy at the time. Adcock had struck out twice and grounded out twice. Now, with the count one ball and no strikes, Adcock hit a high slider toward right center. "I tried to keep a slider down and away," Haddix said later, "but I got it up too high." Virdon dashed back to the wire fence and leaped frantically, but it was no use. The ball dropped over the fence for a homer—end of no-hitter, and of game.

The 19,914 stunned fans watched as Adcock began to circle the bases. However, Aaron, who had touched second base, figured the ball had dropped at the bottom of the fence instead of over it. Assuming that when Mantilla scored the game would be officially over, Aaron headed toward the Braves' dugout while Adcock, running with his head down, reached third base and was declared out for passing Aaron.

Despite the bizarre finale, the game had ended, and Milwaukee had won.

The following day, National League president Warren Giles nullified Aaron's run and ruled that the official score of the game was 1–0. But the score was of no importance to Haddix. "All I knew was that I lost," he says.

September 16, 1960, April 28, 1961

# Warren Spahn: No-hitters at 39 and 40

*Warren Spahn pitches his first career no-hitter.*

It took Warren Spahn nearly a lifetime to realize his greatest ambition. In 15 seasons with the Braves, he had won almost every honor that a pitcher can. Truly one of the greats in the game, Spahn had a dozen 20-game seasons. He finished with the most victories and most shutouts ever registered by a left-handed pitcher. He led the National League in almost every category—victories, complete games, shutouts, strikeouts—but it wasn't until his sixteenth season, when he was nearly 40 years old, that he finally got what he wanted most, a no-hit, no-run game.

He had never before pitched a no-hitter, not even in the minors, and he was beginning to think he never would. In 1953, Richie Ashburn beat out a high hopper to the mound in the seventh inning and ruined what would have been a perfect game for Spahn. Two years earlier, Warren had lost a no-hitter when Al Brazle, the old Cardinals pitcher, nicked him for a pop fly single in back of second base. That one had really hurt.

But there was no stopping the man on September 16, 1960. No one even came close to getting a base hit as Spahn handcuffed the Philadelphia Phillies 4–0. Only two batters reached base, both on passes. Neither got past first. To make the long-sought no-hitter more memorable, Spahn struck out 15 batters, an all-time high for him and all Braves pitchers in nine innings.

The Braves only tough play came on the final out of the game. Bob Malkmus hit a sharp liner back to the mound. Spahn barely got his glove on it, slowing it down for shortstop Johnny Logan, who dashed in, scooped it up, and in the same motion fired to first baseman Joe Adcock. The hurried throw sailed a bit wide, but Adcock gloved it with his foot on the bag. Malkmus was nailed at first base, and Spahn had his first no-hitter.

Spahnie looks back on that day with fond memories. "You know," he says, "I think I've got to give credit for my first no-hitter to my old roomie, Lew Burdette. If he hadn't pitched his no-hitter, I don't think I would have gotten mine."

Burdette, Spahn's closest friend and a fine pitcher himself, had no-hitted the Phillies only a month earlier.

"When Lew pitched his, I just had to go out there and pitch one myself," Spahn explains. "I couldn't let him get away with it. I'm just a copycat, I guess. But you can't blame me too much. It was a long time coming.

"I've always said I'd like at least one no-hitter in my career. It was beginning to look like I'd never get it. Suddenly, when I was just about giving up hope, there she came—right on my twentieth victory in my sixteenth year in the big leagues. The very next year, I got another one. Here I waited nearly a lifetime to get my no-hitter, and no sooner do I get it then I come up with another. That's life."

Spahn's second no-hitter came in only his fifth start of the 1961 season—on April 28 against the San Francisco Giants at Milwaukee. It was the majors' only no-hit game of the year. In every respect Spahn's second masterpiece represented an even greater feat than the first. In the Giants he faced one of the National League's heaviest slugging crews. Not only did he mow them down without a hit, but he faced only 27 batters. He blanked the Giants 1–0. Two walks kept him from a perfect game.

The no-hitter came five days after Spahn observed his fortieth birthday. That made him the second oldest pitcher ever to author a no-hit game in the majors. Only Cy Young, who pitched his at 41, was older.

"It was so easy, it was pathetic," comments Spahn. "Everything went my way, and they kept guessing wrong. But let's face it; I was just plain lucky. I walked a man to start an inning—a cardinal sin with a one-run lead—not once but twice and got away with it."

The two passes, both on four pitches, went to Chuck Hiller in the fourth and Willie McCovey in the fifth. After each, Spahn personally cleaned the bases by starting double plays. Harvey Kuenn hit into the first, Orlando Cepeda the second. Spahn had his closest call in the ninth inning. Catcher Charlie Lau drop-

*Spahn pitches to Philadelphia Phillies pinch hitter Bobby Gene Smith during the ninth inning of the left-hander's first no-hitter.*

ped Ed Bailey's foul fly. Fortunately, Bailey then struck out. On the next play, pinch hitter Matty Alou dragged an almost perfect bunt down the first base line, but in one motion Spahn picked up the ball and tossed it backhanded to retire the fleet-footed runner at first.

For Spahn, the two no-hitters in successive seasons marked another milestone in a career already studded with them.

September 26, 1960

# Ted Williams: Last Time at Bat

**Baltimore**

| | AB | R | H |
|---|---|---|---|
| Brandt, cf | 5 | 0 | 0 |
| Pilarcik, rf | 4 | 0 | 1 |
| Robinson, 3b | 4 | 1 | 1 |
| Gentile, 1b | 3 | 1 | 1 |
| Triandos, c | 4 | 1 | 2 |
| Hansen, ss | 4 | 1 | 2 |
| Stephens, lf | 4 | 0 | 2 |
| Breeding, 2b | 2 | 0 | 0 |
| a Woodling | 1 | 0 | 0 |
| b Pearson | 0 | 0 | 0 |
| Klaus, 2b | 1 | 0 | 0 |
| Barber, p | 0 | 0 | 0 |
| Fisher, p | 4 | 0 | 0 |
| Total | 36 | 4 | 9 |

**Boston**

| | AB | R | H |
|---|---|---|---|
| Green, ss | 3 | 0 | 0 |
| Tasby, cf | 4 | 1 | 0 |
| Williams, lf | 3 | 2 | 1 |
| Hardy, lf | 0 | 0 | 0 |
| Pagliaroni, c | 3 | 0 | 2 |
| Malzone, 3b | 3 | 0 | 0 |
| Clinton, rf | 3 | 0 | 0 |
| Gile, 1b | 4 | 0 | 0 |
| Coughtry, 2b | 3 | 1 | 2 |
| Muffett, p | 2 | 0 | 0 |
| c Nixon | 1 | 0 | 0 |
| Fornieles, p | 0 | 0 | 0 |
| d Wertz | 1 | 0 | 1 |
| e Brewer | 0 | 1 | 0 |
| Total | 30 | 5 | 6 |

a—Hit into force play for Breeding in sixth.
b—Ran for Woodling in sixth.
c—Grounded into double play for Muffet in seventh.
d—Doubled for Fornieles in ninth.
e—Ran for Wertz in ninth.

| Baltimore | 0 2 0 0 1 1 0 0 0—4 |
|---|---|
| Boston | 2 0 0 0 0 0 0 1 2—5 |

Errors—Coughtry, Klaus. Runs batted in—Gentile, Triandos 2, Woodling, Tasby, Williams, Clinton. Two-base hits—Stephens, Robinson, Wertz. Home runs—Triandos, Williams. Sacrifice flies—Clinton, Gentile. Left on base—Baltimore 6, Boston 7. Double plays—Baltimore 1. Bases on balls—Barber 3, Fisher 3. Struck out—Fisher 5, Muffet 4, Fornieles 2. Hits off—Barber, 0 in 1/3; Fisher, 6 in 8 1/3; Muffett, 9 in 7; Fornieles, 0 in 2. Hit by pitch—by Barber (Pagliaroni). Wild pitches—Barber, Muffett. Winner—Fornieles. Loser—Fisher. Umpires—Hurley, Rice, Stevens, and Drummond. Time—2:18. Attendance—10,454.

At the start of the 1960 season, it wasn't expected that Ted Williams would play much, but he overcame the predictions. He played in 113 games, hit 29 home runs, and batted .316. In his first at bat on opening day, he hammered a 500-foot home run off Camilo Pascual. It was the four hundred ninety-third of his career, tying him with Lou Gehrig, behind only Mel Ott, Jimmy Foxx, and Babe Ruth. His neck was bothering him; he still had that pin holding his collarbone together. But the next day, he hit another home run, off Jim Coates of the Yankees. In midseason he hit homer number 510, off Don Lee. Twenty years before, he had hit a home run off Don's father, Thornton Lee.

Wednesday, September 26, was a cold and dreary day in Boston. Facing 42, Ted Williams was an old baseball player at the end of a long season. He had let it be known that this would be his last game in Boston, but everybody except Mike Higgins, the Red Sox' manager, assumed he would make the trip with the Red Sox to New York for the final weekend games of the season.

Ted remembers the day well. "I had had it, and I knew it," he says. "I had gone as far as I could. When I arrived at the park that day, I said to Higgins, 'Mike, this is the last game I'm going to play. I don't want to go to New York.'

"Higgins said, 'All right, you don't have to go to New York if you don't want to.' "

In a ceremony at the plate just before the start of the game, Ted was given a silver bowl and a plaque. His number was retired, and the mayor presented a $4,000 check to the Jimmy Fund, a fund for children with cancer. Williams had been affiliated with the Jimmy Fund since 1947. Curt Gowdy introduced him as "the greatest hitter who ever lived." To tremendous applause Ted stepped to the microphone and took off his cap, probably the first time he'd done that in front of the Boston fans, and thanked them all.

"Despite some of the terrible things written about me by the knights of the keyboard up there," he said, pointing to the press box, "baseball has been the most wonderful thing in my life. If I were starting over again and someone asked me where is the one place I would like to play, I would want it to be in Boston, with the greatest owner in baseball, Tom Yawkey, and the greatest fans in America. Thank you."

Ted didn't take batting practice. The wind was blowing in; it was cold, drizzling, and dark. Steve Barber, a left-hander with a baffling sinker, started for the Baltimore Orioles. He walked Williams on four pitches, and the crowd voiced its disapproval. The next time Williams came to bat, Jack Fisher, a right-hander, was on the mound. Ted hit a one-one pitch high and deep to center field, but Jackie Brandt faded back and made the catch.

*In a fitting close to his career, Williams crashes a home run.*

There were two out in the fifth and the Red Sox were trailing 3–2 when Williams faced Fisher again. This time he caught hold of a fastball and unloaded a tremendous drive to right center. As the ball jumped off the bat, the cry "He did it!" rose from the stands. Right fielder Al Pilarcik took off, pressed his back against the bullpen fence, brought up his hands, and caught the ball close to 400 feet from the plate.

"Damn," Ted muttered when he returned to the bench. "I hit the living hell out of that one. I really stung it. If that one didn't go out, nothing is going out today."

The Red Sox trailed 4–2 as they came to bat in the bottom of the eighth. The Fenway Park lights had been turned on. It was eerie, damp, and so cold that Williams wore his blue jacket in the dugout while waiting for his turn at bat. The cheering began as Willie Tasby came to bat with Ted almost directly behind, heading for the on-deck circle. The cheering reached a peak as Williams stepped into the box and took his stance. Twenty-two years were ending with one time at bat. The fans rose and applauded.

Fisher's first pitch was low. His second pitch was a high fastball. Ted swung viciously and missed. "I knew he was going to try to pump that one past me," Williams remembers. "Sure enough, it was a fastball. I should

have hit it a mile, but I missed the son of a gun, I still don't know how ."

It was home run or nothing now. Everybody in the park knew it, including Jack Fisher. The hard-throwing right-hander couldn't wait to throw the ball. This time Ted swung a little faster. From the moment Ted swung, there was not the slightest doubt that the ball was gone. Jackie Brandt dashed back to the barrier, stopped, turned, and watched. The ball kept going. It sailed over the fence with plenty to spare and landed deep in the right center field

*Ted Williams, playing in his final season, hits the five-hundredth home run of his career, in Cleveland's Municipal Stadium.*

bullpen. It did not seem possible that 10,454 people could make so much noise.

They cheered wildly as Ted trotted around the bases. They cheered as he ducked into the dugout, put on his jacket, and sat down, his head against the wall. They called his name. Ted's teammates pleaded with him to go back out. Even Johnny Rice, the first base umpire, motioned for Ted to come out. But the reserved Williams didn't.

Manager Higgins had already told Carroll Hardy to replace Ted in left field. But he changed his mind. "Ted, go out to left field," he ordered at the start of the ninth. Williams grabbed his glove and sprinted to left field, ignoring the cheers of the fans. No sooner had he gotten there when Higgins sent Hardy to replace him. Ted saw Hardy coming, turned around, and sprinted back to the dugout amid more wild applause. When Ted reached the dugout, he turned, and for a moment it seemed he would acknowledge the fans with a tip of the cap. He hesitated, then ducked his head under the roof.

October 13, 1960

# Mazeroski's Series-winning Home Run

### New York (AL)

| | AB | R | H | PO | A |
|---|---|---|---|---|---|
| Richardson, 2b | 5 | 2 | 2 | 2 | 5 |
| Kubek, ss | 3 | 1 | 0 | 3 | 2 |
| DeMaestri, ss | 0 | 0 | 0 | 0 | 0 |
| d Long | 1 | 0 | 1 | 0 | 0 |
| e McDougald, 3b | 0 | 1 | 0 | 0 | 0 |
| Maris, rf | 5 | 0 | 0 | 2 | 0 |
| Mantle, cf | 5 | 1 | 3 | 0 | 0 |
| Berra, lf | 4 | 2 | 1 | 3 | 0 |
| Skowron, 1b | 5 | 2 | 2 | 10 | 2 |
| Blanchard, c | 4 | 0 | 1 | 1 | 1 |
| Boyer, 3b-ss | 4 | 0 | 1 | 0 | 3 |
| Turley, p | 0 | 0 | 0 | 0 | 0 |
| Stafford, p | 0 | 0 | 0 | 0 | 1 |
| a Lopez | 1 | 0 | 1 | 0 | 0 |
| Shantz, p | 3 | 0 | 1 | 3 | 1 |
| Coates, p | 0 | 0 | 0 | 0 | 0 |
| Terry, p | 0 | 0 | 0 | 0 | 0 |
| Total | 40 | 9 | 13 | x24 | 15 |

### Pittsburgh (NL)

| | AB | R | H | PO | A |
|---|---|---|---|---|---|
| Virdon, cf | 4 | 1 | 2 | 3 | 0 |
| Groat, ss | 4 | 1 | 1 | 3 | 2 |
| Skinner, lf | 2 | 1 | 0 | 1 | 0 |
| Nelson, 1b | 3 | 1 | 1 | 7 | 0 |
| Clemente, rf | 4 | 1 | 1 | 4 | 0 |
| Burgess, c | 3 | 0 | 2 | 0 | 0 |
| b Christopher | 0 | 0 | 0 | 0 | 0 |
| Smith, c | 1 | 1 | 1 | 1 | 0 |
| Hoak, 3b | 3 | 1 | 0 | 3 | 2 |
| Mazeroski, 2b | 4 | 2 | 2 | 5 | 0 |
| Law, p | 2 | 0 | 0 | 0 | 1 |
| Face, p | 0 | 0 | 0 | 0 | 1 |
| c Cimoli | 1 | 1 | 1 | 0 | 0 |
| Friend, p | 0 | 0 | 0 | 0 | 0 |
| Haddix, p | 0 | 0 | 0 | 0 | 0 |
| Total | 31 | 10 | 11 | 27 | 6 |

a—Singled for Stafford in third.
b—Ran for Burgess in seventh.
c—Singled for Face in eighth.
d—Singled for DeMaestri in ninth.
e—Ran for Long in ninth.
x—None out when winning run scored.

| | | |
|---|---|---|
| New York | 0 0 0 0 1 4 0 2 2— | 9 |
| Pittsburgh | 2 2 0 0 0 0 0 5 1— | 10 |

Error—Maris. Runs batted in—Mantle 2, Berry 4, Skowron, Blanchard, Boyer, Virdon 2, Groat, Nelson 2, Clemente, Smith 3, Mazeroski. Two-base hit—Boyer. Home runs—Nelson, Skowron, Berra, Smith, Mazeroski. Sacrifice—Skinner. Double plays—New York 3. Left on base—New York 6, Pittsburgh 1. Bases on balls—Turley 1, Stafford 1, Shantz 1, Law 1, Face 1. Struck out—None. Hits off—Turley, 2 in 1; Stafford, 2 in 1; Shantz, 4 in 5; Coates, 2 in 2/3; Terry, 1 in 1 1/3; Law, 4 in 5; Face, 6 in 3; Friend, 2 in 0; Haddix, 1 in 1. Winner—Haddix. Loser—Terry. Umpires—Jackowski (NL), Chylak (AL), Boggess (NL), Stevens (AL), Landes (NL), and Honochick (AL). Time—2:36. Attendance—36,683.

In this Series the team that couldn't win couldn't lose. The Yankees' victories were lopsided; the Pirates' were razor thin. The Yankees scored 28 more runs than the Pirates, outhit them 91 to 60, outhomered them 10 to 4, and set a Series record for team batting average, .338 (to the Pirates' .256). And they lost. Clearly the Pirates had the help of supernatural elements, for which even the lordly Yankees were no match.

It was a subdued cast of Pirates that hosted the Yankees in the final game of the Series. In the first six games, it seemed that only Elroy Face, the Pirates' bantam relief ace, could handle the relentless New Yorkers. He preserved victories for Vernon Law in games one and four and saved Harvey Haddix's win in game five. In between the Yankees humiliated the Pirates. They amassed 19 hits and 16 runs in game two, the second most productive run-scoring rampage in a Series game. In game three they moderated their assault on Pittsburgh pitching only slightly, accumulating 16 hits and 12 runs as Mickey Mantle knocked in 5 with two homers and Whitey Ford shut out the Pirates on four hits. Then the Yankees' ace reasserted his mastery in game six, and the Yankees inflicted a 12–0 beating on the already ravaged Bucs.

Leading three games to two before the sixth game, the Pirates had felt confident they could win the Series. Now, a day after having absorbed their third pasting, they weren't so sure. On October 13, 36,683 apprehensive partisans gathered at Forbes Field, similarly unsure that they could bear to watch a final decimation of their heroes.

For five innings Vernon Law reassured them as he proficiently worked toward his third Series win. Meanwhile, two Pirate irregulars assaulted the Yankees' Bob Turley for a 2–0 lead. Bob Skinner walked and first base sub Rocky Nelson lifted a two-run homer over the right field screen. In the second the Bucs finished Turley when portly Smokey Burgess lined a single to right and Don Hoak walked. With two outs Bill Virdon singled both of them home off reliever Bill Stafford for a 4–0 advantage. The Pirates' coup seemed to have overthrown the Yankees.

Bill Skowron's homer off Law in the fifth began the Yankees' counter-revolution. An inning later, when Bobby Richardson singled and Tony Kubek walked, Pirates manager Danny Murtaugh brought in the heretofore invincible Face. This time the Yankees turned on the reliever whom they had treated with such deference before. Roger Maris fouled out, but Mantle's skidding grounder rolled past Dick Groat at short for a single. Yogi Berra then golfed a tremendous home run into the second deck in right field, and the Pirates' once-secure lead had become a 5–4 Yankees advantage. In the eighth the Yanks iced the champagne in the clubhouse as they seemed to ice the game on the field. With two out Berra walked, Skowron and John Blanchard singled, and Clete Boyer laced a double down the left field line.

Trailing 7–4, the Bucs appealed to luck and destiny to take up their flagging cause. Apparently their credit was good, and Lady Luck responded bountifully. After Gino Cimoli led off with a pinch-hit single to right center, Bill Virdon slashed an apparent double-play grounder at shortstop Kubek, but the ball struck a pebble, bounced up sharply, and nailed Kubek in the throat. A stunned Kubek sank to the ground.

The Yankees had been similarly wounded. Instead of two out and the bases empty, there were none out and two on. Then Dick Groat singled in a run, and Jim Coates relieved Bobby Shantz, who had pitched five scoreless innings of relief until the eighth. Skinner sacrificed, and Nelson flied out for the second out. With their rally on the verge of extinction, the Pirates received a rare reprieve from the Yanks. Roberto Clemente beat out a slow roller, Virdon scoring, when Coates forgot to cover first. Second-string catcher Hal Smith, subbing for Burgess after Smokey had left for a pinch runner, delivered the inning's coup de grace. Smith clouted the ball over the left field wall, and the Pirates had a five-run inning and a two-run lead, 9–7.

Still unwilling to accept the inevitable, the Yankees went back to work, this time on Bob Friend, regularly a starter, whom they had kayoed twice in the Series already. This time Friend was laboring in behalf of Face, who had saved him so often. The Yankees were not cooperating. Richardson and pinch hitter Dale Long punched singles. Harvey Haddix was quickly summoned, but after retiring Maris, he surrendered a run-scoring single to Mantle, Mickey's third hit of the day. With runners on first and third and one out, Berra blasted a one-bounce smash that threatened to dispatch first baseman Nelson. Fearlessly, Nelson made a spectacular grab, but rather than throw to second to start a double play, he stepped on first. When he spun around to throw to second, he allowed Mantle to scramble back to first and pinch runner McDougald to score from third with the tying run.

No matter. The Pirates were not to be thwarted by their unsophisticated fielding. They had waited since 1925 for this Series triumph, and Bill Mazeroski for one could wait no longer. Leading off the bottom of the ninth, he took ball one from Ralph Terry, the Yanks' fifth pitcher, and then hit the homer that drove Pittsburgh to delirium.

The pitch was a fast slider, letter-high. The stocky second baseman swung and met the ball squarely. As it disappeared over the left center field wall, a hushed crowd erupted. Mazer-

Below: *Bill Mazeroski, hat in hand, waving victoriously, nears home plate and a mob of happy fans and teammates waiting to welcome him.* Right: *Yankees left fielder Yogi Berra stands helplessly as ball clears Forbes Field wall.*

oski, nearing second base, flung his cap in the air, leaped high, and waved his arms. By the time he reached third base, a wildly cheering welcoming committee had all but blocked his path. On a surging river of people, Mazeroski bobbed around third base, touched home plate, and was swept off to a waterfall of champagne in the dressing room. Outside, cars honked, trolley cars clanged, people snake-danced in the streets. For the first time in 35 years, the Pittsburgh Pirates were world champions, and the city embraced the miracle with chaotic celebration. Only the Yankees couldn't understand it, and who could explain it to them?

# Willie Mays: Four Home Runs

*Willie Mays slams his fourth homer of the day.*

Willie McCovey, not an easy fellow to intimidate, was scared half to death. A loud thud had awakened him in the middle of the night. He leaped out of bed, switched on the light, and found his roommate, Willie Mays, lying on the floor. Willie had fallen out of bed and blacked out. McCovey summoned the club trainer, Doc Bowman, who revived Mays, gave him some pills, and got him back into bed.

That was early in 1961. The Giants had arrived in Milwaukee for a three-game series with the Braves, and Willie Mays was in a batting slump. He went hitless in seven times at bat in the first two games. In one of those games, Warren Spahn threw a no-hitter at the Giants. Spahn remarked afterward that he had never seen Mays look so bad at the plate. "I could tell that something was bothering him," Spahn remembers. "He looked like he was having trouble holding up his bat."

Spahn was right. Willie had had a persistent stomachache. Nonetheless, the night before the final game of the series with Milwaukee, he and McCovey went for a midnight snack, and Mays, ignoring his stomach, decided on barbecued spareribs. He should have known better. Afterward, he couldn't fall asleep. He began having sharp pains in his stomach. He became nauseous. That was the night McCovey found him unconscious on the floor.

Mays felt a little better the next day,

but he didn't hit the ball well in batting practice. Joe Amalfitano, a teammate, suggested he try his bat, which was a little heavier than Willie's.

Mays felt a little more comfortable at the plate by the time the game started. Lew Burdette, always a tough pitcher for Mays, was on the mound for the Braves. He threw Mays a slider, and Willie hit it over the fence in left center, 420 feet away. So much for not feeling well. The same thing happened the next time Mays came to bat, in the third inning. This time the ball traveled about 400 feet. When Mays came up for the third time, Seth Morehead was pitching for the Braves. He threw Willie a sinker, and Mays really caught hold of it. The ball landed in dead center, over the fence, out of the park, and beyond the trees. Writers estimated that the ball traveled at least 450 feet.

Moe Drabowsky, a right-hander, faced Mays the fourth time. Willie connected again but didn't get the ball high enough, and it went for a long line drive out to center field. In the eighth inning, Don McMahon, a flame-throwing right-hander, was pitching for Milwaukee. He threw Mays a slider and Willie deposited it in almost the same spot that the third homer had landed.

It was his fourth home run of the game and tied the major league record. Only eight other players since the turn of the century had hit four home runs in a game, only four others in a nine-inning game. Mays drove in eight runs. One homer came with two on base, two with one on base, and one with none on. The last player to hit four homers in a game had been Rocky Colavito in 1959. No player has hit four homers in a game since Mays.

Willie just missed a chance for five. Jimmy Davenport, who batted in front of him, was hitting in the ninth with two out and the crowd yelling for him to get on base. One might have thought they were playing in San Francisco instead of in Milwaukee. Davenport bounced out to end the inning.

"In a way, I'm glad Jimmy didn't get on," Willie says. "I'm not saying I wouldn't have liked a shot at a fifth home run, but I don't think I could have done it. I would have been pressing, knowing I could set a record that might never be equaled. I knew what I had done. I heard it over the loudspeakers.

"That was easily the greatest day of my life. I was already beginning to feel nervous waiting on deck. Funny thing, I wasn't nervous when I hit the fourth home run. That's because I never dreamed I'd hit it. I know I wasn't trying for it. I was just swinging. You're satisfied if you get two in a game, but when you get three, that's something you never expect. Four? That's like reaching for the moon."

Willie's stomachache had gone.

August 11, 1961

# Warren Spahn: The Three-Hundredth Victory

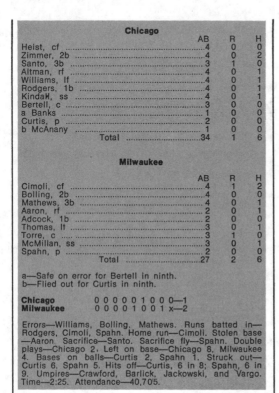

```
                Chicago
                         AB    R    H
Heist, cf ...............4     0    0
Zimmer, 2b .............4     0    2
Santo, 3b ..............3     1    0
Altman, rf .............4     0    1
Williams, lf ...........4     0    1
Rodgers, 1b ............4     0    1
Kindall, ss ............4     0    1
Bertell, c .............3     0    0
a Banks ................1     0    0
Curtis, p ..............2     0    0
b McAnany ..............1     0    0
        Total .........34     1    6

               Milwaukee
                         AB    R    H
Cimoli, cf .............4     1    2
Bolling, 2b ............4     0    0
Mathews, 3b ............4     0    1
Aaron, rf ..............2     0    1
Adcock, 1b .............2     0    0
Thomas, lf .............3     0    1
Torre, c ...............3     1    0
McMillan, ss ...........3     0    1
Spahn, p ...............2     0    0
        Total .........27     2    6
```

a—Safe on error for Bertell in ninth.
b—Flied out for Curtis in ninth.

| | | |
|---|---|---|
| **Chicago** | 0 0 0 0 0 1 0 0 0 | —1 |
| **Milwaukee** | 0 0 0 1 0 0 1 x | —2 |

Errors—Williams, Bolling, Mathews. Runs batted in—Rodgers, Cimoli, Spahn. Home run—Cimoli. Stolen base—Aaron. Sacrifice—Santo. Sacrifice fly—Spahn. Double plays—Chicago 2. Left on base—Chicago 8, Milwaukee 4. Bases on balls—Curtis 2, Spahn 1. Struck out—Curtis 6, Spahn 5. Hits off—Curtis, 6 in 8; Spahn, 6 in 9. Umpires—Crawford, Barlick, Jackowski, and Vargo. Time—2:25. Attendance—40,705.

There is no telling how many games Warren Spahn would have won had not Uncle Sam changed his Boston Braves' uniform for army khaki, which he wore for four years with as much distinction as he was to wear his baseball regalia. (Spahn was commissioned on the field of battle for heroism at Remagen Bridge.)

Because of the four-year hiatus, Spahnie did not win his first game in the major leagues until he was past 25. Consequently, it is all the more remarkable that this extraordinarily durable athlete eventually became the winningest left-hander in the history of the major leagues. His 363 victories, not including those in All-Star and World Series games, ranked him behind only Christy Mathewson and Grover Cleveland Alexander.

Among Spahn's most notable performances were four World Series victories, two no-hitters, 18 strikeouts in an extra-inning game, and 63 shutouts. But the game that gave him his biggest thrill took place on August 11, 1961, when he defeated the Chicago Cubs 2–1 for his three-hundredth major league victory.

"It was fantastic . . . the most exciting game I ever pitched."

A crowd of 40,705 saw him become the first pitcher to join the exclusive 300-victory club since Lefty Grove of the Red Sox gained membership in 1941. The Old Master's bid for num-

*Braves' Warren Spahn goes into his windup during 2–1 victory over the Chicago Cubs in Milwaukee's County Stadium. With the win Spahn became one of 14 hurlers to notch 300 or more victories.*

ber 300 lured the largest County Stadium crowd in two seasons, and he rewarded the fans with a performance typical of one of the game's greatest stars. The veteran left-hander pitched six-hit ball and even drove in one of the two Milwaukee runs with a sacrifice fly.

"That game was even more exciting than the World Series or the two no-hitters," Spahn told reporters, photographers and other well-wishers who crowded around him after the game. "Maybe it was just in my mind. I really don't know. But it was something. Beforehand, I wasn't too excited about winning my three hundredth because I figured it would come eventually. But a few hours before the game, the pressure began to build up. About six o'clock I was wishing we could start the game right then. I wanted to get it over with. I'm relieved that I don't have to go through it again. I've never done anything so tough."

As flash bulbs popped and newspapermen pumped him for something new, Spahn motioned for his teammate Gino Cimoli to join him in posing for pictures. Cimoli had won the game with a home run in the eighth inning and had saved it with a spectacular catch in the ninth. The homer had broken a 1–1 tie in the duel between Spahn and rookie Jack Curtis of the Cubs.

The seventh-place Cubs conceded nothing. They sent their best available

93

pinch hitters to the plate in the ninth inning as they fought Spahn to the final out, which was delayed when Eddie Mathews threw wildly to first base on Ernie Banks's grounder. Hitting for Dick Bertell, Banks reached first on the error. Jim McAnany then swung for Curtis and flied to Henry Aaron for the final out of the game.

That was it. Spahn had his three hundredth, and he gleefully made the rounds of his teammates to shake hands. He went halfway to right field to reach Aaron, who gave him the ball, his most prized souvenir of all. The stands erupted in a manner that recalled the championship days of 1957 and 1958. As he left the field, he waved his cap and blew a kiss to the roaring crowd.

"It was tough," Spahn said elatedly, "but I wouldn't have it any other way."

*Braves right fielder Hank Aaron (44) rushes to congratulate Spahn after the three-hundredth career win.*

July 29–August 20, 1961

# The Phils' Longest Month

One might have thought the Philadelphia Phillies had just won the pennant. In a demonstration that defied logic, hundreds of fans gathered at the Philadelphia airport to give a warm-hearted welcome to the team that had just set a record for most successive losses in modern baseball history.

The loyal fans who poured into Philadelphia's International Airport all evening were accompanied by a five-piece band. It was after 1 A.M. before the Phillies' chartered plane from Milwaukee touched down. The enthusiasm of the greeting had grown rather than diminished with the delay. The people threw confetti at the players. Many held homemade signs, one of which read: "Who said it couldn't be done?" leaving it tactfully unclear whether the sign referred to the team's record losing streak or the long-sought-after streak-snapping victory.

The Phillies of 1961 were one of the least successful representatives of Philadelphia, a city that is no stranger to baseball mediocrity. The Phillies won only 47 games, losing 107, and finished deep in the National League cellar, 46 games off the pace. They hit a horrendous losing streak in midsummer, reviving memory of the worst major league team of all time, Cleveland's National League entry of 1899, which lost 24 in a row.

Cleveland's record losing streak seemed as unassailable as Lou Gehrig's string of 2,130 consecutive games or Joe DiMaggio's record of hitting safely in 56 games in a row. But the '61 Phillies made a noble effort and almost succeeded.

Philadelphia's race for the all-time futility record began on Saturday, July 29, when they dropped a 4–3 decision to the San Francisco Giants. Orlando Cepeda's grand slammer off loser Don Ferrarese in the first inning provided just enough runs for winner Mike Mc-Cormick.

The next three weeks brought steadily mounting anguish to manager Gene Mauch. Loss followed loss as starters Jim Owens, Chris Short, Art Mahaffey, Frank Sullivan, Johnny Buzhardt, and Ferrarese desperately struggled to nail down a victory. Even ailing Robin Roberts, the Phillies' erstwhile ace, returned from the injury list in an attempt to stem the tide. But he, too, failed.

On August 12, the Phils broke their own record for most consecutive losses when Pittsburgh's Vinegar Bend Mizell shut them out 5–0, the fifteenth straight defeat for the hapless team. Four days later, the Phillies lost to Don Cardwell and the Cubs, 9–5, and tied the modern National League record of 19 consecutive losses set by the Boston Braves in 1906 and equaled by the Cincinnati Reds in 1914.

The following day, the Phillies tied the modern major league mark by los-

*Second baseman Bobby Malkus forces Joe Amalfitano of the Giants during Phillies' July 28 win. A long month later the Phils won again.*

ing their twentieth in a row to the Braves in Milwaukee. The Boston Red Sox of 1906 had established that unhappy record, and the Philadelphia Athletics had tied it in 1916 and again in 1943. The Phillies came close to ending their losing string in that game. Going into the eighth, they were leading 6–4, but a two-run homer by Joe Adcock sent the game into extra innings. Al Spangler's single with the bases full drove in the tie-breaking run in the eleventh, and the Phillies had lost another.

On August 18, the Phillies claimed exclusivity in the record book as they bowed to Lew Burdette and the Braves, 4–1, for loss number 21. The next day, still in Milwaukee, they lost number 22, a 4–3 decision to Tony Cloninger. Now there was only one more record left standing—Cleveland's all-time mark. The Phillies had a doubleheader with the Braves on August 20; a double defeat would equal that inglorious achievement.

Chris Short faced Warren Spahn in the opener. The Phils took an early 2–0 lead on Bobby Malkmus's homer, but the Braves tied the score on Frank Thomas's two-run double in the fourth. They added three more runs in the fifth on Eddie Mathews's homer and two Philadelphia errors. Warren Spahn emerged with his three-hundred-second major league victory and the Phils with loss number 23. One more to go.

97

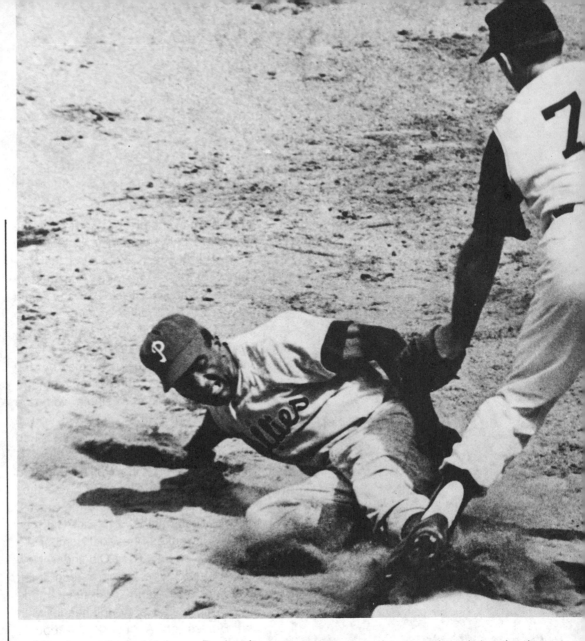

Mauch nominated Johnny Buzhardt, who had pitched Philadelphia's last victory back on July 28, to oppose Carleton Willey, the Braves' starter. Milwaukee took a 1–0 lead on Wes Covington's third-inning homer, but the Phillies went ahead 2–1 in the fourth on run-scoring singles by Clay Dalrymple and Bobby Malkmus. They added another run in the sixth and iced the contest with a four-run outburst in the eighth. Singles by Don Demeter, Ken Walters, Malkmus, and Tony Taylor, a walk, and

Buzhardt's safe bunt produced the decisive tallies off Bob Hendley and Don Nottebart. Roy McMillan and Joe Adcock homered for the Braves in the eighth and ninth, but Buzhardt held fast and finished the game, ending the Phillies' 23-game losing streak.

The Phillies of 1961 may have failed to match Cleveland's mark, but they came out ahead of their 1899 counterparts in fan affection. The Phils received a hero's welcome when they returned to Philadelphia. The '99 Cleve-

*A scene typical of the Phillies' misfortune during their longest month: Pirate Dick Stuart doubles up Phils' Tony Gonzalez in 13–4 debacle.*

land team, aptly known as "the Exiles," was forced to flee town. After winning only 4 of 30 in August, home attendance in Cleveland had become limited to sportswriters, groundskeepers, and lemonade hucksters. The team played its remaining 35 games on the road, losing all but 1. Before the season was over, the itinerant Clevelanders had acquired more nicknames—"the Forsaken," "the Barnstormers" and "the Wanderers." They finished the season, then quietly disbanded.

October 1, 1961

# Roger Maris: The Record

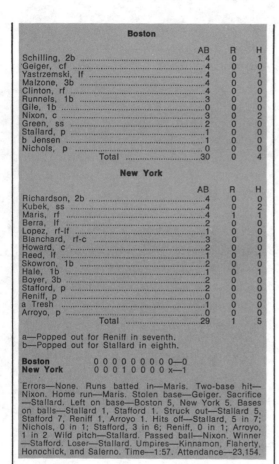

**Boston**

| | AB | R | H |
|---|---|---|---|
| Schilling, 2b | 4 | 0 | 1 |
| Geiger, cf | 4 | 0 | 0 |
| Yastrzemski, lf | 4 | 0 | 1 |
| Malzone, 3b | 4 | 0 | 0 |
| Clinton, rf | 4 | 0 | 0 |
| Runnels, 1b | 3 | 0 | 0 |
| Gile, 1b | 0 | 0 | 0 |
| Nixon, c | 3 | 0 | 2 |
| Green, ss | 2 | 0 | 0 |
| Stallard, p | 1 | 0 | 0 |
| b Jensen | 1 | 0 | 0 |
| Nichols, p | 0 | 0 | 0 |
| Total | 30 | 0 | 4 |

**New York**

| | AB | R | H |
|---|---|---|---|
| Richardson, 2b | 4 | 0 | 0 |
| Kubek, ss | 4 | 0 | 2 |
| Maris, rf | 4 | 1 | 1 |
| Berra, lf | 2 | 0 | 0 |
| Lopez, rf-lf | 1 | 0 | 0 |
| Blanchard, rf-c | 3 | 0 | 0 |
| Howard, c | 2 | 0 | 0 |
| Reed, lf | 1 | 0 | 1 |
| Skowron, 1b | 2 | 0 | 0 |
| Hale, 1b | 1 | 0 | 1 |
| Boyer, 3b | 2 | 0 | 0 |
| Stafford, p | 2 | 0 | 0 |
| Reniff, p | 0 | 0 | 0 |
| a Tresh | 1 | 0 | 0 |
| Arroyo, p | 0 | 0 | 0 |
| Total | 29 | 1 | 5 |

a—Popped out for Reniff in seventh.
b—Popped out for Stallard in eighth.

| | | |
|---|---|---|
| **Boston** | 0 0 0 0 0 0 0 0 0—0 | |
| **New York** | 0 0 0 1 0 0 0 0 x—1 | |

Errors—None. Runs batted in—Maris. Two-base hit—Nixon. Home run—Maris. Stolen base—Geiger. Sacrifice —Stallard. Left on base—Boston 5, New York 5. Bases on balls—Stallard 1, Stafford 1. Struck out—Stallard 5, Stafford 7, Reniff 1, Arroyo 1. Hits off—Stallard, 5 in 7; Nichols, 0 in 1; Stafford, 3 in 6; Reniff, 0 in 1; Arroyo, 1 in 2 Wild pitch—Stallard. Passed ball—Nixon. Winner —Stafford. Loser—Stallard. Umpires—Kinnamon, Flaherty, Honochick, and Salerno. Time—1:57. Attendance—23,154.

Roger Maris holds a special place in American sports. He performed the unprecedented feat of hitting 61 home runs in a single season and has never been forgiven for it. For season-long drama, there was no individual performance during the 1960s that could match the effort Maris made to break Babe Ruth's homer record, which had stood since 1927. The pressures on him were enormous, compounded by the fact that it was not Maris's nature to enjoy the unbelievable attention accorded him.

For those who sympathized with him, it was a painful experience to watch Maris submit to the grinding interrogation of reporters day after day as he closed in on the record. After games, he became a virtual prisoner, jammed against his locker as newsmen surrounded him, pressing home question after question.

The sports world—players, fans, and press—never really understood Maris. Even after he smacked that sixty-first homer on the final day of the season, Maris's detractors said he couldn't match Ruth because the Babe had hit his 60 homers in only a 154-game schedule. To many sports fans around the country, Maris was at best an enigma, at worst, an object of scorn. His crime was bettering the most coveted record of the most popular ballplayer who ever lived. Seven years after he broke Ruth's record, Maris was through as a player, at the relatively youthful age of 33.

"It would have been a helluva lot more fun if I had never hit those sixty-one home runs," Maris says. "Some guys love the life of a celebrity. Some of them would have walked down Fifth Avenue in their Yankee uniforms if they could. But all it brought me was headaches."

Maris is now a beer salesman, and he pays very little attention to baseball. "It's all finished and done," he says. "I don't think the Yankees wanted me to break Ruth's record. They favored Mickey Mantle to break it."

Because Maris hit his 61 homers in a 162-game schedule while Ruth got his 60 in a 154-game schedule, Ford Frick, then commissioner of baseball, placed an asterisk beside Maris's name in the record book. Maris is still bitter. "I didn't make the schedule," he says, "and do you know any other records that have been broken since the hundred-sixty-two game schedule that have an asterisk? I don't. Frick decided on the asterisk after I had about fifty homers and it looked like I'd break Ruth's record."

Maris had 58 home runs when the Yankees flew into Baltimore on Monday, September 18. The Yankees were scheduled for a four-game series with the Orioles, but only the first three fell within the 154-game span that Frick had decreed would be the cutoff point.

A twi-nighter was scheduled for September 19, and a crowd of 31,317 had turned out despite threatening weather to cheer or boo the Rajah's big try. Steve Barber walked him in the first inning and the crowd booed lustily. The left-hander, rankled by the criticism, pitched smartly to Rog after that and retired him the next three times as he recorded a 1–0 victory. Maris was stopped in the second game too, managing a single in five tries against knuckleballers Skinny Brown and Hoyt Wilhelm.

So it came down to one ball game, number 154. Never was the glare of publicity so intensely focused on one man. Papers from Los Angeles, Chicago, Boston, and Washington as well as smaller cities flooded the press box with reporters.

His first time up, facing Milt Pappas, a hard-throwing right-hander, Roger shot a line drive to right field. He hit it solidly but didn't get enough lift. In the third inning, he crashed number 59, a 380-foot line drive into the right field bleachers. Now he needed just one more, and he had three more chances. He came close in his next at bat, slashing a foul that missed being a home run by 10 feet. Then he struck out. He flied out in the seventh, Earl Robinson pulling down the ball in front of the right field bleachers. His last chance came in the ninth, but the best he could do was a little grounder toward

first base, where he was tagged out.

"I gave it all I had," Maris sighed afterward, "but it wasn't enough. I'm glad it's over. The pressure is off."

It wasn't. There were the eight extra games still to play and the chance to surpass the record for one season, regardless of Frick's dictum.

Maris didn't hit a home run off Jack Fisher in the last game in Baltimore, and he was stopped in two games in Boston by right-handers Don Schwall and Bill Monbouquette. After an open date on September 25, it was the Orioles and Fisher again as the opposition in New York. In the third inning,

Roger connected. He drove a tremendous clout that hit the concrete steps of the sixth row of the third deck in Yankee Stadium. Homer number 60.

Maris had attained a pinnacle reached previously only by the immortal Babe. Then the thoroughly unpredictable young man took the next day off! "I need a rest. I'm tired," he explained. "Besides, Barber is pitching against us, and he's always been tough for me. A day's rest will make me stronger."

Maris was stopped the next two games by the same pitchers who stopped him in Boston, Schwall and

Left: *Roger Maris comes home with record-breaking sixty-first home run of the season.*
Below: *Third base coach Frank Crosetti and Orioles' Brooks Robinson watch Maris round third after number 60.*

Monbouquette. But on the final day of the season, Sunday, October 1, in his second time at bat, he broke Ruth's record with a thunderous drive into the lower deck in right field, about 360 feet away, against right-hander Tracy Stallard.

Maris, for once not the stone man, leaped around the bases. The throng of 23,154 screamed in delight. The fans were not satisfied until Rog had taken several bows. "If I never hit another home run," he said with deep satisfaction, "this is one they can never take away from me."

103

May 5, 1962

# Bo Belinsky: A Flash of Greatness

**Baltimore**

| | AB | R | H | PO | A |
|---|---|---|---|---|---|
| Temple, 2b | 4 | 0 | 0 | 2 | 5 |
| Williams, lf | 4 | 0 | 0 | 0 | 0 |
| B. Robinson, 3b | 4 | 0 | 0 | 1 | 1 |
| Gentile, 1b | 2 | 0 | 0 | 10 | 2 |
| Brandt, cf | 3 | 0 | 0 | 2 | 0 |
| Triandos, c | 2 | 0 | 0 | 7 | 0 |
| Nicholson, rf | 4 | 0 | 0 | 0 | 0 |
| Hansen, ss | 3 | 0 | 0 | 1 | 1 |
| Barber, p | 1 | 0 | 0 | 1 | 2 |
| b Breeding | 1 | 0 | 0 | 0 | 0 |
| Stock, p | 0 | 0 | 0 | 0 | 3 |
| Total | 28 | 0 | 0 | 24 | 14 |

**Los Angeles**

| | AB | R | H | PO | A |
|---|---|---|---|---|---|
| Pearson, cf | 4 | 0 | 0 | 3 | 0 |
| Moran, 2b | 4 | 1 | 2 | 1 | 0 |
| Wagner, rf | 4 | 0 | 2 | 1 | 0 |
| Bilko, 1b | 4 | 0 | 0 | 9 | 0 |
| Torres, 3b | 3 | 0 | 0 | 2 | 2 |
| Averill, lf | 2 | 1 | 1 | 0 | 0 |
| a L. Thomas, lf | 0 | 0 | 0 | 1 | 0 |
| Rodgers, c | 3 | 0 | 1 | 8 | 1 |
| Koppe, ss | 3 | 0 | 0 | 2 | 3 |
| Belinsky, p | 2 | 0 | 0 | 0 | 1 |
| Total | 29 | 2 | 6 | 27 | 10 |

a—Ran for Averill in sixth.
b—Struck out for Barber in seventh.

| | | | | | | | | | |
|---|---|---|---|---|---|---|---|---|---|
| Baltimore | 0 | 0 | 0 | 0 | 0 | 0 | 0 | 0 | 0—0 |
| Los Angeles | 1 | 1 | 0 | 0 | 0 | 0 | 0 | x—2 | |

Error—Torres. Runs batted in—Koppe. Two-base hits—Wagner, Rodgers. Sacrifice—Belinsky. Left on base—Baltimore 7, Los Angeles 5. Bases on balls—Barber 1, Belinsky 4. Struck out—Stock 1, Barber 6, Belinsky 9. Hits off—Barber, 6 in 6; Stock, 0 in 2; Belinsky, 0 in 9. Hit by pitch—by Belinsky (Gentile, Barber). Wild pitch —Barber. Loser—Barber. Umpires—Schwartz, Berry, Honochick, and Smith. Time—2:09. Attendance—15,886.

Saturday, May 5, 1962, dawned like any other working day for Robert "Bo" Belinsky. A rookie left-hander with the Los Angeles Angels, Belinsky put on his flashy vest and sports jacket, matched it perfectly with a pair of expensive trousers, climbed into his candy-apple red Cadillac convertible, and drove to Chavez Ravine.

A 25-year-old unpredictable southpaw from Trenton, New Jersey, who only the year before had toiled in the obscurity of Little Rock, Arkansas, Bo was Angels manager Bill Rigney's choice to start against the Baltimore Orioles. A good-sized crowd was expected to watch the young lefty who had won his first three starts without a defeat. Adding to the attraction, Bo was matched against Steve Barber, who also owned a 3–0 record. Barber and Belinsky had been teammates in the Baltimore organization only the year before. Barber had blossomed into a big league star with 18 victories in 1961 while Belinsky labored to a 9–10 record in the Southern Association.

Belinsky knew that only expansion had brought him back to the major leagues. The Los Angeles club had acquired him in the draft from the Orioles and had given him a chance to make it as a starting pitcher, something he was convinced the Orioles never would have done. Quite naturally, he wanted nothing more than to beat the Orioles.

The media had heralded Bo Belin-

sky. The fans at Chavez Ravine had read about " the screwball with the screwball," the self-styled king of the Twist, the pool shark, the devil with the ladies; they had read about his flashy convertible, his Hollywood taste, his squawks for more money. Los Angeles was full of such characters, but for a baseball player, he was a rarity. When they discovered he could pitch too, the fans became curious.

The night was clear. A gentle breeze rippled across the huge ball park. As promised, the fans were treated to a

*Los Angeles Angels left-hander Bo Belinsky,*
*"the screwball with the screwball,"*
*throws a no-hitter against Baltimore.*

pitcher's duel. After seven innings, the Angels held a 2–0 lead. Things looked bright for Bo.

When he came to bat in the bottom of the seventh, the crowd of 15,886 stood and cheered him wildly. Bo didn't have to be reminded that he had not allowed a hit through seven innings. Had he forgotten, the scoreboard in center field was an ever-present reminder.

In the top of the eighth, Belinsky disposed of Dick Williams, Brooks Robinson, and Jim Gentile in rapid succession. The crowd roared with every out, every swing, every pitch. Belinsky, the character who had talked his way into print with his antics and off-beat comments was three outs from pitching a no-hitter.

In the ninth he struck out Jackie Brandt on three pitches. The crowd applauded wildly. Two outs to go. Hard-hitting catcher Gus Triandos bounced out to shortstop Joe Koppe, and only husky Dave Nicholson, a Baltimore bonus outfielder, blocked Bo's bid for baseball fame. Belinsky wound up and fired, and Nicholson swung. The ball arched toward the lights over the Angels' dugout. Third baseman Felix Torres rushed into foul territory, settled under the fly, and squeezed the ball in his glove. Bo Belinsky had accomplished within four games what had evaded many great pitchers in a lifetime. Overwhelmed by Bo's perfor-

mance, the first no-hitter in the American League in four years, the fans stood and gave him a five-minute ovation, firing a barrage of Chavez Ravine seat cushions onto the playing field in salute.

Afterward, in the Angels' boisterous dressing room, Bo was holding court. "I wonder how Paul Richards [Baltimore's manager] liked that," he chortled. "Only thing that man ever said to me the year I was in spring training with the Orioles was, 'Maybe I'll see you again sometime.' Well, he did."

Someone reminded Belinsky of one Alva Holloman, similarly nicknamed ("Bobo"), who pitched a no-hitter for the St. Louis Browns in 1953 only to be banished for good to the minors at the end of the year. Belinsky smiled and said, "Guess I better make another payment on my Cadillac. You never know about this business."

To be strictly accurate, it cannot be said that Belinsky shared the fate of Holloman. He was, after all, still with the club the next year. But, after his meteoric rise (he was 5–0 at one time), his 1962 overall record was a less than glittering 9–10. He was never again to win that many games in a season, and finally, after a 3–9 record with the Houston Astros in 1967, he ended his major league days. Baseball, after all, was hardly Belinsky's most entertaining pastime.

May 30, 1962—September 9, 1965

# Sandy Koufax:
# Four No-hitters

*Koufax was a Dodger for 12 years, his entire major league career.*

There may have been a better pitcher than Sandy Koufax, but in the six years from 1961 through 1966, no one approached this redoubtable left-hander's accomplishments on the mound—not even Walter Johnson, Cy Young, Christy Mathewson, or Lefty Grove. In five of those years, Koufax led the National League in earned run average and struck out 200 or more batters. He led the league in strikeouts four times. He became the first to strike out more than 300 batters in three different years, including 382 in 1956, a National League record. Three times he won the Cy Young Award. He pitched four no-hitters, more than anyone else. The last was a perfect game.

Truly, Koufax's accomplishments bordered on the unbelievable. He pitched with an arthritic elbow, a lingering ailment that forced him to retire at age 30, at the height of his career. But the experts had seen enough. In his first year of eligibility, they voted him into the Hall of Fame; he was the youngest man ever to be selected.

Koufax's four no-hitters came in successive seasons. He pitched his first on Memorial Day, May 30, 1962, against the New York Mets. He struck out 13 but his control was spotty; he walked five and went three and two on eight other batters.

"The first inning of that game," Koufax recalls, "has to be the best I have ever pitched; three strikeouts on nine pitches. Every pitch was exactly where I wanted it."

Koufax's second no-hitter came on May 11, 1963 against the San Francisco Giants. "I didn't have overpowering stuff," says Sandy. "The first batter, Harvey Kuenn, hit a hard line drive to center field that went right to Willie Davis. Five feet either way and my no-hitter would have vanished with the first hitter. I had exceptional stuff in my other no-hitters. In this one it was good but not great. I had only four strikeouts in that game."

Koufax retired 22 straight batters before walking Ed Bailey on a three-two count, spoiling his bid for a perfect game. Willie McCovey walked on four pitches with two out in the ninth, but Koufax got Kuenn to bounce back to the box to preserve no-hitter number two.

Sandy pitched his third no-hitter on June 4, 1964, against the Philadelphia Phillies. "I had tremendous stuff, plus good control," he remembers. "When you've got everything working, you almost can't wait to get started."

With two out in the fourth, he walked Richie Allen on a three-two pitch. Allen was the only batter to reach base. Since he was caught stealing, Koufax faced only 27 batters, the minimum. He struck out 12.

Koufax's fourth no-hitter was one of baseball's most remarkable—not only a perfect game but the only game in major league history with just one hit. Strangely, Lou Johnson's bloop double in the seventh didn't even figure in the lone run the Dodgers managed off the Cubs' Bob Hendley. Overshadowed by Koufax's brilliance and all but forgotten today, Hendley matched the Dodgers' ace pitch for pitch. Only in the fifth did the. Dodgers touch the young lefty for a run, helped considerably by a Cubs defensive lapse. Lou Johnson walked, was sacrificed to second, stole third, and continued home on catcher Chris Krug's high throw.

Meanwhile, facing a lineup stacked with right-handed batters, Koufax mastered the Cubs with only three anxious moments. In the first inning, Glenn Beckert's fly landed just foul in left field; in the second Willie Davis in center grabbed Pidge Browne's hard liner; and in the seventh Sandy momentarily jeopardized his perfect game when he threw three straight balls to Billy Williams before slipping over two strikes and inducing the Cubs' slugger to fly out.

Koufax fanned 14, half of them in the last three innings. "I didn't have particularly good stuff in the beginning," he explained, "—just average. My control was really good, though. My curve was the best I had all year. In the last three innings, my fastball came alive—as good a fastball as I had all year." He had only one anxious moment, a three-one count on Billy Williams in the

108

*Possibly the greatest left-hander the game has ever known, Sandy Koufax of the Dodgers displays imposing form during his perfect game against the Chicago Cubs. Cubs pitcher Bob Hendley gave up just one hit in losing.*

seventh inning. But Williams flied out, and Koufax went on to outdo Bob Feller, another Hall of Famer, by posting his fourth no-hitter. Feller had three.

Koufax had one more season left, his best and most painful. In 1966, he won 27 games, setting a National League record for most victories in a season by a left-hander. His last victory, on the last day of the season, clinched the National League pennant for the Dodgers. He led all pitchers in practically every department, including

victories, complete games, innings pitched, strikeouts, shutouts, and ERA. But for the first time in five years, he failed to notch a no-hitter.

# Maury Wills: 100 Steals

Whether Maury Wills ever joins baseball's immortals in the Hall of Fame is anybody's guess, but one thing is certain. He was one of the most colorful players the game has ever known—and one of the most daring.

At a time when the emphasis was on power, Wills defied the strategists with speed that enabled him in 1962 to accomplish one of the most remarkable feats in modern baseball. He did it with his legs, his eyes, his intuition, his reflexes, his savvy, his cunning—abilities that established him as the game's greatest base stealer.

When Maury stole 50 bases in 1960 for a Dodgers club record, he and everyone else thought that he had reached the ultimate in base stealing. "I didn't see how I could ever improve that. I was even more sure of it the next year, when I stole only thirty-five. Even that was good enough to lead the league," he says.

Wills set a goal of 50 stolen bases for the 1962 season. He would reach that mark in just over 100 games, on July 27.

"I didn't think of the record," Wills says, "until I had upped my figure to seventy-two by stealing three against the Mets on August 26. Then, for the first time, Ty Cobb's record of ninety-six looked like a possibility."

The fever had reached the fans. Wherever Wills and the Dodgers appeared, the fans would yell "Go! Go!

Maury Wills of the Dodgers slides safely into
third for his one-hundred-fourth stolen base.
Hurried throw eludes Giants Jim Davenport.

*Against Houston Wills steals his hundredth base.*

Go!'' whenever Maury got on base. Wills became more daring with every game. The constant chanting gave him renewed strength and confidence. Although he suffered from fatigue bordering on physical exhaustion, he tried to steal at every opportunity.

Each day that Wills came closer to the record, he felt the tension a little more. He worried over the possibility of a batting slump. After all, you have to reach first base before you can steal second. Physically, Wills was in pain. One of his most serious ailments was a pulled hamstring tendon in his right leg, caused by a season of sudden starts and stops. By September his right leg started to bleed internally from the constant pounding. He spent much of his pregame warmup time in whirlpool baths and undergoing diathermy treatments, foot massages, and blood circulating exercises.

As Wills closed in on Cobb's record, he began to steal when he ordinarily would not have. On September 7, he stole four bases against Pittsburgh, giving him 82 for a new National League mark. Bob Bescher of the Cincinnati Reds had posted the old mark of 80 in 1911. Going into the Dodgers' one hundred fifty-fourth game, Wills's stolen base total had risen to 94. He needed only 3 more to break Cobb's 48-year-old record of 96. It didn't appear difficult since the Dodgers had nine games remaining in their 162-game schedule.

Wills's hopes were all but shattered when Commissioner Ford Frick ruled that to break Cobb's mark he must steal those three bases in the one hundred fifty-fourth game, because Cobb had stolen his 96 in a 154-game schedule. Wills was bitterly disappointed, and his resentment has barely diminished.

''I wouldn't have minded so much had Frick made his ruling earlier,'' Wills says now. ''But why did he wait until the last day? Cobb set his record in 1915 when he played in a hundred fifty-six. [Two tie games had to be replayed.] I figured I had three games in which to steal three more bases to

break the record. Had I known earlier, I could have taken some chances in the previous series and maybe could have gotten five or six more stolen bases. At that time I was under the impression that it was a hundred fifty-six games.''

In game number 154, against the Cardinals, Wills stole only one base. That gave him 95, one short of Cobb's record. Then, on September 23, in the Dodgers' one hundred fifty-sixth game, he stole two more to establish a new major league record, regardless of the number of games played. The St. Louis management graciously presented him

with second base, which now rests in the Hall of Fame in Cooperstown, New York. Wills stole two more the next day against the Houston Astros, and on September 27, in the Dodgers' one hundred fifty-ninth game with a cheering crowd of 25,813 looking on, Maury swiped third base in the third inning against the Houston battery of George Brunet and Hal Smith. That made it an even 100. It was his fortieth stolen base in the last 37 games. Maury added four more in the three-game pennant play-off with the Giants, stealing numbers 102, 103, and 104 in the last game.

# Giants–Dodgers: The Second Play-off

With seven games to go, it looked hopeless for San Francisco. The Los Angeles Dodgers led the Giants by four games. If the Dodgers could win but two, the Giants would have to take all seven of their remaining games to win the pennant.

The whittling of the Dodgers' seemingly insurmountable lead began on Sunday, September 23. With Willie McCovey bombing a mighty home run, the Giants swept past Houston 10–3 in Colt Stadium while the Dodgers bowed to St. Louis at home.

Monday was an off day. On Tuesday, Jack Sanford won his twenty-third, whipping the Cardinals at Candlestick Park, 4–2, while the Colts defeated the nervous Dodgers. Two games out with five to go, the Giants seemed less quixotic in their pennant quest. But as good Giants fans are painfully aware, theirs is a team that does not take well to good fortune. As the Dodgers split their next two, so did the Giants. With three games left, the Giants still trailed by two, and only the paranoid Angelinos gave the Giants a chance. The next day, while it rained in San Francisco and the Giants contemplated the strange benificence of their downstate rivals, the Dodgers lost for the fourth time in five games.

In the make-up doubleheader on Saturday, Sanford won his twenty-fourth as the Giants pasted Houston 11–5, but once again frightened by success, they

*Wills slides past the Giants' John Orsino with
the winning run in the Dodgers' 8–7 victory
that tied the play-offs at one game apiece.*

dropped the nightcap, 4–2. Only another Dodgers defeat saved the San Franciscans.

On the final day of the season, a crowd of 41,327 bravely hopeful Giants fans came to watch their skittish heroes and the out-of-town scoreboard. The best they could hope for was a tie—a win by the Giants, a loss by the Dodgers. Willie Mays and Gene Oliver answered their prayers. Willie's homer in the eighth broke a 1–1 tie and gave the Giants a victory. Oliver's homer in the ninth in Los Angeles broke a scoreless tie and gave the Giants a tie for the pennant. Invoking the sainted memory of Bobby Thomson, Giants fans dreamily contemplated the opening of the three-game play-off in San Francisco the next day.

Giants manager Alvin Dark had more devious methods in mind. In an unsubtle effort to slow the running game of Maury Wills, he ordered his groundskeepers to soak the base paths. They responded with such enthusiasm that umpire Jocko Conlan found puddles on the infield dirt when he arrived. With martyred airs the mischievous grounds crew acceded to Conlan's directive to repair the field, but not surprisingly, it was still mushy at game time.

"If the Giants wanted to shake us up," recalls Maury Wills, "they couldn't have picked a better way to do it. We were really demoralized. It even affected our hitting because we were so angry over the mud that we couldn't concentrate properly at the plate."

Having won the psychological battle, the Giants won on the field too, strafing tender-armed Sandy Koufax and the Dodgers 8–0. Billy Pierce continued his masterful pitching at Candlestick, Mays cracked two homers, and disheartened Maury Wills didn't steal a base. A happy band of Giants journeyed to Los Angeles, blissfully unaware that their travails had hardly begun.

Treating the Dodgers' ace right-hander Don Drysdale with the same insouciance they had bestowed on Koufax, the Giants shot into a 5–0 lead. But the Dodgers ended a 35-inning scoreless streak by vengefully pounding across seven runs in the sixth on key hits by Tommy Davis and Frank Howard. Once more, the Giants had found good fortune only to squander it. They tied the score, but handed the game away on three walks and a sacrifice fly in the ninth.

The Giants and Dodgers had played 164 games each. They had, said the cynics, only one more chance to lose the pennant.

In the decisive game, the Giants sent their young right-hander, Juan Marichal against the Dodgers' veteran lefty, Johnny Podres before 45,693 patrons at Dodger Stadium.

Once again, the Giants drew first blood, scoring twice in the third on two singles and two Dodgers errors, and once again, they blew it. In the sixth the Chavez Ravine scoreboard flashed CHARGE in electric lights 18 feet high, and the home team responded nobly. On Duke Snider's single and Tommy Davis's homer, they tied the score. Before the inning had ended, the Dodgers had taken the lead, and in the seventh, they padded it as Maury Wills on the base paths drove the Giants to distraction. Trailing 4–2 going to the ninth, the Giants seemed as unlikely to win the pennant as they had a week earlier. Only the mystics recalled that 11 years before the Giants had entered a fateful ninth inning on the last day of the season trailing by the identical score.

Ed Roebuck began the Dodgers' nightmarish inning by surrendering a single to pinch hitter Matty Alou. Harvey Kuenn forced him at second, but Willie McCovey and Felipe Alou walked, loading the bases. Willie Mays reached for a slider and smashed it off Roebuck's glove for a single, narrowing the Dodgers' lead to 4–3.

Dodgers manager Walter Alston called for Stan Williams to relieve Roebuck. Williams surrendered a sacrifice fly to Orlando Cepeda, tying the score. Then, beset by visions of Ralph Branca perhaps, he panicked. On an errant pitch to Ed Bailey, Alou held at third but Mays took second. When Bailey walked, the Giants had loaded the bases for the third time in the inning.

Jim Davenport stepped up perfectly content to watch the laboring Williams struggle to find the plate. Five pitches later, Davenport stood on first, Williams departed, and the Giants were winning. Before Ron Perranoski could relieve the pressure, the Giants had scored again. To their bitterest rivals, the Dodgers had donated four walks, a wild pitch, two errors, and the pennant. Determined not to tempt fate to indulge in another capricious reversal, manager Dark eschewed his shaky relief corps in favor of Pierce, his ace lefty. Pierce set the Dodgers down in order in the bottom of the ninth, and the Giants had prevailed.

The Dodgers were staggered, but no more so than the victors. Euphoric Giants fans old and sober enough to recall Bobby Thomson's heroic smash in the '51 play-off, decided that the Giants' more modest game- and pennant-winning rally in this play-off was equally satisfying.

117

# The Longest World Series

The day after their improbable pennant winner against the Dodgers, the Giants returned to San Francisco to find the dispassionate Yankees waiting to re-acquaint them with defeat. With businesslike dispatch in the first game, the Yankees disposed of the Giants, 6–2, on Clete Boyer's tie-breaking homer in the seventh. Whitey Ford outpitched Billy O'Dell while the Giants contented themselves with breaking Ford's string of consecutive Series scoreless innings at 33⅔. The Giants seemed to have docilely accepted the forecast that rowdy, error-prone, come-from-behind baseball, so appropriate against the Dodgers, would not be tolerated by the Yankees.

So they changed their style. They won the second game, a model of decorum, 2–0 behind their ace, Jack Sanford. A 24-game winner during the regular season, Sanford limited the Yankees to three hits. The Giants nicked Ralph Terry for six, including Willie McCovey's homer. Terry and Mc-Covey would soon meet again with even more dramatic results.

In New York for game three, the teams battled in a scoreless tie for 6½ innings before Roger Maris doubled to drive in two runs. He then scored a third, the winner. Limiting the Giants to four hits, Bill Stafford bested Billy Pierce, 3–2, despite Ed Bailey's two-run homer in the ninth.

The Giants pulled even the next day,

*San Francisco's Willie McCovey trots home
after seventh-inning home run in the Giants'
2–0 Series victory over the New York Yankees.*

resorting to the slightly off-color tactics they had perfected in the pennant race. Tied 2–2 in the seventh, they loaded the bases on one hit—Matty Alou's double sandwiched between walks to Jim Davenport and pinch hitter Bob Neiman. Harvey Kuenn popped up for the second out, but light-hitting Chuck Hiller lined one of Marshall Bridges's offerings into the right field stands. Hiller's grand slammer, the first in Series history by a National Leaguer, won the game for reliever Don Larsen, who, exactly six years before, had hurled his perfect Series game for the Yankees.

The Yankees recovered the next day. In the first Terry-Sanford rematch, Tom Tresh's three-run homer broke a late-inning tie (the fourth in five games). The Yankees returned to the West Coast on the verge of victory only to be forestalled, first by the weather.

It rained in San Francisco the next three days, delaying the Series and subjecting the Giants' hospitality room at the Sheraton-Palace Hotel to a horde of restless sportswriters. Giants owner Horace Stoneham, who had obviously not anticipated such a crowd at his little reservoir of free booze, now learned to his dismay that there is nothing as unquenchably thirsty as a baseball writer with no baseball to write about. Hundreds of writers huddled day and night around the Palace spa, drowning their self-pity at Stoneham's expense.

On Monday, October 15, before a slightly groggy band of writers, the Series resumed. With one out in the fourth inning of a scoreless game, Felipe Alou singled and Willie Mays walked off Whitey Ford. Alou scored on Ford's errant pickoff attempt, Mays came home on Orlando Cepeda's double, and Cepeda tallied on Davenport's single. Roger Maris homered for

the Yankees, but the Giants got two more in the fifth, leaving them home free on Pierce's three-hitter. Winning 5–2, the Giants evened the Series for the third time.

So it came down to the final game—Ralph Terry versus Jack Sanford for the third time, each having won once. For four innings, neither team scored. In the fifth the Yankees loaded the bases with none out on singles by Moose Skowron and Clete Boyer and a walk to Terry. When Sanford got Tony Kubek to hit into a double play, Skowron scoring, Giants fans gave thanks that the damage had been no worse. In the eighth their team once more approached disaster but once more found reprieve. With the bases loaded and no one out, Billy O'Dell relieved Sanford, got Maris to force Bobby Richardson at the plate, and induced Elston Howard to hit into a double play.

Trailing by a run, the Giants entered the bottom of the ninth and subjected their already ulcerous partisans to 15 more minutes of agony. Pinch hitter Matty Alou led off and beat out a drag bunt. The crowd at Candlestick stirred hopefully, remembering that Alou had started the winning rally in the final play-off game. Their optimism was premature. Terry bore down and struck out both Felipe Alou and Hiller. Now only Willie Mays stood between the Giants and defeat.

He came through. He sent Terry's second pitch, a fastball on the outside, streaking toward the right field corner —surely a double, perhaps a triple. Off with the drive, Alou rounded second at full speed and stormed into third as right fielder Maris caught the bouncing ball on the run and in one lightning motion wheeled and threw. Second baseman Richardson took the throw and held Alou at third. Maris had made a brilliant, game-saving play.

With two out, men on second and third, and Willie McCovey at bat, manager Ralph Houk emerged from the Yankees' dugout to talk to Terry. McCovey had homered off Terry in the second game, but Houk had no thoughts of removing his pitcher. "First base is open," he said. "Do you want to walk him and pitch to Cepeda?"

"I want to pitch to McCovey," said Terry. "I can get him out."

"Go ahead," said Houk, who turned and walked back to the dugout.

Terry later confessed what many suspected: As his manager left, he couldn't help remembering the last inning of the 1960 World Series in Pittsburgh when Bill Mazeroski reached him for the homer that destroyed the Yankees. "A man seldom gets the kind of second chance I did," said Terry. He faced a team that seemed to have had no chance to win the pennant, much less the Series, and now hovered on the verge of another miraculous comeback. But Terry, victimized by such miracles before, had Fate's sympathy this time. McCovey drilled a one-one fastball on a vicious line toward right field. Diminutive Bobby Richardson could hardly have moved had he wanted to. He caught the ball.

No sooner had the game and Series ended than "if onlys" began. If only the outfield grass hadn't been soggy, Maris would not have reached Mays's double in time to hold Alou at third. If only McCovey's drive had been a yard to the left or right. . . . Winners have no patience with such second-guessing. But the Giants, having achieved the impossible twice, could not help but speculate how close they had come to doing it again.

July 13, 1963

# Early Wynn: The Three-Hundredth Victory

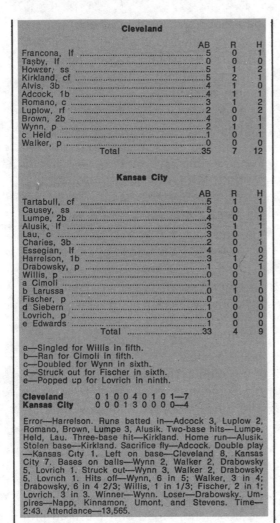

**Cleveland**

|  | AB | R | H |
|---|---|---|---|
| Francona, lf | 5 | 0 | 1 |
| Tasby, lf | 0 | 0 | 0 |
| Howser, ss | 5 | 1 | 2 |
| Kirkland, cf | 5 | 2 | 1 |
| Alvis, 3b | 4 | 1 | 0 |
| Adcock, 1b | 4 | 1 | 1 |
| Romano, c | 3 | 1 | 2 |
| Luplow, rf | 2 | 0 | 2 |
| Brown, 2b | 4 | 0 | 1 |
| Wynn, p | 2 | 1 | 1 |
| c Held | 1 | 0 | 1 |
| Walker, p | 0 | 0 | 0 |
| Total | 35 | 7 | 12 |

**Kansas City**

|  | AB | R | H |
|---|---|---|---|
| Tartabull, cf | 5 | 1 | 1 |
| Causey, ss | 5 | 0 | 0 |
| Lumpe, 2b | 4 | 0 | 1 |
| Alusik, lf | 3 | 1 | 1 |
| Lau, c | 3 | 0 | 1 |
| Charles, 3b | 2 | 0 | 1 |
| Essegian, lf | 4 | 0 | 0 |
| Harrelson, 1b | 3 | 1 | 2 |
| Drabowsky, p | 1 | 0 | 1 |
| Willis, p | 0 | 0 | 0 |
| a Cimoli | 1 | 0 | 1 |
| b Larussa | 0 | 1 | 0 |
| Fischer, p | 0 | 0 | 0 |
| d Siebern | 1 | 0 | 0 |
| Lovrich, p | 0 | 0 | 0 |
| e Edwards | 1 | 0 | 0 |
| Total | 33 | 4 | 9 |

a—Singled for Willis in fifth.
b—Ran for Cimoli in fifth.
c—Doubled for Wynn in sixth.
d—Struck out for Fischer in sixth.
e—Popped up for Lovrich in ninth.

| | | |
|---|---|---|
| **Cleveland** | 0 1 0 0 4 0 1 0 1—7 | |
| **Kansas City** | 0 0 0 1 3 0 0 0 0—4 | |

Error—Harrelson. Runs batted in—Adcock 3, Luplow 2, Romano, Brown, Lumpe 3, Alusik. Two-base hits—Lumpe, Held, Lau. Three-base hit—Kirkland. Home run—Alusik. Stolen base—Kirkland. Sacrifice fly—Adcock. Double play —Kansas City 1. Left on base—Cleveland 8, Kansas City 7. Bases on balls—Wynn 2, Walker 2, Drabowsky 5, Lovrich 1. Struck out—Wynn 3, Walker 2, Drabowsky 5, Lovrich 1. Hits off—Wynn, 6 in 5; Walker, 3 in 4; Drabowsky, 6 in 4 2/3; Willis, 1 in 1/3; Fischer, 2 in 1; Lovrich, 3 in 3. Winner—Wynn. Loser—Drabowsky. Umpires—Napp, Kinnamon, Umont, and Stevens. Time— 2:43. Attendance—13,565.

Winning 300 major league games has become more difficult than it used to be. With the liveliness of the ball, fly balls become homers; the strain of more travel tends to shorten careers; and the rise of the relief pitcher has snatched many a victory from starters.

The living proof of the frustrations that confront a pitcher striving for the magic 300 victories is Early ("Gus") Wynn, who toiled 23 years before attaining that elusive goal. There aren't many modern pitchers who worked as hard as Wynn. He appeared in 691 games and pitched 4,566 innings. He had what was tantamount to two careers, one with Washington and the other with Cleveland and Chicago.

He pitched for bad Washington teams and lost more than he won. Not until he reached Cleveland did he become a winning pitcher. During his years with the Indians, Wynn, Bob Lemon, and Mike Garcia were the Big Three. (Nor was number four an unknown—Bob Feller was soon to become a Hall of Famer.) Wynn won 20 games regularly for the Indians, and in 1959, he registered 22 triumphs for the Chicago White Sox in helping them win their first pennant in 40 years.

Wynn had come a long way since the spring of 1937, when he turned up at the Senators' training camp in Florida in a pair of blue jeans, a beaten-up glove dangling from his belt. After four trips to the minors, he blossomed. He

*Cleveland Indians right-hander Early Wynn
notches his three-hundredth major league victory
in beating the Kansas City Athletics.*

had that good, high hard one, and he was not afraid to challenge the hitters. Later he developed a good curve and change, but the fastball remained his money pitch.

It took Wynn nine years to post his first hundred victories in the majors. His second hundred came in only five years. Eight years later, he was knocking on the door of 300. It was early in September, 1962, while he was with the White Sox, that Wynn won number 299. He had lost 1–0 a few weeks before when Bill Monbouquette of the Red Sox pitched a no-hitter. After he won his two-hundred-ninety-ninth, there were still three weeks left of the season. Early figured to get at least five more starts, and if he couldn't win one of those . . . hell, he knew he'd win at least one.

He didn't. The closest he came was on September 20 against New York. The game was tied 1–1 after nine innings, but in the tenth the Yankees scored and Wynn lost. After two more starts, he was still without that all-important victory. Still, he wasn't terribly concerned. He'd get it next year. He'd be fresh and eager, and the tired arm would have its old snap back.

Then came the shocker. In November he received word from the White Sox that he had been unconditionally released. He was 43 years old, and the club needed to make room for a younger pitcher. Gus tried to latch on with another club as a free agent. He wanted that extra win badly. There were no takers. Wynn went home to Florida brooding, but he kept his arm in shape, throwing to a volunteer catcher in a local gymnasium.

Finally the call came. The Indians, the team with whom he had had some of his best years, sent an SOS. A plague of sore arms and the failure of some of the younger pitchers had made Cleveland manager Birdie Tebbetts desperate. That was in June. Early went to work immediately, but he couldn't find victory number 300, not even after three starts. He lost a 2–0 heartbreaker to the White Sox, when Ron Hansen homered with one on in the ninth. Then he dropped a 2–1 decision to the Yankees.

On Saturday, July 13, Tebbetts sent him out to pitch against the Kansas City Athletics, not one of the better clubs in the league. Obviously, his main idea was to help Wynn in his quest for the elusive three hundreth. His chances didn't appear bright at the start of the day.

"I can't say I was in good shape for that one," Wynn remembers. "I never slept the night before. The gout, which I'd had for ten years, was killing me. The attack got me under the toes of my feet and in the arms. It hurt so bad at times that I couldn't shake hands."

Early wasn't feeling well, and he didn't pitch well, but he hung in. Each club had a run after four innings. The Indians got four runs off Moe Drabowsky in the fifth. Wynn himself ignited the rally with a single, and Joe Adcock and Al Luplow each drove in two runs. That gave Wynn a 5–1 lead going into the Athletics' half of the fifth. It was a lead he couldn't hold. He knew he had to work five full innings to get credit for the victory, but bad things happened quickly. The A's loaded the bases, and Jerry Lumpe doubled to drive in three runs and cut the Indians' lead to 5–4. Luckily, Lumpe was thrown out trying for third, and Wynn threw out the next man for the last out.

That was all for Wynn, just five innings. He couldn't go any more. But the Indians hung on, even getting a couple of more runs. The final score was 7–4. That was number 300, not a well-pitched game but no less a victory. It had taken a long time—exactly 10 months and nine starts— before Wynn recorded number 300. Today the accomplishment appears even more significant, for no one has reached the 300 mark since Wynn did.

August 4, 1963

# Mickey Mantle: Comeback

Mickey Mantle gave much to baseball, and baseball, in turn, gave much to him. Mickey keeps some of his memories alive in the trophy room of his home in North Dallas, Texas. The room harbors 45 plaques, dozens of framed photographs, numerous trophies, and other memorabilia of his great moments in baseball. Prominently displayed in a huge glass-enclosed case are three large hexagonal plaques representing some of Mickey's proudest achievements. They read "Most Valuable Player of the Year," the awards he won in 1956, 1957, and 1962. On a shelf over a desk rest six thick leather-bound gold-stamped books of mounted photographs of special events. The albums were presented to Mickey.
Captions:
• "Dotted line on photo shows flight of ball as it sails into dead center field bleachers for longest measured homer in Yankee history. Blow hit off Ray Herbert in Yankees' 7–3 victory, August 12, 1964. Ball traveled over 500 feet."
• "Trajectory of homer almost hit out of Yankee Stadium vs. Pedro Ramos of Washington, May 30, 1956. Ball struck the facade on right field roof."
• "Longest ball hit at Griffith Stadium in Washington off Chuck Stobbs, April 17, 1953. Measured 565 feet over left field bleachers."
• "Game-winning home run shot off Barney Schultz, Cardinals, ninth inning, third game, 1964 World Series."
There were other reminders of the

*Though he played in pain through most of his career, the Yanks' Mickey Mantle could hit the long ball farther and more often than most healthy men.*

wonderful memories that remained with Mantle when he left baseball after the 1968 season. One in particular still gives him a thrill.

It began in 1963 in Baltimore on a rainy June night when Mantle chased a ball hit by Brooks Robinson right to the chain-link fence. As the ball went over the fence, Mickey went right into it and caught his left foot in the wire mesh. He was carried off the field with a broken bone in his left foot and torn ligaments in his knee. At the hospital, where they put a cast on the foot, doctors told him he'd be lucky if he played again that year. He was on crutches for weeks and as discouraged as he'd ever been. He seriously considered retirement, and thousands of fans anticipated it.

Although he wasn't yet ready to play, Mantle rejoined the Yankees on a road trip after five weeks. Ralph Houk, manager of the Yankees, wanted him with the team. He told writers, "Just having Mickey around gives the guys a lift, and I thought it might give him a lift, too. He can't play, but he makes the other guys play a little harder."

It was August 4, three weeks later. The Yankees were playing a doubleheader at Yankee Stadium against the Orioles. The Birds defeated the Yankees in the opener and were leading 10–9 in the bottom of the ninth of the second game. With pitcher Steve Hamilton due to bat for New York, Houk motioned for Mantle to pinch-hit. Mickey picked up a bat and to a tremendous ovation strode to the batter's box. He hadn't batted in a regular game in two months.

"I was scared," recalls Mantle. "There were forty thousand people in the stands, and when I came out of the dugout, they all stood up and gave me one of the loudest ovations I'd ever heard. It was the first time in my life I ever got goose pimples. I prayed I wouldn't look bad. I said to myself, 'Just meet the ball. Don't strike out whatever you do.'

"I don't remember going to the plate. All I know is I was just hoping that I'd make some contact with the ball. George Brunet was the pitcher, so I batted right-handed. I don't remember whether it was the first pitch or the second, but I hit the ball, and it went for a ride. I thought it would be caught, but it just kept going and landed in the seats for a home run. As I ran around the bases, I said to myself, 'You lucky stiff.' "

The home run tied the score. The Yankees went on to win the game in the tenth inning.

"I hit a lot of balls harder, but I can't say any of them gave me more satisfaction than that one," says Mantle. "I can't express myself well enough to tell you how I felt. My one regret is that my Dad couldn't have lived long enough to share that wonderful moment."

**Willie Mays**
Daniel S. Baliotti

**Tom Seaver**

Melchior DiGiacom

**Bob Gibson**                                    Fred Kaplan

**Willie Stargell**                               Fred Kaplan

Roberto Clemente

Fred Kaplan

**Pete Rose**

Melchior DiGiacomo

**Brooks Robinson**     Fred Kaplan

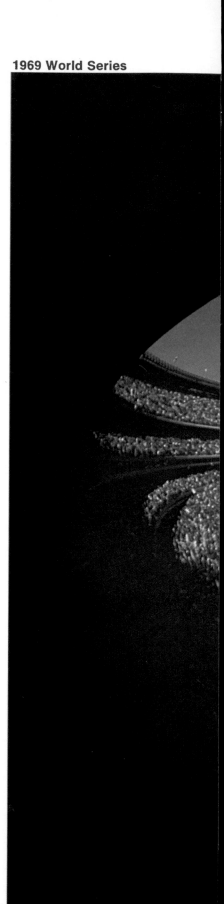

Richard Raphael

Vida Blue

September 29, 1963

# Stan Musial:
# The Last Game

### Cincinnati

|  | AB | R | H |
|---|---|---|---|
| Rose, 2b-lf | 6 | 0 | 3 |
| Harper, rf | 6 | 0 | 0 |
| Pinson, cf | 5 | 0 | 1 |
| Neal, 2b | 0 | 0 | 0 |
| Robinson, lt-cf | 6 | 0 | 0 |
| Coleman, 1b | 5 | 1 | 2 |
| Edwards, c | 2 | 0 | 0 |
| b Keough | 1 | 0 | 0 |
| Pavletich, c | 3 | 1 | 1 |
| Cardenas, ss | 6 | 0 | 2 |
| Kasko, 3b | 5 | 0 | 0 |
| Maloney, p | 2 | 0 | 0 |
| c Skinner | 1 | 0 | 1 |
| O'Toole, p | 0 | 0 | 0 |
| d Green | 1 | 0 | 0 |
| Worthington, p | 0 | 0 | 0 |
| Henry, p | 0 | 0 | 0 |
| h Walters | 1 | 0 | 0 |
| Jay, p |  | 0 | 0 |
| Total | 51 | 2 | 10 |

### St. Louis

|  | AB | R | H |
|---|---|---|---|
| Flood, cf | 7 | 1 | 2 |
| Groat, ss | 4 | 0 | 0 |
| Maxvill, ss-2b | 3 | 0 | 1 |
| Musial, lf | 3 | 0 | 2 |
| a Kolb, rf | 1 | 1 | 0 |
| e Beauchamp | 1 | 0 | 0 |
| Shannon, rf | 1 | 0 | 0 |
| Boyer, 3b | 6 | 0 | 4 |
| White, 1b | 5 | 0 | 2 |
| James, rf-lf | 5 | 0 | 0 |
| McCarver, c | 5 | 0 | 0 |
| Javier, 2b | 3 | 0 | 0 |
| f Altman | 1 | 0 | 1 |
| Buchek, ss | 2 | 0 | 1 |
| Gibson, p | 2 | 0 | 1 |
| g Clemons | 0 | 0 | 0 |
| Taylor, p | 0 | 0 | 0 |
| i Sawatski | 1 | 0 | 0 |
| Broglio, p | 1 | 1 | 0 |
| Total | 51 | 3 | 13 |

a—Ran for Musial in sixth.
b—Struck out for Edwards in seventh.
c—Singled for Maloney in eighth.
d—Popped out for O'Toole in ninth.
e—Struck out for Kolb in tenth.
f—Singled for Javier in ninth.
g—Walked for Gibson in ninth.
h—Popped out for Henry in eleventh.
i—Struck out for Taylor in eleventh.

```
Cincinnati   0 0 0 0 0 0 0 2 0 0—2
St. Louis    0 0 0 0 2 0 0 0 0 1—3
```

Errors—Boyer, Groat. Runs batted in—Cardenas 2, Maxvill, Musial, James. Two-base hits—Flood, Rose, Maxvill. Sacrifice—Harper. Sacrifice fly—James. Double plays—St. Louis 2, Cincinnati 1. Left on base—St. Louis 13, Cincinnati 12. Bases on balls—Maloney 2, Gibson 1, Taylor 2, Broglio 1. Struck out—Maloney 11, Worthington 1, Henry 1, Jay 3, Gibson 11, Taylor 1, Broglio 2. Hits off—Maloney, 5 in 7; O'Toole, 1 in 1; Worthington, 1 in 1/3; Henry, 1 in 1 2/3; Jay, 5 in 3 1/3; Gibson, 7 in 9; Taylor, 1 in 2; Broglio, 2 in 3. Wild pitch—Maloney, Gibson, Broglio 2. Winner—Broglio. Loser—Jay. Umpires Barlick, Weyer, Vargo, and Williams. Time—3:45. Attendance—27,576.

Maybe he should have quit at age 42, with a .330 batting average, but he didn't; he was having too much fun hitting. Besides, the Cardinals wanted him back. The year before, 1962, Stan Musial had played in 135 games, hit 19 home runs and batted in 82 runs. He hit .325 against right-handers and .345 against left-handers. He walked out there, day after day, confident he would hit. It was like old times, so why quit?

Musial began his twenty-second year with a hit, one of two the Cardinals managed off Ernie Broglio of the Giants. On May 8, against the Dodgers, he broke Babe Ruth's career record for extra-base hits with a home run off former teammate Bob Miller. On July 9, he appeared in his last All-Star Game. He went up as a pinch hitter against Jim Bunning. It was his last All-Star appearance, and he wanted badly to bow out with a base hit, but he lined out to Al Kaline in right field.

"I hadn't really made up my mind one way or the other whether I would play another year," Musial recalls. "But I found that I just wasn't able to concentrate at bat as completely as I had previously. My RBI production was good, but my average wasn't. I was taking called third strikes, something I'd rarely done."

Finally, in mid-August, while breakfasting with Bing Devine, the Cardinals' general manager, Musial made up his mind. "This year, Bing, is it," he said.

Musial learned that he had become a grandfather on September 10. His son Dick called to say that his wife, Sharon, had given birth to a boy. Stan celebrated the next day with a two-run homer off Glen Hobbie of the Cubs.

The Cardinals were in the midst of a hot streak, winning 19 of 20 to move within one game of the league-leading Dodgers. St. Louis was pennant happy, and Musial felt like a kid when the Dodgers came to town for a showdown series in late September. In the seventh inning, Musial hit his last home run, number 475, a shot to the pavilion on the roof, tying the score. The fans almost tore the park down. The Dodgers scored twice in the ninth, however, and won 3–1. They won again the next night and swept the series despite two hits by Musial in the finale. The race was over.

The last day of the season was Musial's final game. He had been under great strain for weeks, but it had reached absurd proportions that final weekend. Photographers and cameramen had been practically living with him. September 29, 1963 was a gray day. As Musial arrived at the park, a fan recognized him and called, "I hope you hit a homer today."

Stan grinned. "I'll settle for a little single," he replied.

Inside the clubhouse, Musial was getting into his uniform. "Will you play until you get a hit?" a writer asked.

"Yes," Musial said.

"Do you know what number it will be?"

"No."

"You have thirty-six hundred twenty-eight hits," he was told. "Another hit would be thirty-six twenty-nine."

Musial smiled. "I'd like thirty-six thirty. I like those round figures."

"You mean," the writer said, "you'd like two hits instead of one."

And Musial laughed again. "If I don't get a hit, it's not going to worry me."

Musial dressed, but he did not leave the clubhouse. He wanted to savor every moment. "I guess I'll be expected to say something," he mused. He began scribbling notes.

It was after 12 when he finally walked out on the field. He took his batting practice, drawing cheers with every swing. As the bell clanged to change the teams and Stan ran off, a boy in a box seat held up a sign that read "Stan for President." Musial laughed loudly. He walked over and autographed the sign for the boy.

The pregame ceremonies lasted an hour—presentations, gifts, speeches by Ford Frick, the commissioner; Warren Giles, the league president; Gussie Busch, the club owner; and Ken Boyer, the team captain.

Then, it was Musial's turn. He teetered nervously, nodded, brushed back his hair, rubbed his mouth, and finally spoke. "As long as I live," he said,

Stan Musial of the Cardinals follows through after slashing the six-hundred-fifty-first double of his career, tying Honus Wagner's record.

"this is a day I'll always remember." The start of the game was an anticlimax.

In the first inning, Jim Maloney of the Reds retired the first two batters, then threw a fastball that Musial took for a strike. The game was stopped and the ball was handed to Sid Keener, curator of the Hall of Fame in Cooperstown, New York. Two more pitches, and Musial struck out.

Musial came to bat again in the fourth inning. Maloney hadn't given up a hit. Stan swung at a one-one pitch and slashed hit number 3,629 past Maloney into center field. In the sixth Musial came up for a third time in the still scoreless game. With Curt Flood on second and a count of two balls and one strike, Musial got his second hit, banging a curve ball past first base into right field. The Cards had their first run. In the press box, reporters stood and applauded hit number 3,630 and RBI 1,950, another round figure.

The crowd, Musial, and manager Johnny Keane were satisfied. Gary Kolb came in to run for Musial. The cheers continued as Musial ran off the playing field for the last time.

The Cards won 3–2. Twenty-two years before, on September 17, 1941, Musial had played his first game as a Cardinal. He had made two hits, and the Cards had won 3–2. A writer noted the oddity and wryly remarked, "He hasn't improved at all."

October 5, 1966

# Moe Drabowsky to the Rescue

**Baltimore (AL)**

| | AB | R | H | PO | A |
|---|---|---|---|---|---|
| Aparicio, ss | 5 | 0 | 0 | 4 | 1 |
| Snyder, cf-lf | 3 | 1 | 1 | 2 | 0 |
| F. Robinson, rf | 5 | 1 | 2 | 1 | 0 |
| B. Robinson, 3b | 5 | 1 | 1 | 2 | 1 |
| Powell, 1b | 5 | 0 | 1 | 3 | 0 |
| Blefary, lf | 3 | 0 | 1 | 2 | 0 |
| Blair, cf | 0 | 0 | 0 | 0 | 0 |
| D. Johnson, 2b | 4 | 1 | 2 | 0 | 2 |
| Etchebarren, c | 3 | 1 | 1 | 13 | 0 |
| McNally, p | 0 | 0 | 0 | 0 | 0 |
| Drabowsky, p | 2 | 0 | 0 | 0 | 0 |
| Total | 35 | 5 | 9 | 27 | 4 |

**Los Angeles (NL)**

| | AB | R | H | PO | A |
|---|---|---|---|---|---|
| Wills, ss | 3 | 0 | 0 | 6 | 5 |
| W. Davis, cf | 4 | 0 | 1 | 1 | 0 |
| L. Johnson, rf | 3 | 1 | 0 | 3 | 0 |
| T. Davis, lf | 3 | 0 | 0 | 1 | 0 |
| Lefebvre, 2b | 3 | 1 | 1 | 3 | 5 |
| Parker, 1b | 4 | 0 | 1 | 9 | 0 |
| Gilliam, 3b | 2 | 0 | 0 | 1 | 1 |
| Roseboro, c | 4 | 0 | 0 | 3 | 0 |
| Drysdale, p | 0 | 0 | 0 | 0 | 1 |
| a Stuart | 1 | 0 | 0 | 0 | 0 |
| Moeller, p | 0 | 0 | 0 | 0 | 0 |
| b Barbieri | 1 | 0 | 0 | 0 | 0 |
| R. Miller, p | 0 | 0 | 0 | 0 | 1 |
| c Covington | 1 | 0 | 0 | 0 | 0 |
| Perronoski, p | 0 | 0 | 0 | 0 | 1 |
| d Fairly | 1 | 0 | 0 | 0 | 0 |
| Total | 30 | 2 | 3 | 27 | 14 |

a—Flied out for Drysdale in second.
b—Struck out for Moeller in fourth.
c—Struck out for R. Miller in seventh.
d—Struck out for Perranoski in ninth.

| | | |
|---|---|---|
| **Baltimore** | 3 1 0 1 0 0 0 0 0—5 | |
| **Los Angeles** | 0 1 1 0 0 0 0 0 0—2 | |

Errors—None. Runs batted in—Aparicio, Snyder, F. Robinson 2, B. Robinson, Lefebvre, Gilliam. Two-base hits—Parker, D. Johnson, Powell. Home runs—F. Robinson, B. Robinson, Lefebvre. Stolen base—Wills. Sacrifice—McNally. Left on base—Baltimore 9, Los Angeles 8. Bases on balls—McNally 5, Drabowsky 2, Drysdale 2, Moeller 1, R. Miller 2. Struck out—McNally 1, Drabowsky 11, Drysdale 1, R. Miller 1, Perronoski 2. Hits off—McNally, 2 in 2 1/3; Drabowsky, 1 in 6 2/3; Drysdale, 4 in 2; Moeller, 1 in 2; R. Miller, 2 in 3; Perranoski, 2 in 2. Winner—Drabowsky. Loser—Drysdale. Umpires—Jackowski (NL), Chylak (AL), Pelekoudas (NL), Rice (AL), Steiner (NL), and Drummond (AL). Time—2:56. Attendance—55,941.

Myron ("Moe") Drabowsky survived a checkered career in the major leagues. Never a star, he didn't start a game in his last seven seasons. But he pitched for seventeen years in the big leagues with eight different clubs and witnessed some historic games, albeit not always from a happy perspective.

"I was the pitcher when Stan Musial got his three-thousandth hit," Moe says almost boastfully. "I was the pitcher when Dave Nicholson hit the ball over the left field roof at Comiskey Park, the longest ball ever hit in that park. I was also the losing pitcher when Early Wynn won his three hundredth. And I tied a major league record when I hit four batters in one game."

But the game that will linger longest in Moe Drabowsky's memory is the opening game of the 1966 World Series between the Baltimore Orioles and Los Angeles Dodgers. The Orioles entered that Series, their first in history, as a decided underdog to the redoubtable Dodgers, World Series veterans who had swept the Yankees in four straight and whipped the Twins in seven in their last Series encounters. The two Dodgers pitchers who were mainly responsible for those successes, Don Drysdale and Sandy Koufax, were still at the apex of their careers.

Manager Walter Alston of the Dodgers selected Drysdale to pitch the first 1966 Series game because he had needed Koufax to wrap up the league championship on the final day of the season. Don didn't have it that day. The Orioles jumped him early and decisively. The Robinson boys, Frank and Brooks, bombed Drysdale for two home runs in the first inning. Frank's homer followed a walk to Russ Snyder. The Dodgers never caught up in that game nor in any of the three following games as the Orioles completed an amazing sweep. The first game was the decisive one. The Orioles learned that afternoon they could beat the Dodgers.

Manager Hank Bauer nominated Dave McNally as the Orioles' starting pitcher. The ace left-hander, normally in complete control of his pitches, just couldn't find the strike zone, walking five in 2⅓ innings. When he walked the bases loaded in the third, Bauer called for Drabowsky, whom the Orioles had claimed in the draft the previous year for $25,000 after the St. Louis Cardinals had left him on their Jacksonville farm club roster.

As Drabowsky left the bullpen, he turned to a fellow reliever and said, "I had always dreamed of pitching in a World Series game, but so soon? I still haven't finished dreaming."

Moe was in anything but a trance. His fastball especially was very much alive, sinking and slipping under the Dodgers' bats. With one out and the bases loaded in the third, he took complete control of the game. He struck out Wes Parker, walked Jim Gilliam to force in what proved to be the Dodgers' last run of the Series, and then retired John Roseboro.

In the next inning, the fourth, Drabowsky struck out Jim Barbieri, Maury Wills, and Willie Davis in succession. Then in the fifth inning, he fanned Lou Johnson, Tommy Davis, and Jim Lefebvre, who had homered off McNally in the second. Drabowsky's six strikeouts in a row tied a Series record set by Hod Eller of Cincinnati in 1919.

In 6⅔ innings of superb relief, Drabowsky permitted only one hit, a harmless single, and recorded eleven strikeouts, surpassing the previous World Series strikeout high by a relief pitcher, ten by Jess Barnes of the 1921 Giants. The only hard hit ball by the frustrated National Leaguers was Roseboro's line drive out in the third.

The final score was 5–2. Moe's magic set the pattern for his fellow moundsmen. Jim Palmer pitched the next day and outdueled Sandy Koufax 6–0. Wally Bunker followed with a 1–0 triumph over Claude Osteen, and McNally, in his second outing, extended the Dodgers' scoreless string to 33 consecutive innings with a final 1–0 victory over Drysdale.

Ironically, McNally, Palmer, and Bunker had only one shutout among them during the regular season. "The turning point in that Series," said Bauer afterward, "was when Drabowsky came in to shut the door on the Dodgers."

# Carl Yastrzemski: The Year

It was a year to remember. In the final week of the 1967 season, four teams still had a chance to win the American League pennant. It had been the most fantastic four-team pennant race big league baseball had ever known. Not for a day, a week, or a month but for nearly half a season, each of the four clubs shuffled between first and fourth.

One of the contenders was Minnesota, a sound ball club that had won the pennant only two years before. Another contender, Detroit, boasted a strong lineup and solid pitching. Chicago, although weak at the plate, had the best pitching in the league and a fighting, gambling manager in Eddie Stankey. Finally, Boston, a ninth-place team the year before, had one great pitcher, one great hitter, and a cast of brash young kids imbued with the spirit of manager Dick Williams.

A 100–1 shot at the start of the season, the Red Sox were, in the final weeks of this chaotic pennant race, tied with Detroit, only percentage points behind Minnesota and Chicago.

In the final week, the Red Sox dropped two straight to Cleveland. Two games remained, both with Minnesota at home. The Tigers had four with California, and the White Sox had their two best pitchers, Gary Peters and Joel Horlen, ready for a twi-night doubleheader at Kansas City. It looked bad for Boston until Kansas City stunned Chicago by beating both Peters and Hor-

134

*Boston's Carl Yastrzemski sends a home run over Fenway Park's "Green Monster" wall during his triple crown year of 1967.*

len. Two days later, the White Sox were out of the race.

On the next-to-the-last day, the Red Sox were just one game behind the leading Twins. A sweep of the two with Minnesota would assure them of a tie for first place even if the Tigers won all their remaining games. The entire Red Sox team was living in a sort of dream world, certain that they and nobody else would take a commanding lead. The Red Sox felt they were a team of destiny. Surely their leader, Carl Yastrzemski, was a man of destiny.

A hot hitter all year, Yastrzemski had sizzled in September. Yaz had clinched the RBI title with an amazing streak of 20 RBIs in 15 games. Harmon Killebrew of the Twins and Yaz battled to the final day for the home run title. Each had 43 when the Twins came to Boston for the final two games. Jim Kaat started for the Twins on Saturday. Yastrzemski hit a curve for a single in his first time at bat. Kaat hurt his arm early and was replaced by Jim Perry. The tough, tall right-hander fanned Yaz in the third inning, preserving a 1–0 lead. In the fifth three Red Sox hits tied the score at 1–1. Carl then hit a three-two pitch for another single, scoring Dalton Jones for a 2–1 lead. The Sox still led, 3–2, when Yaz faced Jim Merritt, a left-hander, with two out in the seventh. This time the left-handed slugger caught a fastball and hammered it into the right field seats for his forty-fourth home run. That iced the game for the

Red Sox (they won 6–4) but not for Yastrzemski's home run lead. Killebrew connected with a Gary Bell pitch in the ninth for his forty-fourth.

The victory pulled the Red Sox into a tie for first place with one day left in the season. Unable to restrain their enthusiasm, Boston fans celebrated as if the Sox had won the pennant. On that wild, mad night, people happily indulged in food and drink and toasted the chief object of their affections, Carl Yastrzemski. He had almost single-handedly brought the Red Sox' impossible dream to the verge of reality.

Joe Garagiola dubbed Yastrzemski "Superman." "When do you jump off the Empire State Building and float down to the street on the wings of your cape?" Garagiola asked.

Indeed, there appeared to be nothing that Yaz couldn't do. Game-winning hits became almost routine for him. "I remember saying to my wife," recalls Yastrzemski, "that if we sat down every day and planned situations in which I could be the hero, at bat and on the field, we couldn't have come closer than what actually happened." The base hit, the home run, the great catch, the strong throw, all seemed made to order for Yaz.

Sunday, October 1, the Red Sox were only hours away from a possible pennant. The Tigers, still one-half game behind the Red Sox and Twins, had a chance. While the Red Sox and Twins met in the most important game of the year, Detroit played the California Angels in a doubleheader at Detroit. By winning both games, the Tigers would force a play-off with the winner of the Twins-Red Sox game. If the Tigers split, the winner of the Minnesota-Boston game would be the new champion of the American League.

Fenway Park was filled with Red Sox fans seemingly fixated by Yastrzemski. With the Twins leading 1–0 in the first, Carl faced Dean Chance and managed a lucky hit when he beat out a ground ball that Chance knocked down. The Twins scored again in the third for a 2–0 lead. Chance was still on the mound when Yaz came to bat in the third. This time he slammed a double off the right center field wall, but the Red Sox failed to score. Yaz next came to bat in the fifth inning with the bases loaded and none out. "I was so anxious to hit, I practically ran up to the plate," Yaz recalls. "I was never so sure of myself in my life."

Chance wound up and threw a sinker. Yaz swung and lined a single to center, scoring the tying runs. Before the inning was over, the Red Sox had knocked out Chance, scored five runs, and were enjoying a 5–2 lead. But Yaz wasn't through.

The Twins had two on in the eighth when Bob Allison lined a hit into the left field corner. Yastrzemski backhanded the ball and threw a strike to

*"I was so anxious to hit, I practically ran up to the plate," Yastrzemski recalls. "I was never so sure of myself in my life."*

second base to nip Allison trying for a double. It was the best and most important throw he made all year. It got the Red Sox out of the inning with only one run scoring. Only one inning to go.

Fifteen minutes later it was over. Rich Rollins popped to Rico Petrocelli, and the Red Sox had at least tied for first. When the news came a short time later that the Tigers had lost the second game of their doubleheader to the Angels, the Red Sox were in the World Series, and Carl Yastrzemski had put them there.

The highlights of Yaz's 1967 record: He tied for the league lead in homers with 44 and hit more homers at Fenway Park than any player but Jimmy Foxx. He led the league with a .326 average, his second batting crown. He led the majors in runs batted in with 121. He led the league in hits, runs scored, total bases, and slugging percentage.

Characteristically, he was at his best down the stretch, batting .444 with 26 RBIs in his last 19 games. In his last 13 times at bat, when the pressure was toughest, Yastrzemski had 10 hits.

May 14–June 8, 1968

# Don Drysdale: 58 2/3 Consecutive Scoreless Innings

*Drysdale's menacing look accompanied his sidearm delivery.*

During most of his career with the Los Angeles Dodgers, Don Drysdale pitched well and Sandy Koufax pitched brilliantly. "The big guy," says manager Walter Alston of Drysdale, "in a way, was in a position with us similar to Lou Gehrig's with the New York Yankees in Babe Ruth's heyday. Everybody was paying so much attention to Sandy Koufax, who rated it of course, that Drysdale was badly overshadowed. But no pitcher I've ever seen could hand-cuff right-handed batters the way Drysdale could. And there were days when he was just as overwhelming as Koufax against all types of hitters."

During Drysdale's 13 full seasons, the Dodgers won five flags and three world championships. Drysdale pitched more than 200 innings a season for 12 straight years. Four times he pitched more than 300 innings. He won the Cy Young Award with his 25–9 record in 1962 and led the National League in strikeouts three times. He struck out more than 200 in a season six times. Before he retired, he recorded more victories, pitched more innings, struck out more batters, and notched more shutouts than any other Dodger.

Unlike Koufax, who turned in four no-hitters, Drysdale never pitched one, but the tall right-hander performed an iron-man's feat that ranks with the most unassailable in baseball.

From mid-May through the first week in June of 1968, Big Don did not give up a run through 58⅔ consecutive innings. During this month-long skein, Drysdale wiped out three of the most coveted pitching records. Drysdale's first gem in his record-breaking pitching tiara was the obliteration of King Carl Hubbell's 35-year-old National League standard of 46⅓ consecutive scoreless innings. Then he erased the major league record of five consecutive shutouts, posted by Guy ("Doc") Harris of the Chicago White Sox in 1904. Finally, Drysdale surpassed Walter Johnson's all-time record of 56 straight runless innings, established in 1913, 55 years earlier.

In brushing aside 64 years of history, Drysdale left 11 runners on third and 10 on second. He had to survive three ninth-inning, bases-loaded situations. In one of them, the heavy-hitting San Francisco Giants loaded the bases with none out.

Drysdale began his string on May 14 with a two-hit, 2–0 decision over the Chicago Cubs. Four days later, he blanked Houston, 1–0, on five hits. Then he shut out St. Louis, 2–0, and Houston again, 5–0. That brought Drysdale one shutout away from Harris's 64-year-old mark. Drysdale next faced the Giants on May 31, and more than 50,000 people jammed Dodger Stadium. Going into the Giants' ninth, one inning away from five straight shutouts and having already pitched 44 consecutive scoreless innings, Drysdale was about to face his biggest challenge.

Willie McCovey walked, and Nate Oliver ran for him. Jim Ray Hart singled Oliver to second. A walk to Jim Marshall loaded the bases with none out. That brought Dick Dietz to bat. On a two-two count, Drysdale's pitch hit Dietz. Umpire Harry Wendlestedt, amid protests by the Giants, ruled that Dietz had made no attempt to avoid the pitch. Thus, instead of Dietz reaching first base and forcing in a run, the count merely went full. On the next pitch, Dietz flied to short left. Drysdale then retired the next two batters and came away a 3–0 winner.

On his rush to the record, Drysdale ran his shutout string to six on June 4 with a 5–0 blanking of Pittsburgh. He did not allow a hit against Philadelphia on June 8 until after he had passed Johnson's 56 inning mark, his last remaining goal. When Roberto Pena grounded out opening the third, Drysdale passed Johnson. Finally, in the fifth, he allowed his first run in almost a month. Tony Taylor and Clay Dalrymple singled. With runners on first and third, Drysdale struck out Pena, but Howie Bedell, a little-known outfielder batting for the pitcher, lifted a fly to left field that brought Taylor home from third.

Drysdale's hypnotic pitching spell had ended, but the feat remains legendary today, in an era when pitching six complete games in a row, much less six shutouts, is almost miraculous.

139

July 30, 1968

# Ron Hansen:
# Unassisted Triple Play

Eleven players in the major leagues have pitched perfect games. Nine have hit four home runs in a game. But only eight have made unassisted triple plays. The first was Neal Ball, shortstop for the Cleveland Indians, on July 19, 1906. The last was Ron Hansen, shortstop for the Washington Senators, on July 30, 1968. Between, were six fielders, who, excepting Glenn Wright, were almost as innocuous: Bill Wambsganss, Cleveland, October 10, 1920; George Burns, Boston Red Sox, September 13, 1923; Ernie Padgett, Boston Braves, October 6, 1923; Glenn Wright, Pittsburgh, May 7, 1925; Jimmy Cooney, Chicago Cubs, May 30, 1927; and Johnny Neun, Detroit, May 31, 1927.

Wambsganss's feat was the most famous. It came in the 1920 World Series between the Cleveland Indians and Brooklyn Dodgers. Pete Kilduff led off the fifth inning with a single, and Otto Miller followed with another single. Clarence Mitchell, a good left-handed hitting pitcher who had replaced Burleigh Grimes, took his turn at the plate. Mitchell hit a shot toward center field that looked like a sure hit, but second baseman Wambsganss made a leaping catch. Seeing Kilduff near third and Miller within a few yards of second, Wamby touched second, doubling Kilduff, and then wheeled to throw to first. Then he saw Miller standing next to him, utterly confused. He tagged him for the third out and the only unassisted

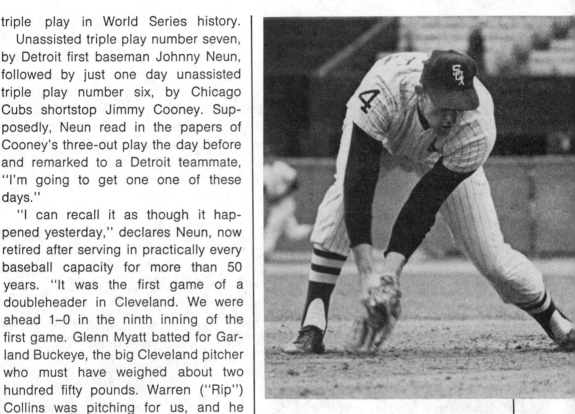

triple play in World Series history.

Unassisted triple play number seven, by Detroit first baseman Johnny Neun, followed by just one day unassisted triple play number six, by Chicago Cubs shortstop Jimmy Cooney. Supposedly, Neun read in the papers of Cooney's three-out play the day before and remarked to a Detroit teammate, "I'm going to get one one of these days."

"I can recall it as though it happened yesterday," declares Neun, now retired after serving in practically every baseball capacity for more than 50 years. "It was the first game of a doubleheader in Cleveland. We were ahead 1–0 in the ninth inning of the first game. Glenn Myatt batted for Garland Buckeye, the big Cleveland pitcher who must have weighed about two hundred fifty pounds. Warren ("Rip") Collins was pitching for us, and he walked Myatt. Then Charlie Jamieson got on with a bunt. Homer Summa came up to bat and tried to bunt twice. Remember, they were trying to push that tying run across. Both bunts rolled foul, so our infield, which had been pulled in, went back to its regular position.

"Summa then socked a line drive right at me. I didn't have to move to catch it, but I had to take at least eight or ten steps to reach first base and retire Jamieson. Meanwhile, out of the corner of my eye, I saw that Myatt

141

was still running toward third and hadn't turned around to see whether the ball had been caught. Charlie Gehringer, our second baseman, yelled for the ball, but I ignored him. I ran to second myself, stepped on the bag, and the game was over—the first time in history that a triple play ended the ball game."

Forty-one years and two months later, on July 30, 1968, the Cleveland Indians met the Washington Senators, who were already well on their way to their accustomed resting place at the bottom of the American League. The Indians had become relatively well acquainted with unassisted triple plays, hitting into two and executing two themselves. Today, while trouncing the Senators 10–1, they would bring a little sunshine to the Senators' dreary season, and a little excitement to an other-

wise tedious, largely familiar pasting.

It happened so quickly that many of those at the ball park didn't realize they had witnessed one of the game's rarest plays. In the first inning, Dave Nelson singled and Russ Snyder coaxed a walk off Washington pitcher Bruce Howard. With a three-two count on Joe Azcue and both runners off with the pitch, shortstop Hansen broke to cover second. When Azcue lined the pitch up the middle, Hansen had merely to catch the ball, touch second, and tag the trapped Snyder steaming into second.

The Cleveland crowd greeted Hansen's first at bat after the triple play with little more enthusiasm than they did his work at the plate (a strikeout). Miffed perhaps by the lack of recognition for his historic feat, Hansen assaulted another record by striking out three more times. His total of four for the game left him one short of the record.

Baseball fortunes, which had risen and crumbled in the 40 years since the previous unassisted triple play, now continued their sometimes whimsical ebb and flow. Two nights later, Hansen crashed a bases-loaded homer for Washington against Detroit. The next day, he was traded to the White Sox for Tim Cullen. That night, playing for the White Sox, Hansen, walked, doubled, singled, and drove in a run against his former teammates.

September 14, 1968

# Denny McLain: 30 Victories

| Oakland | AB | R | H |
|---|---|---|---|
| Campaneris, ss | 4 | 0 | 1 |
| Monday, cf | 4 | 0 | 1 |
| Cater, 1b | 4 | 1 | 2 |
| Bando, 3b | 3 | 0 | 0 |
| Jackson, rf | 4 | 2 | 2 |
| Green, 2b | 4 | 0 | 0 |
| Keough, lf | 3 | 0 | 0 |
| Gosger, lf | 0 | 0 | 0 |
| Duncan, c | 2 | 1 | 0 |
| Dobson, p | 1 | 0 | 0 |
| Aker, p | 0 | 0 | 0 |
| Lindblad, p | 0 | 0 | 0 |
| Donaldson, ph | 0 | 0 | 0 |
| Segui, p | 1 | 0 | 0 |
| Total | 30 | 4 | 6 |

| Detroit | AB | R | H |
|---|---|---|---|
| McAuliffe, 2b | 5 | 0 | 1 |
| Stanley, cf | 5 | 1 | 2 |
| Northrup, rf | 4 | 1 | 0 |
| Horton, lf | 5 | 1 | 2 |
| Cash, 1b | 4 | 1 | 2 |
| Freehan, c | 3 | 0 | 1 |
| Matchick, ss | 4 | 0 | 1 |
| Wert, 3b | 2 | 0 | 0 |
| Brown, ph | 1 | 0 | 0 |
| Tracewski, 3b | 0 | 0 | 0 |
| McLain, p | 1 | 0 | 0 |
| Kaline, ph | 0 | 1 | 0 |
| Total | 34 | 5 | 9 |

| | | |
|---|---|---|
| Oakland | 0 0 0 2 1 0 0 0 1—4 | |
| Detroit | 0 0 0 3 0 0 0 0 2—5 | |

Errors—Bando, Cater, Matchick. Runs batted in—Campaneris, Jackson 3, Northrup, Horton, Cash 3. Home runs—Jackson 2, Cash. Sacrifices—Bando, Donaldson, McLain. Bases on balls—Dobson 2, Aker 1, Segui 2, McLain 1. Struck out—Dobson 4, Lindblad 1, Segui 1, McLain 10. Hits off—Dobson, 4 in 3 2/3; Aker, 0 in 0 (pitched to one batter in fourth); Lindblad, 0 in 1/3; Segui, 5 in 4 1/3; McLain, 6 in 9. Left on base—Oakland 2, Detroit 10. Wild pitch—Aker. Loser—Segui. Umpires—Napp, Umont, Haller, and Neudecker. Time—3:00. Attendance—33,688.

When Denny McLain strode to the mound in Tiger Stadium in Detroit on the afternoon of Saturday, September 14, 1968, the national attention switched from the overriding issues of the day to television's "Game of the Week" and to Denny McLain. Baseball's man of the year, a 24-year-old musician, an extrovert, and a pitcher for the Detroit Tigers, was seeking his thirtieth victory of the season. Only 12 other men in this century had won 30 in a season. Only two others had done it in the last 48 years and none since Dizzy Dean won 30 for the St. Louis Cardinals in 1934.

Just as McLain had this coveted prize within his grasp, so the Tigers, as they faced the Oakland A's, had their first American League pennant since 1945 within grasp. As the Tigers sought to repeat the feat they had last performed when McLain was one year old, the free-wheeling, blithe-spirited, and self-confessed "character" was making good on his boast to become "the greatest pitcher in the world."

Denny started taking organ lessons at the age of 8. At 13 he turned pro, earning $20 one day by playing at a summer fair. But baseball was his first love. He was signed by the Chicago White Sox in 1962 and started his flamboyant career by pitching a no-hitter in the Appalachian League. The next spring, he was claimed on waivers by the Tigers. Two years later, at age

22, he won 20 games. Two years after that, he was going after the magic thirtieth victory.

McLain was neither shy about opening his mouth nor ruffled by putting his foot in it. He had been booed by the Detroit fans, satirized by the Detroit players, and restrained by the Detroit management. His most enduring nickname was "Mighty Mouth." He once

*Denny McLain of the Detroit Tigers works for his thirtieth victory of the 1968 season against Oakland's Bert Campaneris.*

145

called the Tigers a "country-club team." He said the Detroit fans were "the worst in the world," a judgment he later tempered by adding he had meant only some of them. Neither the taunts nor the publicity hampered his pitching, and hitters did only occasionally, as in this game against Oakland.

The Athletics reached McLain for two runs in the fourth inning when Reggie Jackson homered following a single by Danny Cater. The Tigers charged back in the bottom of the inning, knocking out A's starter Chuck Dobson with a three-run rally. Norm Cash's twenty-first home run climaxed the rally after a walk to Jim Northrup and a single by Willie Horton.

After tying the score in the fifth, the A's forged ahead in the ninth when Jackson blasted his second homer of the game. McLain's bid for number 30 seemed thwarted. Diego Segui, who had taken over for the A's in the fifth and pitched scoreless ball since, carried the 4–3 margin to the last of the ninth.

Al Kaline gave the Tigers' partisan crowd some hope by coaxing a lead-off walk from Segui. He held first as Dick McAuliffe fouled out but reached third when Mickey Stanley singled up the middle. With the crowd cheering, A's manager Bob Kennedy went to the mound. After a brief conference, he stayed with Segui and hoped for a double-play grounder.

Segui did his job too well. Jim Northrup managed only a dribbler toward first baseman Danny Cater, who charged halfway to the plate and fielded the ball. With Kaline coming home full tilt from third, Cater's throw on the run sailed past catcher Dave Duncan, and Kaline sprawled over the catcher, gracelessly but emphatically landing on the plate with the tying run.

Stanley raced to third on the error, and Willie Horton stepped to the plate. The Athletics' outfielders, realizing that a sacrifice fly would score the winning run, reluctantly moved in on the powerful Horton. He worked the count to two and two and drilled a long liner to left that sailed over the head of Jim Gosger. Stanley trotted home with the winning run, and the Detroit dugout erupted in a spontaneous celebration for McLain. As soon as Stanley crossed the plate, the Tigers mobbed their garrulous hero and brought him to the dugout steps to receive a standing ovation from the crowd.

One of the 33,688 who cheered was Dizzy Dean, the majors' last 30-game winner, who had come 1,400 miles for the event. With his arms wrapped around McLain, Dean said, "They won't have this much excitement here if they win the World Series," (an assertion soon to be tested).

"I'll never win a bigger one," McLain declared happily. For once, no one disagreed with him.

September 17–18, 1968

# Perry, Washburn: Back-to-Back No-hitters

Two teams exchanging no-hitters on successive days? It did happen. On September 17, 1968, Gaylord Perry of the San Francisco Giants threw a no-hit masterpiece against the St. Louis Cardinals. The next afternoon, less than 24 hours later, Cardinals right-hander Ray Washburn held the Giants hitless, defeating them 2–0.

Perry struck out nine and walked two in winning a 1–0 duel from Bob Gibson. Washburn struck out eight and walked five in outpitching Bob Bolin. A home run by Ron Hunt proved to be the difference in the first game. The homer, only the second of the year for the singles-hitting second baseman, came in the first inning. It was one of only four hits that Gibson permitted.

"It was my first and only no-hitter since I got out of high school," recalls Perry. "I pitched six or seven no-hitters in high school but never was able to get one in professional baseball." Gaylord had come close a month earlier against the Cubs. The only hit off him that day was a single by Glenn Beckert in the seventh inning.

"When I got into the seventh inning against the Cardinals, I couldn't help thinking of Beckert," says Perry. "Nobody on our club mentioned it, but it sure was on my mind. Any pitcher can luck out maybe once in his career. A lot of guys have pitched no-hitters. Mine was a special thrill because it came so soon after that one-hitter."

147

The only Redbirds to reach base against Perry in his great game were Mike Shannon and Phil Gagliano. Shannon walked with two out in the second inning, Gagliano with two out in the eighth. There were no errors and only two difficult plays in the hour, 40-minute classic. Perry made the first, a quick move on a little bouncer by Dal Maxvill in the sixth. The same inning, Willie McCovey made a fine stop of a shot by Bobby Tolan, he fed Perry perfectly, and Gaylord beat the St. Louis speedster to the bag. Perry used three pitches, a fastball, curve, and slider.

This was only the second no-hitter in the 10 years the Giants had inhabited Candlestick Park. Juan Marichal pitched the first one, against Houston in 1963. Then Perry sat in the Giants' dugout the next afternoon, watching Ray Washburn duplicate his performance.

"I was working on Washburn on the rubbing table just before the game," recalls Cardinals trainer Bob Bauman, "and I told him, 'You are going to pitch a no-hitter today because you're going to get even with those guys.' "

Washburn had been under Bauman's special care since a serious muscle tear in 1966 had threatened to end his career. Bauman's care and Washburn's tremendous cooperation paid off. He faced the Giants with a string of seven straight victories, due largely to the addition of an excellent slow curve. "The

curve turned him into a great pitcher," said Johnny Edwards, who caught Washburn that afternoon.

Washburn threw 131 pitches that day; 58 were curve balls. Extra careful at times, he walked five men. Only two balls were hit out of the infield, but there weren't any tough chances. It was Ray's thirteenth victory, a new high for him. Only in the first inning did the Giants push a man past first base, when Washburn walked two men, but he struck out Dick Dietz to end the

threat. The no-hitter was only the fourth by a Cardinals pitcher in this century. Jess Haines, in 1924, Paul Dean in 1934, and Lon Warneke in 1941 had the others.

The back-to-back no-hitters by Perry and Washburn were the first in history. In 1917, Ernie Koob pitched a no-hitter for the Browns against the White Sox. The next day, Koob's teammate, Bob Groom, also pitched a no-hitter against the Sox, but it was in the second game of a doubleheader.

Opposite: *The Giants' Gaylord Perry strikes out the Cardinals' Curt Flood to finish his 1–0 no-hitter.* Above: *The Cards' Ray Washburn gets revenge the following day.*

September 29, 1968

# Pete Rose: A Batting Crown on the Final Day

Matty Alou was hot. Beginning the final week of the 1968 season, he had trailed Pete Rose, the batting leader, by 12 points. Now, with three games left to play for each player, they were tied at .331. Alou had gone nine for 12 and was brimming with confidence. Rose had managed only one hit in 12 at bats and was desperate.

On Friday, September 27, Alou went hitless in four at bats in an afternoon game in Chicago. In 15 innings against the Giants that night in Cincinnati, Rose managed only one hit in seven at bats. Alou and Rose remained virtually dead-locked.

The experts, who are never as endearing or as well remembered as when they are wrong, picked Alou to win. Although Rose had hit over .300 in the last three seasons, Alou had won the title last year in a battle as close as this. Now he had the momentum.

In an effort to regain his faltering batting eye, Rose took 25 minutes of extra batting practice before facing Gaylord Perry the next afternoon. It worked. Rose hit safely the first four times he faced Perry. Unaccustomed to hitters taking such liberties with him, the nettled Giants pitcher approached Rose, who was standing on base after his fourth hit. "Got enough?" asked Perry with no hint that he wanted an answer.

"I'll take another," Rose replied. He did. On his fifth turn at the plate,

*Pete Rose shows muscles that belie his reputation as a singles hitter.*

Pete doubled, his fifth hit. For the first time in nearly two weeks he stopped worrying, fully confident that he had taken care of Matty Alou. But no sooner had he finished congratulating himself than Hal Lanier, the Giants' second baseman, sauntered past and remarked with calculating smoothness, "It's a good thing you got those five hits. He went four for four today."

"Who went four for four?" Rose asked, not sure he wanted to know.

"Matty Alou. You must have heard," answered the ever-helpful Lanier.

Alou's perfect day left him two points behind Rose. Pete began worrying again. "Before I went to bed that night," says Rose, "I had it figured out that I could still win the title if I went one for four and he went two for four."

On the final day, 27,464 fans in Cincinnati gave Rose an ovation as he stepped to the plate the first time. He responded by lashing a double off Ray Sadecki. It was his only hit in three at bats, but Alou went hitless in Chicago. "Charley Hustle" had won the batting title, .335 to .332 for Alou.

It was the first of two consecutive batting titles for Rose. The next year too he would win the crown on the last day of the season, this time over Roberto Clemente. The Pirates' slugger, with three for three on the last day would close to within a point of Pete. But the resourceful Rose, aware of Clemente's threat, would prevail. In his last time at bat, he would, with typical Charley Hustle diligence, lay down a surprise bunt and beat it out, solidifying his lead over Clemente.

Pete's determination and hustle were not rewarded only by the prestigious, but monetarily unsatisfying, twin batting titles. The next year Rose became baseball's first $100,000 singles hitter.

October 2, 1968

# Bob Gibson: 17 World Series Strikeouts

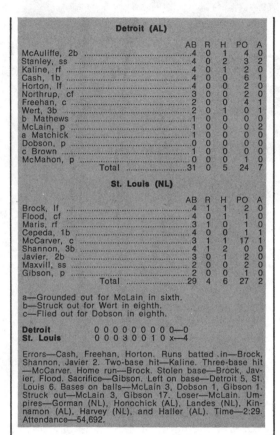

### Detroit (AL)

| | AB | R | H | PO | A |
|---|---|---|---|---|---|
| McAuliffe, 2b | 4 | 0 | 1 | 4 | 0 |
| Stanley, ss | 4 | 0 | 2 | 3 | 2 |
| Kaline, rf | 4 | 0 | 1 | 2 | 0 |
| Cash, 1b | 4 | 0 | 0 | 6 | 1 |
| Horton, lf | 4 | 0 | 0 | 2 | 0 |
| Northrup, cf | 3 | 0 | 0 | 2 | 0 |
| Freehan, c | 2 | 0 | 0 | 4 | 1 |
| Wert, 3b | 2 | 0 | 1 | 0 | 1 |
| b Mathews | 1 | 0 | 0 | 0 | 0 |
| McLain, p | 1 | 0 | 0 | 0 | 2 |
| a Matchick | 1 | 0 | 0 | 0 | 0 |
| Dobson, p | 0 | 0 | 0 | 0 | 0 |
| c Brown | 1 | 0 | 0 | 0 | 0 |
| McMahon, p | 0 | 0 | 0 | 1 | 0 |
| Total | 31 | 0 | 5 | 24 | 7 |

### St. Louis (NL)

| | AB | R | H | PO | A |
|---|---|---|---|---|---|
| Brock, lf | 4 | 1 | 1 | 2 | 0 |
| Flood, cf | 4 | 0 | 1 | 1 | 0 |
| Maris, rf | 3 | 1 | 0 | 1 | 0 |
| Cepeda, 1b | 4 | 0 | 0 | 1 | 1 |
| McCarver, c | 3 | 1 | 1 | 17 | 1 |
| Shannon, 3b | 4 | 1 | 2 | 2 | 0 |
| Javier, 2b | 3 | 0 | 1 | 2 | 0 |
| Maxvill, ss | 2 | 0 | 0 | 2 | 0 |
| Gibson, p | 2 | 0 | 0 | 1 | 0 |
| Total | 29 | 4 | 6 | 27 | 2 |

a—Grounded out for McLain in sixth.
b—Struck out for Wert in eighth.
c—Flied out for Dobson in eighth.

| | | |
|---|---|---|
| **Detroit** | 0 0 0 0 0 0 0 0 0—0 | |
| **St. Louis** | 0 0 3 0 0 1 0 x—4 | |

Errors—Cash, Freehan, Horton. Runs batted in—Brock, Shannon, Javier 2. Two-base hit—Kaline. Three-base hit—McCarver. Home run—Brock. Stolen base—Brock, Javier, Flood. Sacrifice—Gibson. Left on base—Detroit 5, St. Louis 6. Bases on balls—McLain 3, Dobson 1, Gibson 1. Struck out—McLain 3, Gibson 17. Loser—McLain. Umpires—Gorman (NL), Honochick (AL), Landes (NL), Kinnamon (AL), Harvey (NL), and Haller (AL). Time—2:29. Attendance—54,692.

The pitcher who is at his best when the challenge is greatest, who wins the game he must win, is a money pitcher. Year after year, a money pitcher has been the St. Louis stopper. He is the greatest pitcher in the club's history.

Bob Gibson has won more games than any other Cardinals pitcher. The National League's Most Valuable Player in 1968, Cy Young winner in 1970, and author of a no-hitter in 1971, Gibby's finest hour came in the 1968 World Series against the Detroit Tigers. The date was October 2; Gibson's mound opponent was Denny McLain. The duel was one of the most widely heralded pitching match-ups in recent World Series times. McLain, colorful, talkative, and overpowering, had won 31 games during the regular season, the first 30-game winner since Dizzy Dean won that many in 1934 for the Cardinals. Gibson had won "only" 22 games, but more importantly, he'd pitched 13 shutouts and posted a 1.12 earned run average, the lowest ever for a pitcher working 300 or more innings in a season.

Gibson took the mound in the 1968 Series opener at Busch Stadium with a remarkable record. After bowing to Mel Stottlemyre and the New York Yankees in the second game of the 1964 Series, Gibson began a string that reached six consecutive complete-game victories in World Series competition. In this game he would demonstrate why he

Cardinals' Bob Gibson shows his powerful delivery while striking out 17 Detroit Tigers in the opening game of the 1968 Series.

was the number one money man of the mound.

The first inning was unsubtle foreshadowing. Bob began by striking out Dick McAuliffe, and after Mickey Stanley went out, he struck out the Tigers' big hitter, Al Kaline. In the second, he got all three batters on strikeouts—Norm Cash and Jim Northrup swinging, Willie Horton looking. Bill Freehan struck out to start the Detroit third. When McLain bunted foul on the third strike, Gibson had struck out seven of the first nine batters to face him.

Kaline was called out on strikes in the fourth as was Don Wert in the fifth. Gibson got two more in the sixth, Stanley and Cash, both swinging. Two more Tigers, Jim Northrup and Freehan, went down swinging in the seventh. Eddie Mathews batted for Wert to open the eighth and became Gibson's fourteenth strikeout, setting the stage for the record-breaking drama of the ninth inning.

The Cardinals had gotten to McLain in the fourth when Roger Maris and Tim McCarver had walked and Mike Shannon and Julian Javier had singled, producing three runs. A fourth run came across in the seventh when Lou Brock homered off Pat Dobson. Gibson gave up only five hits and one walk. Meanwhile, the strikeouts piled up. Every man in the Detroit starting lineup had fanned at least once.

By the time Detroit batted in the ninth, a partisan St. Louis crowd knew that Gibson was only 1 strikeout from Sandy Koufax's Series record of 15 (against the Yankees in 1963, 10 years after Carl Erskine of the Dodgers had struck out 13 Yankees to set the previous record).

Stanley momentarily thwarted Gibson by singling to open the ninth, but the flame-throwing Redbird right-hander fanned Kaline for the third time, and the crowd roared as the scoreboard flashed number 15.

Three fruitless swings by Cash made Gibson the new World Series strikeout king. A moment later Willie Horton looked at a third strike for the final out of the game. The Cardinals had won, 4–0, and Gibson had fanned his seventeenth.

"It was the greatest pitching performance I've ever seen," said Tigers manager Mayo Smith. There wasn't anyone among the 54,692 paying spectators who didn't agree.

October 3, 8, 10, 1968

# Mickey Lolich: Three World Series Victories

```
                    Detroit (AL)

                              AB  R  H  PO  A
McAuliffe, 2b .................4  0  0   1  3
Stanley, ss-cf ................4  0  1   5  2
Kaline, rf ....................4  0  0   2  0
Cash, 1b ......................4  1  1  11  2
Horton, lf ....................4  1  2   0  0
b Tracewski ...................0  1  0   0  0
Oyler, ss .....................0  0  0   1  0
Northrup, cf-lf ...............4  1  2   1  0
Freehan, c ....................4  0  1   6  0
Wert, 3b ......................3  0  1   0  6
Lolich, p .....................4  0  0   0  2
              Total ..........35  4  8  27 15


                   St. Louis (NL)

                              AB  R  H  PO  A
Brock, lf .....................3  0  1   1  0
Javier, 2b ....................4  0  0   3  2
Flood, cf .....................4  0  2   3  0
Cepeda, 1b ....................3  0  0   7  0
Shannon, 3b ...................4  1  1   1  2
McCarver, c ...................3  0  1   8  0
Maris, rf .....................3  0  0   3  0
Maxvill, ss ...................2  0  0   0  1
a Gagliano ....................1  0  0   0  0
Schofield, ss .................0  0  0   1  0
Gibson, p .....................3  0  0   1  0
              Total ..........30  1  5  27  5

a—Grounded out for Maxvill in eighth.
b—Ran for Horton in ninth.

Detroit       0 0 0 0 0 0 3 0 1—4
St. Louis     0 0 0 0 0 0 0 0 1—1

Error—Northrup. Runs batted in—Northrup 2, Freehan,
Wert, Shannon. Two-base hit—Freehan. Three-base hit—
Northrup. Home run—Shannon. Stolen base—Flood. Dou-
ble play—Detroit 1. Left on base—Detroit 5, St. Louis 5.
Bases on balls—Lolich 3, Gibson 1. Struck out—Lolich
4, Gibson 8. Umpires—Gorman (NL), Honochick (AL),
Landes (NL), Kinnamon (AL), Harvey (NL), and Haller
(AL). Time—2:07. Attendance—54,692.
```

Mickey Lolich has had the misfortune of being upstaged. In 1968, when the Tigers won the pennant, Mickey won 17 games, but Denny McLain had the bad taste to win 31. In 1971, the brilliant Vida Blue won the Cy Young Award as the American League's best pitcher though Lolich won more games than Blue, finished more, pitched more innings, and struck out more batters. In 1972, Lolich won 20 games for the second successive year, but Gaylord Perry won the coveted Cy Young Award.

"Nobody knows I'm around half the time," Lolich once complained. "When my name is mentioned, people look around and say, 'Who's he?' "

In the 1968 World Series, it seemed as if Bob Gibson had the stage to himself. On opening day he beat Denny McLain, won his sixth consecutive World Series game, and set a Series record by striking out 17 batters. Lolich answered with a six-hitter the next day only to watch his club lose the next two, the relentless Gibson winning the fourth game 10–1. The Tigers, down three games to one, looked for a savior in the unheralded Lolich.

He responded nobly (if not yet super-humanly) by outlasting three Cardinals' pitchers en route to a 5–3 victory, his second triumph of the Series. In the next game, the Tigers clawed the Red-birds with 10 runs in one inning and evened the Series. The Tigers had

*Overshadowed by 31-game winner Denny McLain throughout the regular season, Mickey Lolich was the Tigers' hero in the 1968 Series.*

somehow avoided extinction, but now they faced Gibson again, who hadn't lost or failed to complete a World Series game since 1964.

The 32-year-old Nebraskan retired the first 10 Tigers before Mickey Stanley dribbled a base hit to deep short in the fourth inning. Dal Maxvill fielded the ball, but his spikes caught on the edge of the outfield grass and left him unable to throw to first base. By this time Gibson had struck out six men and had broken the Series record of 31. After Stanley's infield single, he retired 10 more batters in a row. Not as spectacular as Gibson, Lolich nonetheless got the same results. The Cardinals threatened in the first when Curt Flood singled with two down and Orlando Cepeda walked, but Mike Shannon flied out to Al Kaline in deep right. In the second Tim McCarver opened with a walk, but Roger Maris grounded sharply into a double play.

McCarver opened the fifth with a single, but Lolich bore down and disposed of the next three batters. In the sixth the Cards wasted their prize opportunity. Lou Brock opened with a single. He had made 11 hits and had stolen seven bases in the first five games. This time, Lolich neatly picked him off first base, and Cash's throw nipped the Cardinals' speedster scampering to second. Julian Javier grounded out, but Flood rapped his second single. Unfazed, Lolich promptly picked *him* off

with a lightning throw to first. That was the end of the Cardinals' vaunted running game.

The teams went to the seventh still scoreless, Lolich pitching a four-hitter and Gibson a one-hitter. Having tamed the Tigers, Gibson seemed merely to be putting them through their paces in the seventh. Stanley obediently took a third strike; Kaline grounded out. Gibson had retired 20 of the 21 batters he had faced. Suddenly, a mild uprising, a disastrous mistake, and Gibson had lost control of the inning, the game, and the Series. Norm Cash lined a single to right, and Willie Horton bounced a single through the left side of the infield. Jim Northrup, who had hit a grand slam the day before, drove the first pitch to deep center field. Flood misjudged the ball. He started in, tried to reverse himself, and slipped. The ball landed behind him for a triple, scoring Cash and Horton. Before Gibson retired the side, another run had scored on Bill Freehan's single.

Gibson was no longer invincible, but Lolich suddenly was. Buoyed by his good fortune, he mowed down the next six Cardinals. In the top of the ninth, singles by Horton, Northrup, and Don Wert gave him a run he didn't need. In the bottom of the inning, he retired Flood on a line drive to Stanley and Cepeda on a foul to catcher Freehan. Shannon ruined his bid for a shutout with a home run into the left field

Below: *Tigers catcher Bill Freehan puts away the final out of the 1968 World Series.*
Bottom: *Finally number one, Lolich celebrates Detroit's championship with Al Kaline.*

stands, but that was only the death cry of the Cardinals. McCarver lifted the next pitch foul toward the Cardinals' dugout. Freehan caught it near the steps, whirled, and threw himself into the arms of Lolich. The neglected left-hander had stopped the Cards on five hits, 4–1, and had become the first lefty to pitch three complete-game victories in the World Series.

"All my life," Lolich said later as the champagne flowed in the Tigers' club-house, "somebody else has been the big star and Lolich was number two. I figured my day would come."

April 9–July 15, 1969

# Rod Carew:
# Seven Steals of Home

Rod Carew's first two years in the American League were outstanding. Twice he was the All-Star second baseman. He was Rookie of the Year in 1967. But the years were lonely ones for Carew. He is as sensitive as he is gifted, and he quickly developed the reputation for being a loner. Some of his teammates privately accused him of being selfish and of not giving 100 percent on the field. Carew became more and more reclusive.

In the winter of 1968, Carew sat down and decided that what was wrong with Rod Carew was Rod Carew. He talked with Billy Martin, manager of the Twins. After two years, Rod Carew finally decided to play baseball with the rest of the Minnesota Twins.

The change in philosophy had a marked effect on his play. He led the league in batting almost from the start and teamed with shortstop Leo Cardenas in threatening the team record for double plays. With constant hustle, he ingratiated himself with his manager and teammates, and he set a record.

Before the season had reached the halfway mark, he had stolen home seven times, an American League record. The seventh came in the first game of a July 15 doubleheader against the Chicago White Sox. Chicago rookie right-hander Gerry Nyman wound up with Carew on third base, and the fleet-footed Panamanian raced past Ty Cobb and Bobby Roth into the record books. "I made up my mind I would go on the first pitch if he wound up," Carew said. "But I was still pretty surprised to see him wind up. I can't remember the last time anybody wound up after the first three or four steals."

Carew's seventh steal of home, his fifteenth stolen base of the year, came in his seventh attempt. (He was also two for two in spring training.) It tied Carew with Pete Reiser, who set the major league record in 1946. But for an injury that sidelined him for more than a month, Carew would probably have broken the tie with Reiser.

The rundown:

- April 9 in Kansas City: In the Twins' second game, Carew stole home against right-hander Roger Nelson to break a 2–2 tie.
- April 19 at home against California: Carew's steal of home in his sixth game tied the score at 5–5 against veteran right-hander Hoyt Wilhelm.
- April 30 at home against Seattle: In his seventeenth game, he stole home against right-hander Darrell Brandon to make it 4–0.
- May 18 at home against Detroit: southpaw Mickey Lolich allowed Carew to steal second, third, and home, making the score 2–2 in Carew's twenty-seventh game.
- June 4 at home against New York: Carew stole home against right-handed reliever Lindy McDaniel to give the Twins a 3–2 lead.

■ June 16 at home against California: right-hander Tom Murphy allowed Carew to tie the American League record that had stood for 52 years. The steal gave the Twins a 2–0 lead in Carew's forty-eighth game.

■ July 16 at home against Chicago: The steal off Gerry Nyman gave the Twins a 6–2 lead in Carew's seventy-fourth game.

Top: *Congenial Rod Carew of the Minnesota Twins before a game.*
Above: *A more combative Rod Carew steals home against the Yankees, upsetting hitter Jim Holt and catcher Jake Gibbs.*

May 1, 1969

# Don Wilson: Vengeance Victory

When Don Wilson marched to the mound in Cincinnati's ancient Crosley Field on the night of May 1, 1969, his Houston teammates knew he was mad. He acknowledged their attempts at conversation with barely audible grunts. He was determined and dead serious.

The source of his anger wasn't the no-hit, no-run game that Jim Maloney had pitched for the Reds the night before. Nor was it the Astros' eight-game losing streak or their terrible start. (They had won only four of twenty-four games since the start of the season.) Wilson's vendetta with Cincinnati stemmed from a 14–0 shellacking the Astros thad taken from the Reds at the Astrodome on April 22, nine days before. The 24-year-old right-hander claimed that in the 14–0 loss, Cincinnati players had tried to humiliate the Astros in front of the home fans.

"They were ahead fourteen to nothing, and Johnny Bench was calling for breaking pitches on three-and-one counts," Wilson charged. "Pete Rose was still running for extra bases. They weren't satisfied to win; they wanted to make us look ridiculous. In the dugout they were laughing at us. They were even sticking out their tongues and turning their caps around backward—making fun of us. You just don't do that in my book. Nobody is going to do that to our club and get away with it."

Wilson had started that game. He was so upset afterward that he called

Don Wilson of the Houston Astros in the final stage of his brilliant no-hit performance against Cincinnati.

the Cincinnati clubhouse to talk to Bench, who told him the Reds were just playing the game the way it had to be played and had no special desire to humiliate the Astros. Wilson wasn't satisfied.

In his next start, he was knocked out of the box in San Francisco. When he arrived at Cincinnati's Crosley Field on the afternoon of May 1, he had worked himself into such a lather that his teammates worried he might not pitch well. After missing a pitch during batting practice, he turned and slammed his bat against the cage.

Once the game started, Wilson funneled his anger and frustration into a flaming fastball. He was wild but effective. He walked six batters and hit another but struck out thirteen. The one he hit was Johnny Bench. No one in the Reds' dugout thought it was an accident. Wilson himself was hit by a Jim Merritt pitch and on two other occasions was forced to evade high hard ones. In the fifth inning, after Wilson had ducked a Merritt delivery, Reds manager Dave Bristol yelled to him, "Gutless! Gutless!"

"You're a gutless bastard, Bristol," Wilson yelled back.

Wilson carried on the verbal feud with the Reds' players throughout the early innings of the game. "They didn't have much to say in the late innings, though," says Wilson. "I was throwing the ball down their throats.

"I was determined to beat them . . . even to pitch a no-hitter against them. I was thinking about it from the first inning on. There were a couple of times my legs were shaking so much I had to step off the mound. I never wanted anything so bad in all my life as to pitch that no-hitter."

Entering the final two innings, Wilson had his no-hitter in sight. Firing as hard as he could, he ran the count to three and two on the first three hitters he faced in the eighth. Pinch hitter Jimmy Stewart walked, and pinch hitter Jim Beauchamp struck out. Pete Rose raised a foul pop-up that catcher Don Bryant staggered under and dropped. Wilson walked Rose, but he got Bobby Tolan and Alex Johnson on the two hardest hit balls of the night, the first to right field and the second to center.

Then came the dramatic ninth. Again Wilson ran the count to three and two on the first three batters. He struck out Tony Perez and retired Bench on a fly to center, but he walked Fred Whitfield. Tommy Helms then stepped to the plate and swinging on the first pitch, hit a sky-high pop to third base. Wilson leaped off the mound and threw up his hands as he saw the ball land in the glove of third baseman Doug Rader. Wilson had his cherished no-hitter and a 4–0 victory over the Reds.

Don's teammates rushed to the mound with congratulations, but Wilson wasn't smiling. He was heading for the Cincinnati dugout snarling, "I'm going to get those bums." Wilson's teammates were forced to restrain him.

"I was pretty far out," he confessed when the incident was recalled to him. "I'm glad the guys stopped me. I hate to think what might have happened had they let me go after them."

"I never saw a guy more psyched up—or more mad—in my life than Wilson was that night," said Harry Walker, manager of the Houston club at the time. "He pitched like he had a personal grudge with every member of the Cincinnati team. He wouldn't talk to anybody on the bench. The guys were afraid to go near him. They left him alone."

The back-to-back no-hitters of Maloney and Wilson, (his second in only two major league seasons) marked the second time in major league history that teams had exchanged no-hitters in successive games. The Giants' Gaylord Perry and the Cardinals' Ray Washburn had done it on September 17 and 18 in 1968 at San Francisco. But theirs was a relatively gentlemanly affair. In Cincinnati on May 2, no one cared to contemplate what would have happened had Wilson lost.

September 15, 1969

# Steve Carlton:
# A Strikeout Record

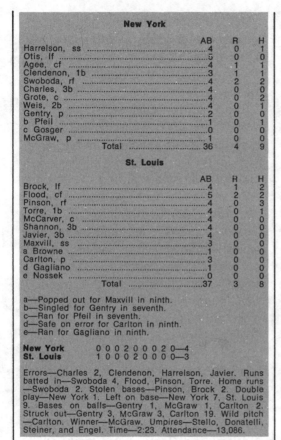

| New York | AB | R | H |
|---|---|---|---|
| Harrelson, ss | 4 | 0 | 1 |
| Otis, lf | 5 | 0 | 0 |
| Agee, cf | 4 | 1 | 1 |
| Clendenon, 1b | 3 | 1 | 1 |
| Swoboda, rf | 4 | 2 | 2 |
| Charles, 3b | 4 | 0 | 2 |
| Grote, c | 4 | 0 | 2 |
| Weis, 2b | 4 | 0 | 1 |
| Gentry, p | 2 | 0 | 0 |
| b Pfeil | 1 | 0 | 1 |
| c Gosger | 0 | 0 | 0 |
| McGraw, p | 1 | 0 | 0 |
| Total | 36 | 4 | 9 |

| St. Louis | AB | R | H |
|---|---|---|---|
| Brock, lf | 4 | 1 | 2 |
| Flood, cf | 5 | 2 | 2 |
| Pinson, rf | 4 | 0 | 3 |
| Torre, 1b | 4 | 0 | 1 |
| McCarver, c | 4 | 0 | 0 |
| Shannon, 3b | 4 | 0 | 0 |
| Javier, 3b | 4 | 0 | 0 |
| Maxvill, ss | 3 | 0 | 0 |
| a Browne | 1 | 0 | 0 |
| Carlton, p | 3 | 0 | 0 |
| d Gagliano | 1 | 0 | 0 |
| e Nossek | 0 | 0 | 0 |
| Total | 37 | 3 | 8 |

a—Popped out for Maxvill in ninth.
b—Singled for Gentry in seventh.
c—Ran for Pfeil in seventh.
d—Safe on error for Carlton in ninth.
e—Ran for Gagliano in ninth.

**New York**  0 0 0 2 0 0 0 2 0—4
**St. Louis**  1 0 0 0 2 0 0 0 0—3

Errors—Charles 2, Clendenon, Harrelson, Javier. Runs batted in—Swoboda 4, Flood, Pinson, Torre. Home runs —Swoboda 2. Stolen bases—Pinson, Brock 2. Double play—New York 1. Left on base—New York 7, St. Louis 9. Bases on balls—Gentry 1, McGraw 1, Carlton 2. Struck out—Gentry 3, McGraw 3, Carlton 19. Wild pitch —Carlton. Winner—McGraw. Umpires—Stello, Donatelli, Steiner, and Engel. Time—2:23. Attendance—13,086.

In 1972, when Steve Carlton came to Philadelphia and performed record-breaking heroics for the hapless Phillies, he was no stranger to futility. Two years earlier, as a member of the St. Louis Cards, he had won only 10 games and lost 19, the most in the league. Eight of those defeats were by one run, and in four of his other losses, his troops deserted; they did not score a run for him.

Perhaps the most poignant defeat of his career came the year before, on September 15, 1969. That night he became the first pitcher in modern major league history to strike out 19 batters. Steve made 152 pitches in that game. Only two were mistakes. Ron Swoboda, the New York Mets' outfielder, hit both into the seats for two-run homers. Final score: Mets 4, Cardinals 3.

Carlton, who had pitched the pennant-winning victory in Houston the previous year, arrived at the ball park for the game against the Mets feeling a bit feverish. He had a sore back, which required a rubdown and pain-killing pills. But once the game began, after a 26-minute rain delay, and once it resumed, after a 54-minute delay in the first inning, Carlton transferred most of his ailments to the Mets' hitters.

Carlton struck out the first three batters he faced. At the end of seven innings, he had registered fourteen strikeouts. He had at least one in each inning and had fanned the side three times as he went to the eighth inning protecting a 3–2 lead. The Mets had taken a 2–1 lead in the fourth when Swoboda followed a walk to Donn Clendenon with his first home run. But the Cards regained the lead in the fifth, scoring two runs off Gary Gentry on singles by Lou Brock, Curt Flood, Vada Pinson, and Joe Torre.

Carlton registered his fifteenth and sixteenth strikeouts in the eighth but not before Tommie Agee had singled and Swoboda had followed with his second homer. Still, Carlton was within reach of two strikeout marks, and he knew it. He needed two more strikeouts to better the team record of seventeen set by Dizzy Dean in regular season competition and matched by Bob Gibson in the 1968 World Series. And he needed three more to break the major league record of eighteen shared by Bob Feller, Sandy Koufax, and Don Wilson.

To surpass the latter marks, Carlton had to fan three batters in the last inning. He got relief pitcher Tug McGraw on a one-and-two fastball to start the ninth. Switch-hitter Bud Harrelson was next. On another one-and-two count, plate umpire Dick Stello waved him out on a fastball that hit the inside corner. That strikeout tied the record of 18. Now it was rookie Amos Otis, whom Carlton had struck out three times. "At that time," recalls Steve,

"I felt I'd rather see Otis get a hit instead of fouling out or grounding out. I had made up my mind when I went into the ninth that I would go all out for the record."

The count on Otis went to two and two. Then Otis went fishing for a slider in the dirt. Catcher Tim McCarver had to throw out Otis, but it was a strikeout nonetheless, and Carlton had achieved a feat that had eluded Walter Johnson, Christy Mathewson, Lefty Grove, Rube Waddell, and every other major league strikeout pitcher.

"When I look back to that night," said Carlton, "it seems like a dream. It was so unreal. I felt so strong; I had so much confidence. It's as if I knew I was going to strike all those guys out."

Every man in the Mets' all-right-handed starting lineup went down on strikes at least once. Besides striking out Otis four times, Carlton victimized Harrelson, Agee, Swoboda, Ed Charles, Al Weis, and Gentry twice each; Clendenon, Jerry Grote, and McGraw once each.

The man who made the final putout, first baseman Joe Torre, quipped, "It was Carlton's own fault for making things so tough for himself. If he hadn't picked that man off first base, he'd have had a chance for twenty strikeouts."

October 11–17, 1969

# The Miracle Mets

**Baltimore (AL)**

| | AB | R | H | PO | A |
|---|---|---|---|---|---|
| Buford, lf | 4 | 0 | 0 | 1 | 0 |
| Blair, cf | 4 | 0 | 0 | 0 | 0 |
| F. Robinson, rf | 3 | 1 | 1 | 0 | 0 |
| Powell, 1b | 4 | 0 | 1 | 9 | 1 |
| b Salmon | 0 | 0 | 0 | 0 | 0 |
| B. Robinson, 3b | 4 | 0 | 0 | 4 | 0 |
| Johnson, 2b | 4 | 0 | 1 | 0 | 0 |
| Echebarren, c | 3 | 0 | 0 | 8 | 0 |
| Belanger, ss | 3 | 1 | 1 | 2 | 1 |
| McNally, p | 2 | 1 | 1 | 0 | 0 |
| a Motton | 1 | 0 | 0 | 0 | 0 |
| Watt, p | 0 | 0 | 0 | 0 | 0 |
| Total | 32 | 3 | 5 | 24 | 5 |

**New York (NL)**

| | AB | R | H | PO | A |
|---|---|---|---|---|---|
| Agee, cf | 3 | 0 | 1 | 4 | 0 |
| Harrelson, ss | 4 | 0 | 0 | 1 | 6 |
| Jones, lf | 3 | 2 | 1 | 3 | 0 |
| Clendenon, 1b | 3 | 1 | 1 | 8 | 0 |
| Swoboda, rf | 4 | 1 | 2 | 5 | 0 |
| Charles, 3b | 4 | 0 | 0 | 0 | 1 |
| Grote, c | 4 | 0 | 0 | 5 | 0 |
| Weis, 2b | 4 | 1 | 1 | 1 | 2 |
| Koosman, p | 3 | 0 | 1 | 0 | 1 |
| Total | 32 | 5 | 7 | 27 | 10 |

a—Grounded out for McNally in eighth.
b—Ran for Powell in ninth.

| | | |
|---|---|---|
| **Baltimore** | 0 0 3 0 0 0 0 0 0—3 | |
| **New York** | 0 0 0 0 0 2 1 2 x—5 | |

Errors—Powell, Watt. Runs batted in—F. Robinson, McNally 2, Clendenon 2, Swoboda, Weis. Two-base hits—Koosman, Jones, Swoboda. Home runs—McNally, F. Robinson, Clendenon, Weis. Stolen base—Agee. Left on base—Baltimore 3, New York 6. Bases on balls—McNally 2, Koosman 1. Struck out—McNally 6, Watt 1, Koosman 5. Hits off—McNally, 5 in 7; Watt, 2 in 1; Koosman, 5 in 9. Hit by pitch—by McNally (Jones). Loser—Watt. Umpires—DiMuro (AL), Weyer (NL), Soar (AL), Secory (NL), Napp (AL), and Crawford (NL). Time —2:14. Attendance—57,397.

In their formative years, the Mets were noted for finding fascinating ways to "snatch defeat from the jaws of victory." It is therefore sometimes overlooked that the Mets were also accredited masters of the mundane defeat, not daringly seized but simply swallowed, with the placid regularity of a hot dog glutton at Shea Stadium. In 1962, their first year, the Mets gorged themselves on defeat—120 losses, more than any other club in the twentieth century. Even in 1968, by which time most of the misfits who comprised the original Mets had left, the club escaped the cellar by only one game.

Such regular and prolific failure, for all the ingenious ways the Mets accomplished it, made it difficult for their fans to adjust to the unexpected—victory. Many of the Mets' dedicated followers had already been badly shaken when the Dodgers and Giants jilted them in 1957. Prone to giddiness whenever the Mets won, they became delirious in 1969. For nothing in the Mets' improbable past had prepared them for the greatest improbability of all—the Mets winning the pennant and the World Series.

A ticker tape parade greeted the Mets' three-game sweep of the playoff series with Atlanta for the pennant. Hardly had the city streets been cleared when the mighty Baltimore Orioles and Mike Cuellar disposed of the Mets and Tom Seaver like so much debris, 4–1.

The cynics predicted a Baltimore sweep, but the Mets were undaunted. In the second game, they took a 1–0 lead when Donn Clendenon homered off Dave McNally in the fourth and maintained it as Jerry Koosman held the Orioles hitless for six innings. Koosman surrendered the tying run in the seventh when Paul Blair singled, stole second, and scored on Brooks Robinson's single. But in the ninth, the Mets' singles hitters asserted themselves. Ed Charles singled past Brooks Robinson at third base and raced to third on a single by Jerry Grote. This flurry brought up Al Weis, the utility infielder filling in at second base for Ken Boswell. Never known for robust hitting, Weis cracked his second single and drove in his second run, sending the Mets ahead 2–1. Koosman retired the first two batters in the ninth, but at last disconcerted on the verge of victory, he walked Frank Robinson and Boog Powell. Manager Gil·Hodges called for Ron Taylor, who got Brooks Robinson on a grounder, and the Mets had their first Series win.

The third game was Tommie Agee's. The first batter to face Jim Palmer, the hard-hitting center fielder crashed a home run and thereafter saved the game with his fielding. In the Orioles' fourth, with two on, two out, and the Mets ahead 3–0, Elrod Hendricks lashed a drive to left center that appeared certain to reach the wall. Hav-

ing shifted toward right for the left-handed hitting catcher, Tommie now had to scamper some 40 yards toward left just to reach the ball. At full speed he snared the ball backhanded in the very edge of his webbing. Agee had saved two runs with a catch that ranked with the Series catches of Willie Mays, Sandy Amoros, and Al Gionfriddo. And then he did it again.

In the seventh inning, the Orioles loaded the bases with one out. Hodges excused starter Gary Gentry and brought in Nolan Ryan to pitch to Blair. The Orioles' center fielder connected with a fastball and rocketed it down the right center field alley. This time, Agee raced to his left, dived headfirst, and caught the ball just before his body crashed to the turf. He skidded 15 feet but held on to the ball. Had he missed, Blair would have had a triple and the Orioles three runs.

"The second one was easier," ex-

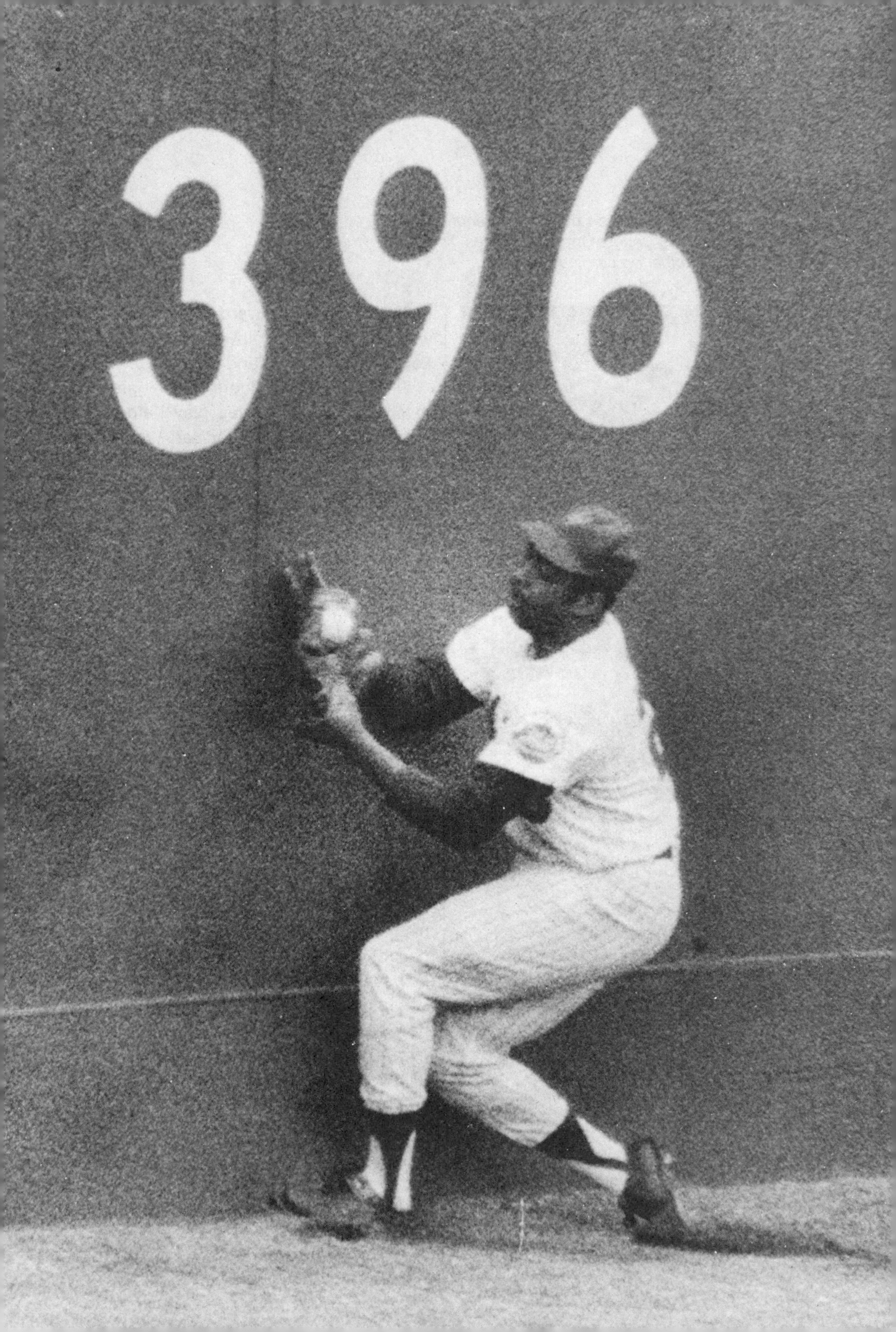
396

plained Agee afterward, "because it was away from my glove. But the wind kept taking it away, and I had to dive."

"I've seen outfielders make great catches in World Series play before," groaned Orioles manager Earl Weaver, "but I've never seen two such catches by the same player in the same game." Demoralized, the Orioles surrendered the game 5–0.

Some of Agee's daring apparently rubbed off on Ron Swoboda, the Mets' outfielder who in former years had battled fly balls with only modest success. The next day, he made Agee's feats seem almost routine. Tom Seaver was nursing a 1–0 lead in the ninth (Clendenon had homered in the second off Mike Cuellar) when Frank Robinson singled and went to third on Boog Powell's single.

With one out and runners on first and third, Brooks Robinson followed with a sinking line drive to right center. Swoboda thundered in, dove forward, his glove arm extended to his right, and caught the ball backhanded a few inches from the ground. The catch was astounding. Some say it should never have been attempted, for had Swoboda missed, the ball would have rolled to the wall for a triple and at least two Orioles runs. But the Mets had clearly transcended "shoulds" and "would haves." As it was, Frank Robinson scored from third after Swoboda's tremendous catch, tying the score,

and the game went into extra innings.

In the bottom of the tenth, the Mets solidified their claim to being Destiny's children. Jerry Grote reached second when Don Buford misjudged his fly to left. A walk to Weis brought up J. C. Martin, who plunked a bunt in front of the plate. Pete Richert, who had relieved Cuellar, pounced on the ball, whirled, and threw to first, but the ball hit Martin on the left wrist and ricocheted toward second base. Rod Gaspar, running for Grote, did not stop until he had crossed the plate with the winning run.

Facing elimination, the Orioles returned to New York for the fifth game, determined to prevent baseball's biggest upset. In the third inning, Mc-

Nally, the pitcher, hit a two-run homer off Koosman, and shortly thereafter, Frank Robinson unloaded a tremendous drive over the left field wall to make it 3–0.

For the time being, the Mets spurned such conventional baseball. In the top of the sixth, Robinson was struck on the thigh by a pitch from Koosman, but home plate umpire Lou DiMuro said Frank had fouled the pitch and refused to give him first base. After a five-minute delay for treatment, Robby returned to the plate and struck out. Not content with that little triumph, the Mets made more mischief in the bottom of the sixth. With the Orioles still grousing over DiMuro's call in the top of the inning, Cleon Jones hopped away from a sharply dipping curve thrown by Mc-Nally and claimed that it had hit his foot. DiMuro ordered Cleon back to the plate. Out of the dugout came Gil Hodges, holding the ball, which had conveniently skittered into the Mets' dugout. "Lou," Hodges said slowly, "the ball hit him."

DiMuro looked at Hodges, who handed him the ball for inspection. Sure enough, there was a smudge of shoe polish on it. The fans tensed, aware that Earl Weaver had been losing arguments all week and was ready to explode if the decision was reversed. DiMuro gave the ball a thorough examination. Then, with the precarious resolve of a judge letting a guilty defendant go free on a technicality, he straightened up, took a deep breath, and thrust out his right arm, index finger pointing to first base. The 57,397 spectators roared in approval.

Surprisingly, plaintiff Weaver did not hotly contest the circumstantial evidence. DiMuro assured him that the shoe polish was Jones's and that the shoe-polished ball was the game ball. Having been found in contempt and ordered from the premises the previous day, Weaver was not anxious for another ejection. Up in the press box, the boys recalled the only other trial-by-shoe-polish in World Series history and agreed that DiMuro had followed precedent. In 1957, the home plate umpire ruled that a pitch by the Yankees' Ryne

Duren had bounced off the foot of Nippy Jones of Milwaukee.

Now the Mets began the final and most glorious comeback of their eight years. With Cleon Jones on first, Clendenon hit his third Series homer, this one into the second deck in left field, bringing the Mets to within a run. In the bottom of the seventh, Al Weis, who had in the second game been satisfied with a game-winning single, whacked a 375-foot homer into the temporary left field stands, tying the score at 3–3. And finally, the Mets broke it open. With Eddie Watt pitching in relief for the Orioles in the eighth, Jones doubled over the head of center fielder Blair. Clendenon grounded out, but Ron Swoboda drove a soft liner down the left field line. Desperately, Bufford tried a backhand stab of the ball. When he failed, Jones scored and Swoboda raced to second. After Ed Charles grounded out, Boog Powell fumbled Grote's grounder and Swoboda scored.

The Mets dallied no longer on the brink of their miracle. In the ninth Frank Robinson walked, but Powell grounded out, Brooks Robinson flied out, and Dave Johnson raised a high fly to Jones in left field. Shea Stadium erupted as Jones squeezed the ball and made a dash to the dugout to escape the fans, who after eight years of repression rampaged on the field like the Mongol hordes. The New York Mets were champions of baseball.

April 22, 1970

# Tom Seaver: 19 Strikeouts

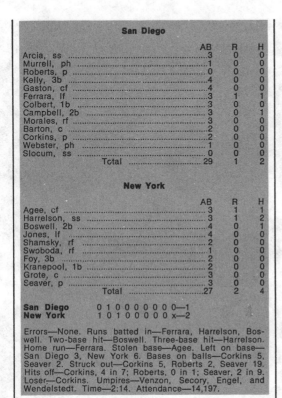

**San Diego**

| | AB | R | H |
|---|---|---|---|
| Arcia, ss | 3 | 0 | 0 |
| Murrell, ph | 1 | 0 | 0 |
| Roberts, p | 0 | 0 | 0 |
| Kelly, 3b | 4 | 0 | 0 |
| Gaston, cf | 4 | 0 | 0 |
| Ferrara, lf | 3 | 1 | 1 |
| Colbert, 1b | 3 | 0 | 0 |
| Campbell, 2b | 3 | 0 | 1 |
| Morales, rf | 3 | 0 | 0 |
| Barton, c | 2 | 0 | 0 |
| Corkins, p | 2 | 0 | 0 |
| Webster, ph | 1 | 0 | 0 |
| Slocum, ss | 0 | 0 | 0 |
| Total | 29 | 1 | 2 |

**New York**

| | AB | R | H |
|---|---|---|---|
| Agee, cf | 3 | 1 | 1 |
| Harrelson, ss | 3 | 1 | 2 |
| Boswell, 2b | 4 | 0 | 1 |
| Jones, lf | 4 | 0 | 0 |
| Shamsky, rf | 2 | 0 | 0 |
| Swoboda, rf | 1 | 0 | 0 |
| Foy, 3b | 2 | 0 | 0 |
| Kranepool, 1b | 2 | 0 | 0 |
| Grote, c | 3 | 0 | 0 |
| Seaver, p | 3 | 0 | 0 |
| Total | 27 | 2 | 4 |

| | | |
|---|---|---|
| **San Diego** | 0 1 0 0 0 0 0 0 0—1 | |
| **New York** | 1 0 1 0 0 0 0 0 x—2 | |

Errors—None. Runs batted in—Ferrara, Harrelson, Boswell. Two-base hit—Boswell. Three-base hit—Harrelson. Home run—Ferrara. Stolen base—Agee. Left on base—San Diego 3, New York 6. Bases on balls—Corkins 5, Seaver 2. Struck out—Corkins 5, Roberts 2, Seaver 19. Hits off—Corkins, 4 in 7; Roberts, 0 in 1; Seaver, 2 in 9. Loser—Corkins. Umpires—Venzon, Secory, Engel, and Wendelstedt. Time—2:14. Attendance—14,197.

"I may never come this close again," Tom Seaver remembers saying to himself as he stood on the mound at Shea Stadium that afternoon of April 22, 1970. "I may as well go for it." And with that, Seaver buzzed a low fastball past Al Ferrara. The San Diego outfielder swung and missed, and that was that. Seaver had earned a niche in the record book with one of the greatest daylight performances in major league history. It was his nineteenth strikeout of the game and tenth in a row.

Some people might discount 19 strikeouts against an expansion club. Besides, Steve Carlton of the Cardinals had already struck out 19, in 1969. But no one can knock 10 in a row. "He was like a machine those last few innings," said catcher Jerry Grote incredulously.

In the stands sat Johnny Podres, one of four pitchers who had struck out eight in a row, the previous record. Max Surkont of the old Milwaukee Braves, Jim Maloney of the Reds, and Don Wilson of the Astros were the others.

"He was fantastic, outstanding," recalls Podres. "There was no doubt in my mind he would break the record. He had perfect rhythm. As hard as he was throwing, he was still hitting the spots. If you didn't swing, it was a strike."

Jack Lang, the veteran baseball writer for the *Long Island Press* who has covered the Mets from their incep-

Below: *Young Tom Seaver represented the Mets in the 1968 All-Star game in Houston.*
Opposite: *Seaver strikes out San Diego's Al Ferrara for his tenth consecutive strikeout and his nineteenth of the day.*

tion in 1962, recalls that watching Seaver work the last couple of innings in that game was like "watching an artist create a masterpiece on canvas."

"As Ferrara took a third strike to end the sixth inning," Lang said, "there was no hint of the record-breaking performance that was about to unfold. At that point, Tom had only ten strikeouts. Carlton's record was the last thing in anyone's mind. It was still a 2–1 ballgame, and although Seaver had allowed only two hits, he did not appear that overpowering. But he got it late. He just kept building up as the game went on."

Nate Colbert, the Padres' clean-up hitter, was the first to face Seaver in the seventh. Seaver struck him out. Dave Campbell looked at a third strike as did Jerry Morales. That made it four in a row. Bob Barton struck out looking to open the eighth. Pinch hitter Ramon Webster missed a third strike. That was number 15, tying Nolan Ryan's club record, and the news was flashed on the message board.

"I wasn't really aware I had that many strikeouts," Seaver said. "I thought I had ten or eleven. But when I had fifteen, I tried for sixteen. I have to admit I also tried for nineteen. But those were the only two strikeouts I really tried for."

Ivan Murrell, a pinch hitter, became Tom's sixteenth strikeout victim. The last out in the eighth, Murrell went down swinging for the club record and Sea-

ver's seventh strikeout in a row. The Mets had hardly gone out in their half of the eighth when the crowd began chanting for Seaver to tie the record of eight straight. Seaver wasted no time obliging the 14,197 customers, striking out Van Kelly to open the ninth. Three pitches later, he had wiped out the record by getting Clarence Gaston on a called third strike. That made it nine in a row.

Finally, Ferrara. Seaver's first pitch, a slider, nicked the outside corner, and umpire Harry Wendelstedt's arm recorded the strike. Another slider for a ball was followed by a fastball for a swinging strike. Only one strike to go for a 2–1 victory and the record.

"I might have thrown a different pitch in a situation like this," Seaver remembered. "The pitch probably should have been a slider outside. . . . I was thinking about Ferrara as far back as the eighth inning. I remember he had hit a home run off my fastball earlier. I was still worried about him, but I had to challenge him. So I just let the fastball rip. I was that close, and I wanted it."

May 10, 1970

# Hoyt Wilhelm: The Thousandth Appearance

### St. Louis

| | AB | R | H |
|---|---|---|---|
| Cardenal, cf | 5 | 0 | 1 |
| Ca. Taylor, rf | 5 | 0 | 0 |
| Maxvill, ss | 0 | 0 | 0 |
| Brock, lf | 4 | 1 | 1 |
| Allen, 3b | 4 | 1 | 2 |
| Torre, 1b | 4 | 2 | 3 |
| Javier, 2b | 4 | 1 | 2 |
| Gagliano, 1b | 3 | 0 | 1 |
| Davalillo, ph-rf | 1 | 1 | 1 |
| Ramirez, ss | 3 | 0 | 0 |
| Hague, ph-1b | 1 | 0 | 0 |
| Torrez, p | 2 | 0 | 0 |
| Rojas, ph | 1 | 0 | 0 |
| McCool, p | 0 | 0 | 0 |
| Johnson, p | 0 | 0 | 0 |
| Lee, ph | 0 | 0 | 0 |
| Campisi, p | 0 | 0 | 0 |
| Total | 37 | 6 | 11 |

### Atlanta

| | AB | R | H |
|---|---|---|---|
| Jackson, ss | 3 | 0 | 0 |
| Millan, 2b | 4 | 1 | 1 |
| H. Aaron, rf | 4 | 0 | 0 |
| Carty, lf | 4 | 1 | 1 |
| Lum, lf | 0 | 0 | 0 |
| Cepeda, 1b | 4 | 0 | 0 |
| Boyer, 3b | 4 | 1 | 1 |
| Gonzalez, cf | 3 | 2 | 2 |
| King, c | 2 | 0 | 1 |
| Didier, c | 0 | 0 | 0 |
| Garr, ph | 1 | 0 | 0 |
| Stone, p | 3 | 0 | 0 |
| Priddy, p | 0 | 0 | 0 |
| Wilhelm, p | 0 | 0 | 0 |
| Aspromonte, ph | 0 | 0 | 0 |
| Total | 32 | 5 | 6 |

| | | |
|---|---|---|
| St. Louis | 0 0 0 2 0 0 0 0 4 | —6 |
| Atlanta | 0 0 0 4 0 0 1 0 0 | —5 |

Errors—None. Runs batted in—Cardenal 2, Allen 2, Torre 2, Carty, Gonzalez 3, King. Two-base hit—King. Home runs—Gonzalez, Torre, Allen. Stolen bases—Brock, Jackson. Double plays—St. Louis 1, Atlanta 1. Left on base—St. Louis 5, Atlanta 5. Bases on balls—Torrez 2, McCool 1, Campisi 2, Wilhelm 1. Struck out—Torrez 3, Johnson 1, Stone 6. Hits off—Torrez, 4 in 6; McCool, 2 in 2/3; Johnson, 0 in 1 1/3; Campisi, 0 in 1; Stone, 8 in 8 (pitched to two batters in ninth); Priddy, 2 in 0 (pitched to two batters in ninth); Wilhelm, 1 in 1. Winner—Johnson. Loser—Priddy. Umpires—Burkhart, Sudol, Weyer, and Olsen. Time—2:31. Attendance—23,166.

Hoyt Wilhelm has consistently amazed teammates, opponents, and fans. Each time he walked to the mound in the latter days of his career, he set a record for appearances. He was nearly 47 in 1970, and he could have been home in Columbus, Georgia, drawing his baseball pension. But he was in his nineteenth season, making his thousandth major league mound appearance. He had long ago set the record for most appearances for a pitcher, but he had not yet fulfilled his great ambition. Above all else, he wanted to be the first pitcher in the history of baseball to still be throwing at age 50. He missed by four months.

With a knuckleball that became legendary, Wilhelm pitched 21 years in the big leagues, dividing his time among nine clubs. He made 1,070 mound appearances, all but 52 in relief, won 143 games, had 226 saves and holds a plethora of records for relief pitchers. He spent the 1973 season in the minors, in his first venture as a manager, passing on his trade secrets.

Hoyt Wilhelm's longevity is even more remarkable for the fact that he was almost 29 before he even reached the major leagues. He had been buried in the obscurity of the Class D leagues for years, passed over and apparently condemned to a life of oblivion. The Giants finally drafted him, but Wilhelm took four more years to reach the varsity, after ten years in the low minors.

*Hoyt Wilhelm, at 46, pitches in his one-thousandth major league game. Relieving in the ninth inning, Wilhelm throws to Cardinals pinch hitter Carl Taylor, who eventually grounded into an inning-ending double play.*

That was in 1952. Since then, he has pitched against eight teams that no longer exist: the Brooklyn Dodgers, the New York Giants, the Boston Braves, the Milwaukee Braves, the Kansas City Athletics, the Seattle Pilots, the original Washington Senators, and the expansion Washington Senators. During his major league career, no less than eighteen teams came into existence: the Los Angeles Dodgers, the San Francisco Giants, the San Diego Padres, the Milwaukee Braves, the Atlanta Braves, the Montreal Expos, the Houston Astros, the Kansas City Athletics, the Oakland A's, the Baltimore Orioles, the California Angels, the Minnesota Twins, the expansion Washington Senators, the Kansas City Royals, the Seattle Pilots, the Milwaukee Brewers, the New York Mets, and the Texas Rangers.

Wilhelm credits his longevity to his knuckleball, which he claims is easy to throw. When he first started out, his manager told him he'd never get anywhere because of "that darned knuckleball." Fortunately, Wilhelm persisted.

The trouble with Hoyt Wilhelm is that he has no sense of drama. If he had, the greatest of all relief specialists would have reversed the roles he played in his nine hundred ninety-ninth and one thousandth major league games.

On May 9, 1970, Luman Harris, then manager of the Atlanta Braves, brought in Wilhelm from the bullpen to protect a 5–3 lead against the St. Louis Cardinals. It was the knuckleballer's nine hundred ninety-ninth appearance in a big league game. The Redbirds had the bases loaded in the seventh inning with only one out. Wilhelm faced Richie Allen and Joe Torre, the most feared hitters in the Cardinals' lineup, and struck out both of them. In the ninth the Cards had two runners on base with the same two batters coming up. Hoyt fanned them again.

The next day, Sunday, May 10, was a day to remember for Hoyt Wilhelm—and a day to forget. Just two months shy of his forty-seventh birthday, Hoyt made his one thousandth appearance, against the Cardinals again, but the result was not as pleasant. When Wilhelm was called into the game to a standing ovation of 23,166 fans, the Braves led 5–3, but the Cardinals had loaded the bases with none out. With Wilhelm on the mound, one run scored on an infield out, and pinch hitter Leron Lee walked, loading the bases again. Then José Cardenal ripped a two-run single to beat the Braves 6–5 and halt their winning streak at 11 games.

Wilhelm shrugged off the defeat. "That's the way it goes," he said. "My arm felt good, and the knuckleball was jumping around. The difference between yesterday and today is that yesterday they didn't hit it. Today they did."

May 12, 1970

# Ernie Banks: Number 500

**Atlanta**

| | AB | R | H |
|---|---|---|---|
| Jackson, ss | 4 | 1 | 0 |
| Millan, 2b | 5 | 1 | 1 |
| Aaron, rf | 4 | 0 | 0 |
| Carty, lf | 3 | 0 | 3 |
| Garr, ph | 0 | 0 | 0 |
| Wilhelm, p | 0 | 0 | 0 |
| King, ph | 1 | 0 | 0 |
| Priddy, p | 0 | 0 | 0 |
| Cepeda, 1b | 4 | 0 | 0 |
| Boyer, 3b | 4 | 1 | 2 |
| Gonzalez, cf | 4 | 0 | 0 |
| Tillman, c | 2 | 0 | 0 |
| Lum, lf | 1 | 0 | 0 |
| Jarvis, p | 3 | 0 | 0 |
| Didier, c | 1 | 0 | 0 |
| Total | 36 | 3 | 6 |

**Chicago**

| | AB | R | H |
|---|---|---|---|
| Kessinger, ss | 5 | 1 | 3 |
| Beckert, 2b | 5 | 0 | 1 |
| Williams, lf | 4 | 1 | 1 |
| Santo, 3b | 5 | 1 | 2 |
| Callison, rf | 4 | 0 | 0 |
| Banks, 1b | 3 | 1 | 1 |
| Hickman, cf | 3 | 0 | 0 |
| Martin, c | 2 | 0 | 0 |
| Hall, ph | 1 | 0 | 0 |
| Hiatt, c | 1 | 0 | 1 |
| Holtzman, p | 2 | 0 | 0 |
| Smith, ph | 1 | 0 | 0 |
| Abernathy, p | 0 | 0 | 0 |
| Popovich, ph | 1 | 0 | 0 |
| Regan, p | 0 | 0 | 0 |
| Total | 37 | 4 | 9 |

| | | |
|---|---|---|
| Atlanta | 2 0 0 0 0 1 0 0 0 0—3 | |
| Chicago | 0 1 0 0 0 0 1 0 1 0 1—4 | |

Error—Martin. Runs batted in—Banks 2, Williams 1, Santo 1. Two-base hits—Boyer, Santo. Home runs—Banks, Williams. Sacrifice fly—Banks. Double plays—Atlanta 1, Chicago 2. Left on base—Atlanta 4, Chicago 6. Bases on balls—Jarvis 1, Priddy 1, Holtzman 3, Regan 1. Struck out—Jarvis 6, Wilhelm 2, Holtzman 4. Hits off —Jarvis, 4 in 8; Wilhelm, 2 in 2; Priddy, 3 in 0 (pitched to four batters in eleventh); Holtzman, 5 in 8; Abernathy, 1 in 2; Regan, 0 in 1. Wild pitch—Holtzman 3. Winner —Regan. Loser—Priddy. Umpires—Venzon, Secory, Engel, and Wendelstedt. Time—2:45. Attendance—5,264.

Of the thousands of homers that have rocketed out of Wrigley Field since the stadium was built in the Federal League days, three will be forever remembered. One was belted by Babe Ruth in the third game of the 1932 World Series, the homer that Babe called in advance, according to a persistent legend. The second was Gabby Hartnett's homer, in September, 1938, against the pennant-contending Pirates. The third was hit by Mr. Cub himself, Ernie Banks, in the waning days of his fabulous career.

Ernie was 22 years old when the Cubs purchased him from the Kansas City Monarchs in September, 1953, for an estimated $10,000. Experts immediately tabbed the skinny 150-pound shortstop "good-field-no-hit." They weren't all wrong—the newcomer *could* field. As for hitting, Banks converted the skeptics with unseemly haste. Two years after he arrived, he smashed 44 home runs, drove in 117 runs, and batted .295. In 13 of his 19 seasons as a Cub, Banks hit 20 or more home runs; in 5 seasons he topped the 40-homer mark. His highest totals came in 1958 and 1959, when he hammered 47 and 45 homers, respectively. He was voted the National League's Most Valuable Player in each of those years. By then he had long since passed Hartnett as the Cubs' greatest home run hitter.

In 1969, when he hit 23 home runs and batted in 106 runs, Banks was 38 years old and in his seventeenth sea-

*Chicago's "Mr. Cub," Ernie Banks, twice the National League's MVP, terrorized pitchers for more than a decade.*

son. His home run production that year boosted his career total to 497. Just short of 500, a mark only eight others in baseball history had attained, Banks took 13 days at the start of the 1970 season before hitting number 498. It came off Jim Bouton of the Astros. Number 499 came 12 days after that, on May 9, off Gary Nolan of the Cincinnati Reds.

Tuesday, May 12, was Senior Citizens Day in Chicago. The weather had not favored the promotional venture. The day was dark and threatening, the field soggy from an all-night downpour. In an expression of unwarranted optimism, 5,264 fans showed up for a game. Inexplicably, the clouds lifted somewhat, and the Cubs began the final game of their series with the Atlanta Braves.

In the second inning, with two out and nobody on base, the sun came out in the person of Ernie Banks. Never one to countenance gloom, whether its cause was meterological or human, the genial veteran connected with a one-one pitch from Pat Jarvis and drove it just over the left field wall. The ball struck the concrete below the second row in the bleachers and caromed back to the field. After circling the bases for this, his five hundredth homer, Banks had to emerge twice from the Cubs' dugout to acknowledge the standing ovation of the sparse crowd.

Ernie's longtime buddies, Billy Wil-liams and Ron Santo, got the message. There was to be no dreariness this day. With a homer in the ninth, Williams tied the game, and with a bases-loaded single in the eleventh, Santo won it. Ernie's friends had provided an appropriately happy conclusion to that happy afternoon for the Cubs fans.

"There was no way we were going

to lose that game and spoil Ernie's day for him," said Williams.

Later, Banks was asked what he was thinking about when he was trotting around the bases. "I was thinking about my mother and dad," he said. "I was thinking about all those people in the Cubs' organization that helped me and about the wonderful Chicago fans who have come out all these years to cheer me on."

Someone told him that May 12 was Senior Citizens Day in Chicago. Ernie laughed. "Wouldn't you know it?" he cracked. "Old man Banks hit number five hundred on Senior Citizens Day. Fitting." There was no more grousing about the weather.

May 17, 1970

# Hank Aaron: 3,000 Hits

**Atlanta**

| | AB | R | H |
|---|---|---|---|
| Jackson, ss | 7 | 0 | 1 |
| Millan, 2b | 6 | 3 | 2 |
| H. Aaron, rf | 5 | 2 | 3 |
| Carty, lf | 3 | 0 | 0 |
| Gonzalez, lf | 2 | 1 | 0 |
| Cepeda, 1b | 6 | 0 | 1 |
| Lum, cf | 6 | 0 | 0 |
| Boyer, 3b | 5 | 0 | 2 |
| Didier, c | 6 | 0 | 0 |
| Stone, p | 3 | 0 | 0 |
| Wilhelm, p | 0 | 0 | 0 |
| Garr, ph | 1 | 0 | 0 |
| Kline, p | 0 | 0 | 0 |
| Jaster, p | 1 | 0 | 0 |
| King, ph | 1 | 0 | 0 |
| Neibauer, p | 0 | 0 | 0 |
| Total | 52 | 6 | 9 |

**Cincinnati**

| | AB | R | H |
|---|---|---|---|
| Rose, rf | 7 | 1 | 1 |
| Woodward, 2b | 4 | 0 | 1 |
| Chaney, 2b | 3 | 0 | 1 |
| Gullett, p | 1 | 0 | 1 |
| Perez, 3b | 7 | 2 | 5 |
| Bench, c | 7 | 2 | 2 |
| May, 1b | 6 | 1 | 3 |
| McRae, lf | 3 | 0 | 0 |
| Tolan, cf | 3 | 0 | 1 |
| Corrales, c | 2 | 0 | 0 |
| Stewart, 2b | 3 | 0 | 0 |
| Concepcion, ss | 7 | 1 | 2 |
| Simpson, p | 2 | 0 | 0 |
| Ward, ph | 1 | 0 | 0 |
| Granger, p | 1 | 0 | 0 |
| Helms, ph | 1 | 0 | 0 |
| Carroll, p | 0 | 0 | 0 |
| Bravo, ph-lf | 1 | 0 | 0 |
| Total | 59 | 7 | 17 |

```
Atlanta      1 0 2 0 0 0 0 0 3 0 0 0 0 0—6
Cincinnati   0 0 0 0 2 0 1 0 3 0 0 0 0 1—7
```

Errors—Concepcion, Cepeda, Boyer, Chaney, Perez. Runs batted in—H. Aaron 3, Cepeda, Rose, Gullett, Bench 2, May 3. Two-base hits—Perez, Tolan, May. Three-base hits—Concepcion. Home runs—H. Aaron, Rose, Bench, May. Stolen bases—Perez, Tolan. Sacrifices—Millan, Bravo. Double plays—Atlanta 1, Cincinnati 3. Bases on balls—Stone 1, Wilhelm 1, Jaster 1, Neibauer 2, Simpson 2, Granger 4, Gullett 2. Struck out—Stone 3, Wilhelm 2, Jaster 1, Neibauer 1, Simpson 2, Granger 1, Gullett 4. Hits off—Stone, 9 in 7; Wilhelm, 0 in 1; Kline, 3 in 1; Jaster, 2 in 3; Simpson, 4 in 7; Granger, 4 in 3; Carroll, 3 in 1; Gullett, 0 in 2. Hit by pitch—by Simpson (Cepeda). Winner—Gullett. Loser—Neibauer. Umpires—Venzon, Secory, Engel, and Wendelstedt. Time—3:55. Attendance—33,317.

Hank Aaron slept very little on Saturday night, May 16. Well-wishers kept the hotel's night switchboard operator busy plugging into Henry's room. In fact Aaron had had very little rest in the past few days, as he neared one of the milestones in his career. Sixteen years after he hammered his first major league hit, off the Cardinals' Vic Raschi in 1954, he was about to become only the ninth player in the 101-year history of the game to get 3,000 hits. The strong, silent slugger of the Atlanta Braves had begun the 1970 season 44 hits shy of 3,000. He had gotten 43 of those hits in the first 33 games.

Despite the lack of sleep, he felt good on the morning of May 17. He read in the paper that Jim Merritt, a left-hander, would be the Reds' starting pitcher in the opening game of the doubleheader that day. Aaron dearly wanted to get number 3,000 in the first game because it was to be televised home to Dixieland. His parents lived in Mobile, Alabama, and his wife and four children were in Atlanta. Also, he knew that Stan Musial, the last man to reach the 3,000-hit plateau, would be on hand for the game, and he wanted to perform well before his longtime idol.

More than great batting skill, it takes a combination of consistency, durability, and good luck to reach 3,000 hits. Henry clearly was consistent and durable. Today he wanted a little luck.

Luck failed him in the first game. Jim

*Called "Bad Henry" because he's so good,*
*Hank Aaron makes amends for a weak three-thousandth*
*hit by sending number 3,001 for a ride.*

Aaron slams his six-hundredth career homer,
victimizing the San Francisco Giants.

Merritt, a pitcher who relied on cunning and guile to redeem the lack of a fastball, held him hitless in four appearances at the plate. Although deeply disappointed, Aaron lauded Merritt for his fine pitching.

"No, I wasn't overanxious," he replied to a question later. "Merritt simply outsmarted me. I kept looking for one pitch, and he kept throwing me another. He's a good pitcher."

Musial, an interested observer, saw it differently. "Hank was pressing," he said sympathetically. "He'll get one early in the second game, and just watch it—it will relax him."

In his first time at bat, against Wayne Simpson, the Red's firing right-hander, Henry topped a grounder past the mound and beat it out for an infield hit. No sooner had Aaron crossed the bag than the crowd of 33,317 stood up and cheered. Stan Musial, seated behind the Braves' dugout, hopped the railing and headed toward Aaron. "Congratulations, Hank," said Stan as he shook Henry's hand.

"Thanks," replied Aaron, "I really appreciate your coming. It means a lot to me."

It was not exactly the kind of hit Aaron had dreamed of as fitting to be his three thousandth. Perturbed, he slammed a homer on his next time at bat, as if to emphasize another of his special achievements. Not only had he become the first player to enter the 3,000 hit portals since Musial made it in 1958, but he was the first in the history of the game to register 3,000 hits and 500 home runs. (Willie Mays was later to join him.)

At 36, Aaron was the youngest to reach 3,000 since Ty Cobb did it at the age of 35 in 1922. Honus Wagner and Napoleon Lajoie arrived at the 3,000 summit in 1914. Tris Speaker and Eddie Collins did so in 1925. Paul Waner got his three thousandth in 1945. Stan Musial achieved his 13 years later. Adrian ("Cap") Anson was the first to reach 3,000 hits, before the turn of the century.

Unfortunately, from Aaron's standpoint, the Braves lost both ends of the doubleheader, bowing in 15 innings in the second game 7–6, but not before Henry had collected a third hit. In the Braves' clubhouse after the game, a representative of the Hall of Fame requested that the ball be enshrined forever in Cooperstown, New York. Aaron handed it over. "I'm not used to this attention," he said with a smile.

June 21, 1970

# Cesar Gutierrez:
# Seven for Seven

### Detroit

| | AB | R | H |
|---|---|---|---|
| Stanley, cf | 6 | 1 | 2 |
| Gutierrez, ss | 7 | 3 | 7 |
| Kaline, 1b | 6 | 1 | 1 |
| W. Horton, lf | 6 | 1 | 3 |
| Northrup, rf | 5 | 2 | 2 |
| Maddox, 3b | 6 | 0 | 0 |
| I. Brown, 2b | 3 | 0 | 0 |
| G. Brown, ph | 1 | 1 | 1 |
| Freehan, c | 1 | 0 | 0 |
| Price, c | 1 | 0 | 0 |
| Cash, ph | 1 | 0 | 0 |
| Hiller, p | 0 | 0 | 0 |
| Wert, ph | 1 | 0 | 1 |
| Timmerman, p | 1 | 0 | 0 |
| Kilkenny, p | 0 | 0 | 0 |
| Patterson, p | 2 | 0 | 0 |
| Nagelson, ph | 1 | 0 | 0 |
| Scherman, p | 0 | 0 | 0 |
| McAuliffe, 2b | 3 | 0 | 0 |
| Total | 51 | 9 | 17 |

### Cleveland

| | AB | R | H |
|---|---|---|---|
| Heidemann, ss | 5 | 1 | 1 |
| Leon, 2b | 5 | 1 | 1 |
| Uhlaender, cf | 6 | 2 | 3 |
| Fosse, c | 6 | 1 | 2 |
| T. Horton, 1b | 5 | 1 | 4 |
| Foster, lf | 4 | 0 | 0 |
| Lasher, p | 0 | 0 | 0 |
| Rollins, ph | 1 | 0 | 0 |
| Ellsworth, p | 0 | 0 | 0 |
| Klimchock, ph | 1 | 0 | 0 |
| Hennigan, p | 0 | 0 | 0 |
| Hinton, rf-lf | 6 | 1 | 3 |
| Nettles, 3b | 3 | 1 | 3 |
| Austin, p | 1 | 0 | 0 |
| Higgins, p | 1 | 0 | 0 |
| Pinson, rf | 3 | 0 | 0 |
| Total | 47 | 8 | 17 |

```
Detroit      1 0 4 0 0 0 2 1 0 0 0 1—9
Cleveland    5 1 0 0 1 1 0 0 0 0 0 0—8
```

Error—T. Horton. Runs batted in—Stanley, Gutierrez, Kaline 2, Northrup 5, Heidemann, Uhlaender, T. Horton 5, Hinton. Two-base hits—T. Horton, Fosse, Gutierrez, G. Brown. Home runs—T. Horton, Hinton, Uhlaender, Kaline, Northrup 2, Stanley. Sacrifice—Higgins. Sacrifice flies—T. Horton, Heidemann. Double plays—Detroit 1, Cleveland 1. Left on base—Detroit 13, Cleveland 11. Bases on balls—Kilkenny 1, Patterson 1, Hiller 1, Timmerman 2, Austin 2, Higgins 2, Lasher 1, Ellsworth 1, Hennigan 1. Struck out—Kilkenny 2, Patterson 3, Hiller 1, Timmerman 1, Austin 3, Higgins 5, Lasher 1. Hits off—Kilkenny, 5 in 2/3; Patterson, 4 in 4 1/3; Scherman, 2 in 2; Hiller, 2 in 2; Timmerman, 4 in 3; Austin, 5 in 2 1/3; Higgins, 4 in 4 2/3; Lasher, 3 in 2; Ellsworth, 3 in 2; Hennigan, 2 in 1. Wild pitch—Scherman. Passed ball—Price. Winner—Timmerman. Loser—Hennigan. Umpires—Napp, Rice, Springstead, and Barnett. Time—4:00. Attendance—23,904.

In 1892, before baseball's modern era, Wilbert Robinson, a catcher with the Baltimore Orioles, then in the National League, hit safely seven times in seven at bats in a single game. In the next 78 years, some 10,000 major league players failed to duplicate that mark. A number of players got six straight hits in a game but never seven. Then came a lightly regarded player, virtually unheard of, who astounded the baseball world by collecting six singles and a double in seven trips to the plate.

Cesar Gutierrez was an unlikely candidate for baseball fame. The 5-foot, 8-inch, 150-pound infielder from the Venezuelan town of Coro had been obtained by the Detroit Tigers from San Francisco, where twice he had failed to make a favorable impression on the Giants. The Pirates had given up on him earlier.

He landed a berth with the Tigers by default. Tommy Tresh and Dick Tracewski had shared the shortstop job for the Tigers in 1969, and both were gone the next year, Tresh a victim of injuries and Tracewski a victim of age. Mickey Stanley, who had helped out at shortstop, was back in the outfield. In desperation Tigers manager Mayo Smith had turned to Gutierrez, who in 50 games in the major leagues, had hit .222. He was down to .211 when Smith decided that Ken Szotkiewicz might do better. He was wrong.

While Cesar warmed the bench on

*Detroit Tigers unknown Cesar Gutierrez achieved a certain measure of fame by going 7 for 7 in one game against Cleveland.*

June 21, 1970, the Tigers lost the first game of a doubleheader to Cleveland and shortstop Szotkiewicz failed to get the ball out of the infield in four trips to the plate. Resigned, manager Smith turned back to Gutierrez, not for his hitting, but because he could run and throw better than Szotkiewicz.

Gutierrez was grateful for the opportunity to win back the regular shortstop job. Facing Rick Austin in the first inning, he looped a single to center. He singled again in the third and once again in the fifth. Encouraged by his first three-hit game of the year but apparently bored with singles, Cesar doubled to left in the seventh. It was

the first time in his brief major league career that he had collected four safeties. Gutierrez was far from through. In the eighth he slapped a single to right, and in the tenth he bounced a single behind second base for his sixth hit.

"After I got my sixth hit," said the jubilant Venezuelan later, "Wally Moses [the Tigers' batting coach] told me I was close to a record. I didn't know what he meant, but I knew I had six hits. So I said, 'Okay, I try for seven.'"

It came in the twelfth. With the score tied 8–8, Cesar, batting left-handed against the right-handed Phil Hennigan, slashed a hard grounder off the pitcher's glove and beat it out for his seventh hit of the game (and his third infield hit).

"Sometimes you have to be lucky," said Cesar philosophically. "The shortstop made a diving stop of my ball in the tenth but couldn't make the play. I hit the pitcher's leg in the twelfth, and he couldn't make the throw in time."

The seven hits boosted Gutierrez's batting avearge 38 points to .249 and earned him the regular job for the remainder of the season. He played in 135 games for the Tigers that year, batting .243. That was the honeymoon. The following year, after his avearge shrunk to .189 in 38 games, the Tigers handed him the pink slip, and he was gone from the big leagues. He may never come back, but devotees of the record book will not forget him.

# Willie Stargell:
# Five Extra-base Hits

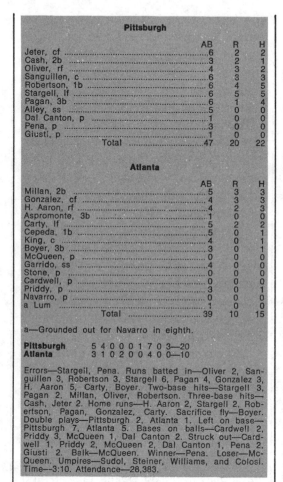

**Pittsburgh**

| | AB | R | H |
|---|---|---|---|
| Jeter, cf | 6 | 2 | 2 |
| Cash, 2b | 3 | 2 | 1 |
| Oliver, rf | 4 | 3 | 2 |
| Sanguillen, c | 6 | 3 | 3 |
| Robertson, 1b | 6 | 4 | 5 |
| Stargell, lf | 6 | 5 | 5 |
| Pagan, 3b | 6 | 1 | 4 |
| Alley, ss | 5 | 0 | 0 |
| Dal Canton, p | 1 | 0 | 0 |
| Pena, p | 3 | 0 | 0 |
| Giusti, p | 1 | 0 | 0 |
| Total | 47 | 20 | 22 |

**Atlanta**

| | AB | R | H |
|---|---|---|---|
| Millan, 2b | 5 | 3 | 3 |
| Gonzalez, cf | 4 | 3 | 3 |
| H. Aaron, rf | 4 | 2 | 3 |
| Aspromonte, 3b | 1 | 0 | 0 |
| Carty, lf | 5 | 2 | 2 |
| Cepeda, 1b | 5 | 0 | 1 |
| King, c | 4 | 0 | 1 |
| Boyer, 3b | 3 | 0 | 1 |
| McQueen, p | 0 | 0 | 0 |
| Garrido, ss | 4 | 0 | 0 |
| Stone, p | 0 | 0 | 0 |
| Cardwell, p | 0 | 0 | 0 |
| Priddy, p | 3 | 0 | 1 |
| Navarro, p | 0 | 0 | 0 |
| a Lum | 1 | 0 | 0 |
| Total | 39 | 10 | 15 |

a—Grounded out for Navarro in eighth.

| | | |
|---|---|---|
| **Pittsburgh** | 5 4 0 0 0 1 7 0 3 | —20 |
| **Atlanta** | 3 1 0 2 0 0 4 0 0 | —10 |

Errors—Stargell, Pena. Runs batted in—Oliver 2, Sanguillen 3, Robertson 3, Stargell 6, Pagan 4, Gonzalez 3, H. Aaron 5, Carty, Boyer. Two-base hits—Stargell 3, Pagan 2, Millan, Oliver, Robertson. Three-base hits—Cash, Jeter 2. Home runs—H. Aaron 2, Stargell 2, Robertson, Pagan, Gonzalez, Carty. Sacrifice fly—Boyer. Double plays—Pittsburgh 2, Atlanta 1. Left on base—Pittsburgh 7, Atlanta 5. Bases on balls—Cardwell 2, Priddy 3, McQueen 1, Dal Canton 2. Struck out—Cardwell 1, Priddy 2, McQueen 2, Dal Canton 1, Pena 2, Giusti 2. Balk—McQueen. Winner—Pena. Loser—McQueen. Umpires—Sudol, Steiner, Williams, and Colosi. Time—3:10. Attendance—28,383.

Willie Stargell is an itinerant apostle of the long long ball. He spreads the gospel as prodigiously in Los Angeles and Montreal as in Pittsburgh, his home base. While spectators gasp like the faithful at a revival meeting, Willie pounds more home runs farther than anyone.

One of the most awesome challenges to long-ball hitters used to be the right field roof of old Forbes Field in Pittsburgh. A pavilion hovered over a double-decked grandstand that stood 86 feet high. Babe Ruth was the first to hit the ball over that roof, in 1935, 10 years after it was erected. The feat was repeated 17 times, 7 times by Stargell.

On August 6, 1969, he walloped a ball out of Dodger Stadium farther than anyone ever had before. In Montreal's Jarry Park barely a few months after it opened, Stargell hammered one that left the park in right field and landed in the middle of a swimming pool.

He is particularly fond of hitting home runs in clusters. He was the first man to hit three home runs in a game at Dodger Stadium, a renowned pitchers' ball park. Four times he hit three home runs in a game. Only Johnny Mize, Ernie Banks, and Ralph Kiner have done it that often. Three times he has made four extra-base hits in a game, tying a National League record. But during the first half of the 1970 season, he could hardly buy a base hit, let alone a home run.

For almost four months, the Pirates carried Willie Stargell and his slumping bat. Only occasionally would he break out in a show of power. That was not enough for manager Danny Murtaugh and the Pirates. Willie Stargell was the power guy who was supposed to carry the Bucs. Reluctantly, in July Murtaugh began to platoon Stargell. But when Roberto Clemente was sidelined with a bruised right wrist, Murtaugh was forced to reinstate Stargell on full-time duty. He couldn't afford to have both Clemente and Stargell out of the lineup at the same time. Though his batting average remained below .250, Stargell returned on a daily basis.

Willie gave signs of snapping out of his slump in a three-game series in Cincinnati, but not until the Pirates reached Atlanta did Stargell really wake up. Atlanta had always been a live town for him. There he twice hit three home runs in a game. Against the Braves he had tied a National League record by hitting eleven home runs in a season.

Atlanta didn't disappoint Stargell. Batting for the first time in the game on August 1, the left-handed hitting Stargell lined a double off southpaw George Stone in the first inning. In the five more times he came to bat in the game, Stargell smashed two pitches out of the park for homers and two against the fence for doubles. That gave him five extra-base hits, tying a major league record for most extra-base hits in a game. Lou Boudreau hit four doubles and a home run for Cleveland against the Red Sox on July 14, 1946, and Joe Adcock clubbed four home runs and a double for Milwaukee against the Dodgers on July 31, 1954.

"It was the greatest show I've ever seen," said a delighted Murtaugh. "We've waited a long time for Willie to come out of it. With Willie, you're willing to wait because you know how much he means to a ball club. The big thing about Stargell is that he never got down on himself. The younger players on the team look up to him. He showed them the importance of being a team man."

*Pirate Willie Stargell does his thing.*

August 22–23, 1970

# Roberto Clemente: 10 Hits in Two Games

Roberto Clemente's brilliant 18-year major league career, which included four National League batting titles, was composed of many outstanding days. Twice he hit three home runs in a single game, once he batted in all seven of his team's runs, once he smashed three triples in a game, and twice he scored five runs in a game.

Clemente had so many sparkling games at bat that it is difficult to select his best. In the 1971 World Series, his 12 hits, .414 average, and flawless play in the field picked up the Pirates and led them to the world championship after they had lost the two opening games to Baltimore. That was the Series in which the four-time batting champion and perennial Golden Glove winner and All-Star finally became a household name throughout the entire nation.

The Pittsburgh star himself once volunteered that the game that gave him the most satisfaction was the one in which he slammed three home runs and a double and drove in seven runs against the Cincinnati Reds. His self-satisfaction stemmed from the fact that he had set out before the game to hit home runs—to prove that he could if he wanted to. After that, he went back to his regular style of making other hits as well.

Though that may have been Clemente's finest single day in baseball, other players have hit three or more

*Possibly the greatest right fielder of all time, Pittsburgh's Roberto Clemente loses a battle with Wrigley Field's ivy.*

homers and have driven in seven or more runs in a single game. But no player in modern times has had two consecutive days such as Clemente enjoyed on August 22 and August 23, 1970.

Pittsburgh and Los Angeles were locked in a 1–1 confrontation from the third inning through the fifteenth at Dodger Stadium on the night of August 22. Bob Moose of the Pirates and Don Sutton of the Dodgers had started this pitching duel, but both had long since departed. The Pirates had managed but nine hits against Los Angeles pitching, and Clemente had four of them. One of these, a single in the third inning, had driven in Bill Mazeroski with the run that offset the Dodgers' tally in the first. Pete Mikkelsen, the Dodgers' third pitcher, easily disposed of the first two Pirates in the sixteenth, but Clemente rapped his fifth hit, a line single to right. Roberto then stole second and rode home with the lead run on a single by Milt May. Bruce Dal Canton protected the one-run margin in the bottom of the inning, and the Pirates trudged wearily off the field with a 2–1 triumph that had taken them four hours and 21 minutes to accomplish.

The players did not get back to their hotel until 2 A.M. and then had to wake up early for a 1 P.M. game Sunday. Normally, Clemente, who had turned 36 the previous Tuesday, would have been rested in a day game following a night

contest, especially after a marathon night game. But Willie Stargell, the Pirates' clean-up hitter, was still nursing an injured leg. Manager Danny Murtaugh needed Roberto's big bat in the lineup.

In the first inning, facing Alan Foster, Clemente singled and scored. In the second he batted in a run with a single. In the fourth, with Fred Norman pitch-

*As accomplished at bat as he was in the field, Clemente compiled a remarkably high lifetime batting average of .317.*

drove in four, raising his batting average to .363 and wresting the league batting leadership from Atlanta's Rico Carty. The victories, coupled with New York's split with Cincinnati, increased the Pirates' first-place lead over the Mets to three games.

An interested onlooker during Clemente's record spree was Al Campanis, the Dodgers vice-president. He recalls today that back in 1953 he was sent to Puerto Rico to scout a young ballplayer. "He looked like the best prospect I have ever seen," Campanis says. "I think we signed him for ten thousand." The prospect was Roberto Clemente, who, after a .257 year at the Dodgers' Montreal farm in 1954, was drafted by the Pirates for $4,000.

"I hated to see anybody beat the Dodgers," Campanis muses, "but if it was going to happen, it was kind of nice to see Clemente do it. He was the most complete ballplayer I ever saw, and I'll always be proud of the fact that I signed him."

Danny Murtaugh still looks back to Clemente's feat with awe. "Roberto really should not have played that second game," recalls Murtaugh. "He was so tired from the previous night's game and lack of sleep, that he passed up batting practice. But he played all twenty-five innings within a twenty-hour period. . . . Man, when I was playing, it would take me three or four weeks to get that many hits."

ing, he doubled in a run and later scored. In the seventh he singled before Al Oliver's home run. He climaxed his batting barrage in the eighth with a booming home run off rookie Charlie Hough for his second straight five-hit game. The Pirates won 11–0.

Roberto's 10 hits included two doubles, seven singles and his tenth homer of the season. He scored five runs and

# Vida Blue: Double Gem

Rarely, if ever, has a youngster stormed into the big leagues with such fire and fury—and such a blazing fastball. Less than a year out of De Soto High, where he was more renowned for his ability to throw touchdowns than strikes, Vida Blue, Jr., of Mansfield, Louisiana, was being measured for the mantle of superstar. Before another year had elapsed, they were calling him "the Blue Blade," "the Blue Streak," and "the Black Koufax." Charles Finley, owner of the Oakland Athletics, who had personally signed him, even tried to get the youngster to change his name to "True Blue," without success. Vida was drawing accolades customarily reserved for the Seavers, the Gibsons, and the Marichals.

Why not? Six weeks into the 1971 season, the youngster had become baseball's first 10-game winner and had lost only once. He led the American League in ERA, shutouts, complete games, and strikeouts. He was helping Oakland to maintain a sizable lead in the American League Western Division. By the All-Star break, he had won 16 of 19 decisions, and when the season came to an end, he captured the league's Most Valuable Player Award and the Cy Young Award. The 6-foot, 190-pounder with the explosive fastball had become the most talked about pitcher in baseball.

Blue won 24 games in 1971, his first full year in the major leagues. He per-

The American League's MVP and Cy Young Award winner in 1971, Oakland's Vida Blue prepares to deliver his blue blazer.

mitted only 209 hits in 312 innings, hurled eight shutouts and struck out 301 batters. His earned run average was an amazing 1.82. It was only his first full year in the majors, but already they were comparing him with south-paw legends Lefty Grove, Rube Wad-dell, and Sandy Koufax. None of them had such a spectacular start.

After his first season in professional baseball, Blue suddenly found himself in the big leagues following a 10–3 1969 season with Birmingham in the Southern Association. Although he split two decisions in the majors, he obviously wasn't ready yet. The kid was rocked for 13 home runs in 42 innings. Al Kaline hit three straight homers off him, and Harmon Killebrew slammed one with the bases loaded.

Blue returned to the minors in 1970, swept up every prize in the American Association with a 12–3 mark at Iowa, and came back to the A's for another chance. This time he was ready. He made his first start in Chicago's White Sox Park on Labor Day. The A's won, but Blue did not receive credit for the victory. He was nervous, and the White Sox knocked him out in the fifth inning. His greatest contribution was, of all things, a three-run homer. "I was try-ing too hard," he explained later.

Four nights later, Vida started in Kansas City against the Royals, who had run off four straight victories. Blue retired 11 batters before walking Amos

Otis in the fourth. In the fifth he hit Ellie Rodriguez with a pitch and walked Dick Severson but struck out Wally Bunker to end the threat. In the sixth he walked Pat Kelly. In the eighth Sev-erson flied out, and Hawk Taylor, a pinch hitter, struck out. Just as every-body started thinking no-hitter, Kelly lined a clean single, spoiling Vida's bid. That was the Royals' only hit as Blue pitched his first big league shut-out, 3–0.

It was just a warm-up. Ten days later, in his fourth start of the year, Blue faced Minnesota in Oakland. The Twins expected to clinch the Western Division title in the American League, eliminating the A's. Champagne was chilling on ice in the Minnesota dress-ing room. Jim Perry, the 23-game win-ner who would win the Cy Young Award as the league's best pitcher that year, was pitching for the Twins. He had hurled 12 straight victories over the A's and had not lost to them in four years.

Blue began by retiring 11 in a row, and 4, including Harmon Killebrew, on strikeouts. Only occasionally did he tease the Twins with a curve. He was throwing fastballs nine pitches out of ten. The A's had staked their rookie pitcher to a 1–0 lead in the first when Bert Campaneris tripled and scored on a grounder.

In the fourth Vida got Tovar on a grounder and Cardenas on a fly, but too careful with Killebrew, he walked him on a three-one curve. Killebrew was the first Twin to reach base. Blue then retired Oliva on a ground out, ending the inning.

"Killebrew was one man I was afraid of," said Blue later. "He hits the ball a long way. We were only one run ahead at the time, and I didn't want him to tie it with a homer."

In the fifth, after Blue had disposed of the first two batters, George Mitterwald slammed a drive toward left center, but Campaneris, darting to his left, made a leaping, one-handed stab of the liner. In the sixth Danny Thompson popped up, Perry grounded out, and Tovar popped a foul that catcher Gene Tenace caught after nearly falling into the Twins' dugout. After a perfect seventh inning, the players and the fans were thinking no-hitter again, but nobody said a word. "I was thinking about it, too," admitted Blue. "How could I help it? I remembered losing the other one, and I tried to push it out of my mind."

In the eighth Alyea struck out, Renick grounded out, and Mitterwald banged a hard grounder to third. Bando knocked it down and recovered in time to throw out the slow-moving catcher. The A's were inspired. They left the rookie free to concentrate on the no-hitter by scoring five times in their half of the eighth. Campaneris struck the key blow, a three-run homer.

Three men now stood between Blue and his no-hitter. The small crowd of 4,284 was making enough noise for 40,000. Blue didn't appear to hear as he came out blazing in the ninth. He struck out Thompson. Bob Allison, a pinch hitter, came up, and he too struck out, number nine for Blue. Now it was Tovar, a tough man to fool. Vida got a strike past him. Then another. On the third pitch, a fastball, Tovar raised a high pop foul outside first base. Don Mincher, the first baseman, moved nervously under it and caught it for the third out. Not yet 21, with less than a full season in the majors, Vida Blue had his no-hitter.

A few minutes later, Charles Finley was on the phone, excitedly calling him from Chicago. The generous Oakland owner congratulated Blue with a $2,000 bonus and even had $1,000 for Gene Tenace, the catcher of the no-hitter.

"He gives little awards like that for no-hitters, perfect games, and other such feats," acknowledged a smiling Blue. "I hope to get more phone calls like that."

September 22, 1963–September 2, 1970

# Billy Williams:
# 1,117 Consecutive Games

Ever hear of a ballplayer begging a manager to take him out of the lineup? Billy Williams, the National League's endurance king, had to do it before Leo Durocher finally paid heed. A stroke of Leo's pen that left Williams out of the lineup on September 3, ended Williams's National League record consecutive game total at 1,117.

"I had played seven years without missing a game," recalls Williams, "and slowly it began to dawn on me I actually had no place to go as far as breaking Lou Gehrig's record—not unless I played every game for seven more years. Imagine that!"

That left the Chicago Cubs' outfielder third on baseball's all-time list of iron men, far behind the almost unapproachable record of 2,130 games held by the legendary Gehrig of the New York Yankees. Second, at 1,307, is Deacon Scott of the Boston Red Sox and Yankees.

"It took a long time to get me out of there," states Williams, "but it had to happen. I wasn't getting the bat around, I wasn't performing at the plate. It was a good time to end the streak, and it could have helped my career in the long run. I felt I was hurting the club by staying in there. I was physically spent, and I knew I needed a rest. A ballplayer can tell when everything isn't just right. You can feel it in your legs when you have to go from first to third and you don't push off the bag at sec-

*Agility as well as luck enabled Billy Williams to play 1,117 consecutive games.*

ond the way you should. You can feel it in your hands when you grip the bat. You can tell.''

Durocher remembers the day vividly. ''Billy talked a long time about ending his streak,'' he recalls, ''but I paid no attention. Twice before I scratched his name off the starting lineup, but I got him into the game, once as a pinch hitter, the other time for defensive purposes. On this day, I didn't decide to take him out until I made out the lineup card before the game.''

''Leo and I talked about it quite a bit,'' explains Williams, ''and we both agreed that it would be better for me and the ball club if this thing wasn't hanging over our heads. Once the decision was made, I was just afraid I'd change my mind before the game was over, or Leo would. I did everything possible to stay away from Leo. I didn't want him to look around for a pinch hitter and see me. So I went into the clubhouse and listened to the game on the radio.''

So the streak, which had begun on September 22, 1963 against the Milwaukee Braves and had lasted almost seven seasons, finally came to an end in Wrigley Field on September 3, 1970. Williams, a Cubs starter since he won National League rookie honors in 1961, had moved into third spot on June 29, 1969. That day, in a doubleheader against the St. Louis Cardinals, Williams played his eight hundred ninety-fifth and ninety-sixth games, breaking the National League consecutive game record of 895 held by the Cards' Stan Musial.

''When the streak reached a thousand, I said I'd be satisfied to end it right there,'' Williams says, ''but at that time I felt good, and there was no reason to stop then. The day it ended, there was every reason to stop. I was tired. Really tired. If I had to do it over again, I wouldn't go for a consecutive record. It just isn't worth it because it hurts you as well as the ball club. Too often you are out there playing when you shouldn't be, because you are not anywhere near one hundred percent. I can remember distinctly three times during the streak when I was hurt and certainly was far below par. And there were other times when I was under the weather, feeling bad, or just so tired I couldn't do my best.

''In 1964, I was hit on the shoulder and hardly could swing a bat. In 1965, I had a bad back, and in 1969, I hit myself on the right foot with my own foul ball. I could hardly walk, let alone run. But the skipper kept my streak going by having me pinch hit. You know, that kind of record isn't anything they pay off on. You get paid for performance, not for how many games you played in a row. When contract time comes, the man looks at what you did with the bat and what you did on the field.''

Left: *Williams shows form.* Below: *Breaks Musial's record.* Bottom: *After a game-winning home run.*

October 10–15, 1970

# Brooks Robinson: One-Man Show

When other memories of the Baltimore Orioles' 1970 conquest of the Cincinnati Reds have faded, Brooks Robinson's legacy will still sparkle. With teammate Paul Blair, Brooks tied a five-game record by collecting nine hits. He tied another record with four hits in a game (the fourth). His 17 total bases (two homers, two doubles, and five singles) broke a record. And though statistics adequately recount his superior performance at the plate, they barely hint at his heroics in the field. In short, the 1970 World Series belonged to Brooks Robinson.

In the first game, he made three exemplary plays at third base. The finest was his lunging stop of Lee May's smash. In foul territory 25 feet behind third base, he recovered the ball and threw out May at first base. Earlier he had made a backhand stab of Bernie Carbo's drive down the third base line. Having saved the game in the field, Brooks won it at bat with a home run in the seventh inning.

In game two Brooks demonstrated that his legerdemain in the field is a daily routine, a fact Baltimore fans have long since taken for granted. He made a diving stop of Bobby Tolan's smash in the first inning and turned it into a force play. Two innings later, he again robbed Lee May, again with a diving backhand grab. This one he turned into a double play. Slightly less conspicuous at bat this day, he merely drove in

The defensive star of the 1970 World Series,
Baltimore's Brooks Robinson makes a diving
stop, robbing the Reds' Johnny Bench of a hit.

the tying run in the fifth with a single.

Lee May had apparently been convinced of the futility of pulling the ball down Robinson's way. Now it was Johnny Bench's turn. After Tommy Helms failed to faze Robinson in the second with a swinging bunt, which Brooks bare-handed and threw to first in one motion for the out, Bench tried a more forceful approach. He smashed a low line drive between third and short in the sixth, but an airborne Brooks stretched full length and nabbed it in the end of his glove's webbing. Then he stepped to the plate in the bottom of the inning, lined his second double of the day (his first drove in two runs), and trotted home moments later on pitcher Dave McNally's grand slam, the first by a pitcher in World Series play. That made it three in a row for Baltimore, and the dazed Reds needed no further convincing. Reds manager Sparky Anderson flatly called Robinson the best third baseman he had ever seen. Johnny Bench marveled, "I never saw Pie Traynor play, but if he was better at playing third than Brooks, he had to be inhuman."

Trying their best to ignore the balding hero, the Reds eked out a 6–5 victory in the fourth game despite the distraction of Robinson's four hits, including a homer. By now everyone had conceded Brooks the automobile, awarded each year to the Series' outstanding performer. As the Birds trounced the Reds the next day, he made it official with a final backhand nab of a Bench smash. Johnny couldn't help wondering if there was another way to deal with Brooks. "If we'd known he wanted a car so badly," mused the Reds' slugger, "we'd have chipped in and bought him one."

*Brooks Robinson practices his craft on Lee May. Cincinnati's sluggers spent the Series witnessing what Baltimore fans routinely expected.*

June 26, 1970

# Frank Robinson: Back-to-Back Slams

## Baltimore

| | AB | R | H |
|---|---|---|---|
| Buford, lf | 5 | 3 | 4 |
| Blair, cf | 4 | 2 | 1 |
| F. Robinson, rf | 4 | 2 | 2 |
| Powell, 1b | 4 | 1 | 2 |
| B. Robinson, 3b | 4 | 0 | 1 |
| Johnson, 2b | 5 | 1 | 0 |
| Hendricks, c | 5 | 0 | 1 |
| Belanger, ss | 4 | 1 | 1 |
| McNally, p | 2 | 2 | 0 |
| Total | 37 | 12 | 12 |

## Washington

| | AB | R | H |
|---|---|---|---|
| Brinkman, ss | 3 | 0 | 1 |
| Comer, cf | 4 | 0 | 1 |
| Howard, lf | 4 | 0 | 0 |
| Reichardt, rf | 2 | 2 | 2 |
| Rodriguez, 3b | 3 | 0 | 0 |
| Unser, pr | 0 | 0 | 0 |
| Epstein, 1b | 4 | 0 | 1 |
| Casanova, c | 4 | 0 | 1 |
| Cullen. 2b | 4 | 0 | 0 |
| Coleman, p | 1 | 0 | 1 |
| Grzenda, p | 0 | 0 | 0 |
| Nen, ph | 1 | 0 | 0 |
| Shellenback, p | 0 | 0 | 0 |
| Stroud, ph | 1 | 0 | 0 |
| Pina, p | 0 | 0 | 0 |
| Total | 31 | 2 | 7 |

| | | |
|---|---|---|
| **Baltimore** | 0 0 1 0 4 5 0 0 2 | —12 |
| **Washington** | 0 0 0 0 0 0 1 0 1 | — 2 |

Errors—None. Runs batted in—F. Robinson 8, Buford 3, Belanger 1, Reichardt 2. Two-base hits—Blair, Powell 2, Epstein. Home runs—Buford, F. Robinson 2, Reichardt 2. Double plays—Baltimore 3, Washington 1. Left on base—Baltimore 8, Washington 6. Bases on balls—McNally 2, Coleman 5, Grzenda 2, Shellenback 1, Pina 2. Struck out—McNally 4, Coleman 5, Shellenback 2. Hits off—McNally, 7 in 9, Coleman, 6 in 4 1/3; Grzenda, 3 in 1 2/3; Shellenback, 0 in 2; Pina, 3 in 1. Hit by pitch—by McNally 2, (Reichardt, Rodriguez). Loser—Coleman. Umpires—Chylak, Goetz, Denkinger, and Frantz. Time—2:33. Attendance—13,194.

Few players in the history of major league baseball have enjoyed as much success as Frank Robinson has. He is the only player ever to have won the Most Valuable Player award in both the American and National Leagues. He is the only player to have led both leagues in slugging percentage. He is one of the few who played on the All-Star team in both leagues. He is one of a handful to have captured the triple crown (that is, to have led his league in home runs, runs batted in, and batting average). He has homered in more major league ball parks than any other player.

However, the night of June 26, 1970, loomed as the most dismal of off-nights for Robbie as he and the Orioles arrived at Robert F. Kennedy Stadium in Washington for a game against the Senators. He had sprained his back the previous afternoon in making a sensational game-saving catch against the Red Sox in Boston. During batting practice before the game against the Senators, he could swing only gingerly, so great was the pain when he put his body into the swing. Hampered by the pain, he was even more concerned about his seven-year-old son, Kevin, who had a sore throat and a 104-degree temperature. The night before, Robinson had sat up until 4 A.M. with his son. When he arrived at the ball park, he had had only five hours sleep at most.

Below: *An MVP in both leagues, Frank Robinson has homered in more big league parks than anyone.* Opposite: *Robinson takes a mighty cut.*

In the fifth inning, having been stifled by Joe Coleman twice before in the game, Robinson suddenly forgot his troubles. After Dave McNally had walked, Don Buford had singled, and Paul Blair had walked loading the bases, Robinson walloped a grand slammer over the right field wall. "The pitch was a little outside," Robinson explained later. "Normally, I would have taken it, but I had two strikes, and I was afraid it might nick the corner. . . ."

Robinson was less defensive the next inning against Joe Grzenda. McNally had once again walked, Buford had once again singled, and Blair had once again walked, once again loading the bases. Hardly the one to ruin such a productive pattern, Robbie crashed a Grzenda fastball into the upper stands in left center for one of the longest homers of his career and

205

*Pausing to savor the sight of a home run hit deep over the left field wall.*

his second grand slam in two innings. "The count was two balls and no strikes," said Robinson. "I knew he had to come right down the middle, and he did." Only six other players had ever hit two grand slams in a game, and only two, Jim Gentile and Jim Northrup, had done it in successive times at bat. None had done it in successive innings.

Frank almost hit a third. The Orioles later loaded the bases with Paul Blair at bat and Robbie in the on-deck circle, but Blair flied out to end the inning. Still, Frank's contribution of two grand slammers and eight RBIs to the Orioles 12–2 decimation of the Senators served as a successful palliative for Frank's aching back. "It hurts, but it didn't hurt enough for me to stay out," reasoned Frank.

July 15, 1971

# Pittsburgh versus San Diego: A Seesaw Battle

### San Diego

|  | AB | R | H |
|---|---|---|---|
| E. Hernandez, ss | 7 | 0 | 1 |
| Mason, 3b-2b | 7 | 1 | 1 |
| Gaston, cf | 6 | 1 | 1 |
| Severinsen, p | 0 | 0 | 0 |
| Dean, ph | 1 | 0 | 1 |
| Coombs, p | 0 | 0 | 0 |
| Colbert, 1b | 7 | 0 | 0 |
| Stahl, lf | 7 | 0 | 1 |
| Brown, rf | 6 | 0 | 2 |
| Barton, c | 4 | 0 | 2 |
| Norman, pr | 0 | 0 | 0 |
| Kendall, c | 3 | 0 | 0 |
| Campbell, 2b | 2 | 0 | 0 |
| Lee, ph | 0 | 0 | 0 |
| Jestadt, 3b | 1 | 0 | 0 |
| Spiezio, ph-3b | 3 | 0 | 0 |
| Roberts, p | 3 | 0 | 0 |
| Bravo, ph | 1 | 0 | 0 |
| Miller, p | 0 | 0 | 0 |
| Murrell, ph-cf | 2 | 1 | 1 |
| Total | 60 | 3 | 10 |

### Pittsburgh

|  | AB | R | H |
|---|---|---|---|
| Mazeroski, 2b | 8 | 0 | 3 |
| Clines, cf | 8 | 0 | 4 |
| Clemente, rf | 8 | 1 | 1 |
| Stargell, lf | 6 | 1 | 1 |
| Sanguillen, c | 6 | 0 | 0 |
| Robertson, 1b | 3 | 0 | 0 |
| Davalillo, ph-1b | 3 | 1 | 1 |
| Pagan, 3b | 4 | 0 | 1 |
| J. Hernandez, 3b | 0 | 0 | 0 |
| Hebner, ph-3b | 3 | 1 | 1 |
| Alley, ss | 6 | 0 | 2 |
| Blass, p | 2 | 0 | 0 |
| Stennett, ph | 1 | 0 | 0 |
| Giusti, p | 1 | 0 | 0 |
| Oliver, ph | 1 | 0 | 0 |
| Grant, p | 0 | 0 | 0 |
| Sands, ph | 0 | 0 | 0 |
| Ellis, pr | 0 | 0 | 0 |
| Veale, p | 0 | 0 | 0 |
| Nelson, p | 1 | 0 | 1 |
| Totals | 61 | 4 | 15 |

```
San Diego   0 0 0 0 0 0 1 0 0 0 0 0 1 0 0 1 0—3
Pittsburgh  0 0 0 0 0 0 0 1 0 0 0 0 1 0 0 1 1—4
```

Error—Barton. Runs batted in—Murrell, Clemente, Stargell, Hebner, Alley. Two-base hit—Alley. Home runs—Murrell, Stargell, Hebner, Clemente. Stolen bases—Alley, Davalillo. Sacrifice fly—Alley. Bases on balls—Roberts 1, Severinsen 2, Blass 2. Double plays—San Diego 1, Pittsburgh 1. Left on base—San Diego 8, Pittsburgh 13. Struck out—Roberts 9, Miller 1, Severinson 2, Coombs 3, Blass 7, Giusti 4, Grant 3. Hits off—Roberts, 7 in 9; Miller, 2 in 3; Severinsen, 3 in 3; Coombs, 3 in 1 1/3; Blass, 4 in 8; Giusti, 1 in 4; Grant, 2 in 2; Veale, 2 in 1 1/3; Nelson, 1 in 1 2/3. Hit by pitch—by Roberts (Sanguillen). Wild pitch—Nelson. Passed ball—Sanguillen. Winner—Nelson. Loser—Coombs. Umpires—Sudol, Williams, Colosi, and Stello. Time—4:12. Attendance—17,405.

As every pickup softball player knows, baseball is a game of last licks—no stalls, no freezes, no running out the clock. Get the other guy out in his inning, or you can't win. Lest the baseball public forget that most basic baseball truth, the Pirates and Padres took it on themselves to demonstrate it. Before their 17-inning marathon had ended, the Padres had three times sent the hometown Pirates to what should have been their last licks, and three times the Pirates had wriggled out of it. And then, as if to brandish baseball's copyright on sudden death, the game ended with a crashing home run.

It began innocently, as these struggles usually do. Through eight innings, San Diego southpaw Dave Roberts muffled the Pirates' powerful bats. Three times the Pirates put runners in scoring position for the heart of their batting order, but each time Roberts escaped without damage. A strong pitching performance by Steve Blass appeared wasted as the Pirates came to bat in the last of the ninth inning trailing 1–0.

A walk, a single, a sacrifice fly, and suddenly the game was tied. The Pittsburgh crowd, which had sat in moody silence for eight innings, now suddenly came to life. Two innings later, it sensed victory when with two out and the winning run in scoring position, Richie Hebner worked Padres reliever Al Severinsen for a full count. Not yet ready to submit, Padres manager Preston Gomez motioned to his pitcher to issue an intentional fourth ball. Severinsen nodded his assent, then threw a fastball over the heart of the plate. A bewildered Hebner swung belatedly and missed, ending the threat.

In the thirteenth the Padres teetered on the brink of victory for the second time only to skittishly back away. Pinch hitter Ivan Murrell connected with one of Mudcat Grant's fastballs and lined it over the left field wall for a 2–1 San Diego lead. Then Severinsen disposed of the first two Pirates in the bottom of the inning. But Willie Stargell, who had struck out four times already and who later observed, "I was beginning to think I might catch up with my record [of seven]," brought the defeatists back from the exits with a towering home run into the left field seats.

Chastened, the Padres waited two more innings before their next flirtation with victory. Singles by Don Mason and pinch hitter Tommy Dean off veteran left-hander Bob Veale, Pittsburgh's fourth pitcher, put Padres on first and third with one out. Pirates manager Danny Murtaugh sought relief in Jim Nelson, but the rookie right-hander promptly uncorked a wild pitch, permitting Mason to cross the plate with the lead run.

The Pirates didn't take long to brusquely answer this tentative claim. Richie Hebner atoned for his strikeout in the eleventh by furiously assaulting a curve ball from southpaw Danny Coombs, the Padres fourth pitcher. Hebner drove the ball over the fence, tying the score again.

It fell to Roberto Clemente to conclude the wearying affair. The brilliant outfielder had been frustrated in seven previous trips to the plate, but in the bottom of the seventeenth, he took pity

*Pittsburgh's Manny Sanguillen (35) and Roberto Clemente (21) congratulate Richie Hebner after his game-saving home run.*

on the groggy fans and writers, lagging in their determination to see the end of the contest. Again Coombs was the victim. Roberto leaned on another hanging curve and lambasted it into the left field seats. Stifling their yawns of weariness, 17,405 Pittsburgh partisans left satisfied and lulled themselves to sleep by contemplating the infinite baseball game.

# Amos Otis: It Takes a Thief

The ability fo steal bases is a valuable asset in a player's arsenal. The threat of a stolen base can disrupt the strategy of both the pitcher and the catcher. The pitcher may concentrate more on the runner than on the batter, and the catcher may be more inclined to call for fastballs so that he can get the ball away faster in the event the runner decides to steal. It all gives the batter a decided edge.

Ty Cobb, of course, was a master at upsetting the opposing battery whenever he got on base, which was quite often. In recent years, the best base stealer was Maury Wills, whose running was an essential part of the Dodgers' drives to the pennant in 1962, 1963, 1965, and 1966.

The best in this returning art today are Lou Brock of the St. Louis Cardinals and Bert Campaneris of the Oakland A's. Other fine base stealers include Joe Morgan and Bobby Tolan of the Cincinnati Reds, Willie Davis of the Los Angeles Dodgers, Bobby Bonds of the San Francisco Giants, Freddy Patek of the Kansas City Royals, Tommy Harper of the Boston Red Sox, and Cesar Cedeño of the Houston Astros. Before the 1973 season, Brock led the National League in six of seven years. Campaneris paced the American League in six of eight. Both have exceptionally high stolen base percentages, but neither owns the highest percentage of players in the last 40 years

Kansas City's Amos Otis, always a threat to
steal, dives back toward first as Detroit's
Norm Cash prepares to take the throw.

who have stolen 100 or more bases. (Stolen base percentages, steals divided by attempts, weren't recorded before 1930.) That honor belongs to Bonds, followed closely by Amos Otis of the Royals.

Otis gave no evidence of his base stealing ability during his apprenticeship with the New York Mets, but once he got the chance to play regularly, with the Kansas City team, there was almost no stopping him. In 1970, his first season with the Royals, the young outfielder failed only twice in 35 attempts. Not since Max Carey stole 51 bases in 53 tries for the Pirates in 1922 has a base stealer been as successful. In 1971, Otis stole 52 bases in 60 attempts, leading the American League in the number of steals as well as in percentage. That same year, Otis's

teammate, Freddy Patek, stole 49 bases. (In 1972, the Reds' Joe Morgan, 58, and Bobby Tolan, 42, stole 100 bases between them, one less than the Otis-Patek total.)

Otis's greatest day on the base paths was September 7, 1971, against the Milwaukee Brewers in Kansas City. The fleet-footed center fielder excelled at the plate too, hitting safely in all four appearances. He singled off Marty Pattin in the first, third, and fifth innings and stole second each time. Darrell Porter was catching for the Brewers. Otis capped his performance by scoring the winning run in the seventh. With Ken Sanders on the mound, he beat out an infield hit, stole second and third, and came home on an overthrow by Porter. The final score was Kansas City 4, Milwaukee 3.

Otis's five stolen bases in one game fell one short of the major league record, set by Eddie Collins of the Philadelphia Athletics in 1912. Nonetheless, Amos was the first to steal five since Johnny Neun did it for Detroit in 1927. Dan McGann of the 1904 New York Giants and Clyde Milan of the 1912 Washington Senators are the only others since the turn of the century to steal five bases in a game.

The least impressed by Otis's base stealing exploits is Otis himself. "I never wanted to be known as a base stealer," he says. "I want to be known as an all-around player."

September 29, 1971

# Ron Hunt: HBP

There is not a manager in the National League, with the possible exception of Ron Hunt's, who believes that Ron makes an earnest effort to avoid being hit by pitched balls. On the contrary they are convinced that Hunt has perfected the art of being nicked not only by close pitches but even by pitches that would have been strikes had they reached the catcher. For more than a decade, the battle-scarred infielder has been making a living in the major leagues by leaning away from, yet somehow into, pitched balls.

Hunt, of course, denies that he deliberately gets hit. "I have always stood straight up at the plate, leaning into the pitch," he maintains. "When the pitch tails in, it's too late for me to get out of the way. I can't afford to change my hitting style just to avoid being hit. If I start bailing out, I just don't hit. If the ball is coming in, I roll around, but I don't fall back."

His explanation has not satisfied National League managers. Leo Durocher, who doesn't need much provocation to develop dilated blood vessels, almost burst one when umpire Augie Donatelli awarded Hunt first base after a pitch by Milt Pappas of the Cubs nicked him on the left shoulder. "He didn't even try to get out of the way," shouted Leo. "He actually leaned into the ball. That Hunt is making a mockery of the rule. He's a G-- d--- faker."

Two weeks later, on August 7, 1971,

Below: *"Everything worthwhile in life demands a price."* Opposite: *Ron Hunt, as a member of the San Francisco Giants, suffers a concussion after being hit by Tom Seaver.*

Sparky Anderson had similar cause for distress. The Reds' Jim McGlothlin had just plunked Hunt, Ron's thirty-second HBP of the season (bettering the National League record set by Steve Evans of the St. Louis Cardinals in 1910). "He leaned into the pitch!" complained the Reds' manager, but no one listened.

Hunt's peculiar batting style has enabled him to set an all-time career record for being hit the most by pitched balls. At the end of the 1972 season, his body had absorbed 219 pitches. He passed Minnie Minoso's old mark of 192 on July 23, 1972.

Hunt admits it hurts to get hit, but he has disciplined his mind not to think about pain. "Everything worthwhile in life demands a price," he says. "Some people give their bodies to science; I give mine to baseball." Then he speaks seriously. "Actually, a player who lacks certain skills should try to find some way to compensate for his shortcomings. With me it's HBPs."

Hunt's most satisfyingly painful year was 1971. Entering the final three games, Ron had been hit by 48 pitches, just shy of the major league single-season record of 49, established by Hughie Jennings of the old Baltimore Orioles in 1896. Hunt collected number 49 the first day when Bill Bonham of the Cubs got him Twenty-four hours later, on September 29, in a night game at Jarry Park, Hunt was hit for the

fiftieth time in one season, eclipsing the record that had stood for 75 years. The pitcher was Milt Pappas.

The Chicago right-hander, who had also contributed number 27 in the Hunt collection, cried foul. "Hey, Ken," he shouted to plate umpire Ken Burkhart, "he didn't even try to get out of the way. That pitch was right over the plate. He got hit by a strike."

"Quit beefing," Hunt answered with a grin. "I got you into the record books, didn't I?"

That was the sixth inning. In the ninth, with the record assured, Hunt decided to hit the ball instead of letting it hit him. He singled in the winning run in the Expos' 6–5 victory.

May 14–21, 1972

# Willie Mays:
# The Triumphant Return

They disbelieved when they first heard that Willie Mays was coming home after 14 long years in the camp of the enemy. They wanted to believe it. But how could it be? For years they had hoped for this miracle, that Willie Mays would come back to finish his glorious career in New York, where he began it so long ago. Now at long last their dream had come true.

Willie Mays had indeed returned to the town that made him famous, and returned with a flourish. In his very first game, on Sunday, May 14, the kid out of the past hit his first home run— first for the New York Mets, that is— and it won the ball game. That's what Willie Mays is all about.

In 1951, Mays, only 19 years old, slammed his first hit as a major leaguer in his first game at the Polo Grounds. Naturally, it was a home run, off Warren Spahn. Of course, it won the game. Twenty-one years later, almost to the day, the Say Hey Kid had done it again.

The return of Willie Mays to New York was greeted with near sellout crowds. There were those, however, who questioned whether the Mets were wise to trade for Mays, age 41, obviously slowed down and beset by aches and pains. But in the eyes of Mrs. Joan Payson, the owner of the Mets, the acquisition of Mays was the realization of a decade-old dream. Thousands of fans shared her sentiments.

Willie Mays' career of 23 glorious seasons began and ended in New York.

*Willie Mays beats his old team with a homer in his first game as a New York Met.*

Willie Mays, of course, was not the Willie Mays of 1951, but he could still exhibit flashes of brilliance that made him one of the most electrifying players in the history of the game. And he wasted no time proving it.

Willie joined the Mets on Thursday, May 11. Friday he donned the orange-and-blue-trimmed doubleknits and sat on the bench as the Mets eked out a 2–1 decision over the Giants. Many in the crowd of 44,271 at Shea Stadium called for Willie instead of John Milner to pinch hit in the ninth inning. Again on Saturday, Mays sat in the dugout while his new mates set back the Giants, 1–0 this time.

But on Sunday, May 14, Mays did break into the lineup at first base, and he broke in in style. He walked to open the game and later scored on Rusty Staub's grand slam home run. Then, with the score tied at 4–4 in the last of the fifth inning, Mays laid into a Don Carrithers slider and parked it into the visiting team's bullpen. It was home run number 647, his first homer as a Met and a game-winning one at that.

Thursday, May 18. Idle since his starring role Sunday, Mays went to center field for the first time as a Met, replacing Tommie Agee. This time it was his legs and savvy that won the game. Mays walked in the first inning and raced around the bases on a long drive by Ted Martinez. He slowed up rounding third to coordinate his and the ball's arrival at the plate, then jarred the ball loose from catcher John Boccabella's bare hand. As the ball rolled into the Montreal dugout, Martinez trotted in from third with the run that gave the Mets a 2–1 victory.

Saturday, May 20. The Mets defeated the Phillies 3–1. Mays drove in the first run with a double into the left field corner.

Sunday, May 21. The Mets won their eleventh straight, equalling the longest string in Mets history. With the Phillies leading 3–0, Mays led off the sixth with a double off Steve Carlton and rode home on Agee's home run. In the eighth, after Jim Beauchamp pinch hit a single, Mays lined the first pitch for his second home run as a Met and the six hundred forty-eighth of his career. Mays had won his third game of the week for the Mets.

The incomparable outfielder had left no doubt in anyone's mind that at 41, in his twenty-first season in the big leagues, he was still quite a ballplayer.

August 1, 1972

# Nate Colbert: Five Home Runs

"Sooner or later Nate Colbert will hit fifty home runs in a season. And if he were playing in Atlanta, where the ball carries to all fields, he'd have a helluva shot at the home run record." The speaker was Sparky Anderson in 1959, when Sparky was coaching at San Diego and Colbert was breaking in as a rookie first baseman with the Padres.

Colbert has yet to fulfill Anderson's prophecy, but don't bet that he won't. Nate is still young. He's already hit 38 homers in a season, not once but twice. In his first four major league seasons, Colbert hammered 127 home runs, a better pace than those of such recognized sluggers as Henry Aaron, Willie McCovey, Richie Allen, and Willie Stargell.

On August 1, 1972, Colbert reminded onlookers of Anderson's three-year-old prediction. In a doubleheader at Atlanta Stadium, the huge first baseman made his mark in the baseball record book by smashing five home runs and driving in thirteen runs. In the first game, he hit two home runs and two singles and drove in five runs. In the second he clouted three more home runs, one a grand slammer, and knocked in eight runs. Each of the five home runs came off a different pitcher. The Padres swept the doubleheader 9–0 and 11–7.

Colbert's 13 runs batted in erased the major league mark of 11, shared by three American Leaguers—Cleveland's

Earl Averill in 1930, Boston's Jim Tabor in 1939, and Baltimore's Boog Powell in 1966. He cracked the National League mark of 10 set by St. Louis's Enos Slaughter in 1947.

Colbert's five home runs in a doubleheader tied the major league record set by Stan Musial of the Cardinals in 1954. His 22 total bases broke Musial's mark of 21 in a twin bill. Stan set the record on May 2, 1954, the day he hit five homers.

"Stan Musial has been my hero since I was a kid in St. Louis," says Colbert. "You know, I was in Busch Stadium the day Musial got those five home runs. I don't remember the exact day, but I know it was a Sunday, and I remember marveling at the hitting exhibition."

Colbert was listed as a doubtful starter on August 1, 1972. He had injured his knee in a collision at home plate the previous week and was forced to miss a couple of games. On the flight from Houston to Atlanta, manager Don Zimmer asked him if he wanted to give his ailing knee more rest by sitting out the twin bill against the Braves. "I said it didn't matter how I felt because I wanted to play in the Braves' park," Colbert says. "Any well hit fly ball in Atlanta has a chance of going out."

Colbert had hit four home runs when the Padres came to bat in the ninth inning of the final game. The right-hander Cecil Upshaw quickly retired the first two batters, and it appeared Colbert wouldn't get a shot at Musial's record. But Larry Stahl punched a seeing-eye single past second baseman Larvell Blanks, and Colbert stepped to the plate to face the sidearmer "who always gave me trouble." Colbert smacked Upshaw's first pitch, a high, inside fastball, over the left field fence, drawing a standing ovation from a few thousand Braves' fans who had stayed to the end.

"I was shocked when I hit it," recalls Colbert. "I wasn't thinking home run when I went up against Upshaw. I don't like to bat against him. I was just thinking about a base hit. But he threw me a high fastball, and I hit it. I couldn't believe it when I saw it go over the fence. It was unreal.

"When I approached second base, the umpire [Bruce Froemming] said to me, 'I don't believe this.' I told him, 'I don't either.' "

September 30, 1972

# Roberto Clemente: The Last Hit

### New York

| | AB | R | H |
|---|---|---|---|
| Garrett, 3b | 4 | 0 | 0 |
| Boswell, 2b | 4 | 0 | 1 |
| Milner, lf | 3 | 0 | 0 |
| Staub, rf | 3 | 0 | 0 |
| Rauch, p | 0 | 0 | 0 |
| Marshall, ph | 1 | 0 | 0 |
| Kranepool, 1b | 3 | 0 | 1 |
| Fregosi, ss | 3 | 0 | 0 |
| Schneck, cf | 3 | 0 | 0 |
| Dyer, c | 2 | 0 | 0 |
| Nolan, c | 1 | 0 | 0 |
| Matlack, p | 2 | 0 | 0 |
| Hahn, ph-rf | 0 | 0 | 0 |
| Total | 29 | 0 | 2 |

### Pittsburgh

| | AB | R | H |
|---|---|---|---|
| Goggin, 2b | 4 | 0 | 2 |
| Stennett, cf | 4 | 0 | 0 |
| Clemente, rf | 2 | 1 | 1 |
| Mazeroski, ph | 1 | 0 | 0 |
| Davalillo, rf | 1 | 0 | 0 |
| Stargell, 1b | 3 | 1 | 1 |
| Zisk, lf | 1 | 2 | 0 |
| Sanguillen, c | 3 | 1 | 1 |
| Pagan, 3b | 3 | 0 | 0 |
| Hernandez, ss | 3 | 0 | 1 |
| Ellis, p | 2 | 0 | 0 |
| Clines, ph | 1 | 0 | 0 |
| Johnson, p | 0 | 0 | 0 |
| Total | 28 | 5 | 6 |

| | | |
|---|---|---|
| **New York** | 0 0 0 0 0 0 0 0 0—0 | |
| **Pittsburgh** | 0 0 3 0 2 0 0 x—5 | |

Error—Garrett. Runs batted in—Sanguillen, Hernandez 2. Two-base hit—Clemente. Three-base hit—Hernandez. Left on base—New York 5, Pittsburgh 4. Bases on balls—Matlack 5, Ellis 2. Struck out—Matlack 5, Rauch 1, Ellis 5, Johnson 1. Hits off—Matlack, 5 in 6; Rauch, 1 in 2; Ellis, 1 in 6; Johnson, 1 in 3. Passed balls—Dyer, Nolan. Winner—Ellis. Loser—Matlack. Umpires—Crawford, Harvey, Kibler, and Pulli. Time—2:10. Attendance—13,117.

Fate, which frustrated Roberto Clemente for so long and was so cruel at the end, was kind to him in one way. Clemente's final hit of the 1972 season and of his life was the three thousandth of his career. With that he joined his old rivals, Henry Aaron and Willie Mays, as the only active major leaguers at that exalted level. Soon after, he was dead.

Roberto had already surpassed the legendary Honus Wagner as the Pittsburgh club record holder in games played, at bats, hits and total bases, and he had broken Pie Traynor's club RBI mark. Now there was this most coveted of all milestones; one more base hit was all he needed.

On September 29, the Pirates played host to the New York Mets at Three Rivers Stadium. Some 24,000 fans cheered robustly as Roberto Clemente strode to the plate to bat against Tom Seaver. Most of them were there to see Roberto hit number 3,000. It was a happening. After all, only 10 other men had made 3,000 big league hits.

Clemente seemed to rise four inches off the ground when he hit the ball. He swung very hard but hit the ball softly. It took a high bounce over the pitcher's leap, took three or four smaller bounces toward second, and skipped off the glove of Ken Boswell.

The crowd looked impatiently to the scoreboard. Nothing. The people were puzzled. The press box was in angry

*"I give this hit [number 3,000] to the fans of Pittsburgh and to the people of Puerto Rico."*

confusion. The official scorer had made
his decision immediately—"Error, second baseman. Error Boswell"—but the
message was not getting through to
the level above, where a crew operated
the electronic scoreboard in center
field. Suddenly, hesitantly, inexplicably,
just once, the "H" blinked. The crowd
went wild. Streamers of toilet tissue
floated into the outfield. The umpire
flipped the ball to first baseman Ed
Kranepool, who flipped it to Roberto
Clemente, who flipped it to first base
coach Don Leppert, who gave Roberto
a congratulatory pat on the backside.

Meanwhile in the press box, somebody was clicking the phone frantically,
trying to reach the scoreboard crew.
The official scorer was yelling, "What
the heck's the matter?"

The call finally got through, and the
"E" flashed on the big board. The
crowd booed, its celebration aborted,
then settled back to await the historic
hit in Roberto's next at-bats. It didn't
come. Tom Seaver handled him surprisingly well. Only in the ninth did he
hit the ball solidly. "I'm glad they didn't
call it a hit," Clemente said afterward.
"I want to get it without any taint."

Clemente was not to be denied the
next night, however. He went out the
first time, but in the fourth inning, he
boomed a double, one hop off the wall
in left center. The number 3,000 lit up
the entire scoreboard. Umpire Doug
Harvey handed the souvenir ball to

Roberto who shook his hand. The
crowd stood and cheered. Clemente,
one foot on second base, raised his
batting helmet in reciprocal appreciation. Jon Matlack, the pitcher, held the
ball for a full minute, keeping Willie
Stargell in the batting box, allowing
Clemente to soak up the full measure
of his fame.

It was better this way, no doubt. That
hit belonged in the company of Ty

Cobb, Tris Speaker, Honus Wagner, Eddie Collins, Napoleon Lajoie, Paul Waner, Stan Musial, Adrian Anson, Henry Aaron, and Willie Mays, the exclusive 3,000-hit club.

Extremely self-conscious and embarrassed by public demonstrations, Clemente was nevertheless deeply touched by the reaction of the crowd. "I give this hit to the fans of Pittsburgh and to the people of Puerto Rico," he said.

Three months later, this very special, very private, very proud person was dead. An airplane carrying him on a mercy mission to help people left homeless by a Nicaraguan earthquake, crashed and snuffed out his life at 38. Baseball won't be the same without him. He gave much to the game, and he gave his life for his fellow man. He will long be remembered by all who knew him.

October 20, 1972

# The Magnificent Deception: Johnny Bench Strikes Out

"The great American game of baseball is a fraud, a treachery and un-American. It offers a regrettable example to the nation's youth, is populated by cheats, thrives on sneaky tricks, and teaches Fagin values to thousands of Little Leaguers. It is corruptive and should be repressed. And as sometimes played by major leaguers, it is . . . fascinating.

"In the third World Series game, there was a rip-off to delight all admirers of the Brinks heist and the Great London Train Robbery. With exquisite execution, the thoroughly unprincipled Oakland A's pulled it against Johnny Bench, the National League's home run king and Most Valuable Player, who mistakenly assumed he was competing against men of honor."

That is how *Washington Post* columnist Shirley Povich described the magnificent deception of October 20, 1972.

In the top of the eighth inning, the Cincinnati Reds were threatening to add to their skimpy 1–0 lead at the expense of Vida Blue, who had replaced John ("Blue Moon") Odom. With one out Blue walked Joe Morgan, who raced to third on Bobby Tolan's single up the middle. In came Rollie Fingers, the A's relief specialist. Tolan easily stole second as Fingers worked carefully to Johnny Bench. The count went to three and two.

Enter Dick Williams, stage left. The A's manager called time, walked to the

*"Bench stood there transfixed. . . . .*
*'I guess that made me look like the goat.' "*
*But Cincinnati won the game 1–0.*

mound, and belabored the obvious: With first base open, the A's would not risk a good pitch to the Red's dangerous clean-up hitter. Catcher Gene Tenace and third baseman Sal Bando joined the discussion. Then, with the subtlety of a mustachioed villain in a silent movie, manager Williams twice pointed to first base, apparently instructing Fingers to walk Bench on the next pitch.

Impresario Williams could not resist an additional flourish. He pointed to the next hitter, Tony Perez, in the on deck circle. The charade anesthetized Bench, but the A's had not yet finished introducing the small town Oklahoman to big city theater. Catcher Tenace trudged dutifully back to home plate, waited for Bench to step back into the batter's box, and not only held his mitt at arm's length in anticipation of the fourth ball, but also began the ritual of moving a step toward first, as catchers always do when a deliberate pass is coming.

Too late, Bench's teammates discovered the ruse. As Fingers delivered the ball, Joe Morgan yelled to Bench from third, "Be ready, John! They're gonna pitch to you."

Alex Grammas, the Reds' third base coach, had seen the play in the minors, as had Morgan. "I started to holler, but all I got out was 'uh,' " Grammas says, "and by that time, the ball was on the way."

The denouement was crushing and swift. Tenace quietly eased into his regular catching position, and Fingers, without much windup, delivered a splendid slider that clipped the strike zone about knee high. Bench stood there transfixed, his bat on his shoulder. "I guess that made me look like the goat," he said sheepishly.

It could have been worse. Though the Reds' failed to score in the inning, they held the A's and won 1–0. Still, Fingers relished his dramatic debut. "I tried to be relaxed," he explained later. "I just came up real nonchalant and let the ball go. . . . I couldn't have thrown it better if I had taken fifteen minutes."

227

September 27, 1973

# Nolan Ryan: 383 Strikeouts

Above and opposite: *Nolan Ryan grimly fires away in his quest for the strikeout record.*

In New York, where Nolan Ryan toiled for four years with the Mets, a movie-going fan dubbed Nolan's fastball "Ryan's Express," after a train in a movie of a similar name. But like the train in the movie, not to mention the trains of the fun city where he pitched, Ryan's Express fell victim to inconsistency and even breakdowns. Disillusioned by two also-ran years after the miraculous championship in 1969, and impatient with child pitching prodigies who didn't produce, the Mets' management peddled Ryan to the California Angels. In exchange, the Mets received Jim Fregosi, a proven major leaguer who, it was believed, would solve the New Yorkers' hitting and fielding woes at third base. Ryan for Fregosi: it was supposed to be a trade of promise for performance.

Records aren't made to be broken and trades aren't made to be swindles. It just often works out that way. In 1972, while Fregosi flopped and irate Met fans bestowed on the management the wrath they usually reserve for the mayor, Ryan achieved in his first year at Anaheim the success his blazing fastballs had long heralded.

In one season Ryan set or tied 14 club records, won 19 games, and led the major leagues with 329 strikeouts. Once he struck out 17 in a game. Twice he fanned 16. In a game against

the Red Sox, Ryan not only struck out 8 in a row, setting an American League record, but also struck out the side on nine pitches. For the season he limited the opposition to a .168 batting average, second only in stinginess to Luis Tiant, who held the hitters he faced to a .167 average. Finally, Ryan set the record for the lowest average of hits allowed per nine innings—5.26.

With the 1973 season barely a month old Ryan and his popping fastball announced that '72 had been no accident. On May 15, he beat the Kansas City Royals with a no-hitter so overpowering that for the most part, his defense could have taken the night off. Said the Royals' John Mayberry of Ryan, "He was throwing the ball harder than any man I ever saw. . . ."

Exactly two months later, the 26-year-old, 5-year veteran did it again, this time against the Tigers in Detroit's Tiger Stadium. The 62-year-old arena, renowned as a hitters' ball park, hadn't witnessed a no-hitter for 21 years, until Kansas City's Steve Busby stifled the home team early in '73.

Before an awe-struck audience of 41,411 that must have longed for the sound of bat meeting ball, Ryan threw third strikes past 12 of the first 14 Tigers he faced. One of the victims, Norm Cash, trudged to the plate in the fifth inning with a paddle, as much in desperation as in jest. Undaunted when plate umpire Ron Luciano threw the

paddle out of the game, the Tigers' inventive slugger returned to the plate in the ninth carrying a piano leg wrapped in tape—a "beggar's bat."

A reasonable man, Cash had apparently realized the futility of using a conventional batting style against Ryan.

After seven innings, Ryan had recorded 16 strikeouts, including 5 in a row at one point. He had struck out the side in the second, fourth, and seventh, and had not only a second no-hitter in his sights but the major league strikeout record as well. After fanning Ed Brinkman in the eighth for his seventeenth strikeout of the game, Ryan needed only two more to tie the mark.

His teammates unwittingly did him in. Jittery with only a 1–0 lead, they obtusely concluded that Ryan needed insurance runs. In their half of the eighth, they scored five, turned the game into a 6–0 rout, and kept Ryan on the bench for 20 minutes. There his arm stiffened, and in the ninth, although he completed the no-hitter, he notched no more strikeouts.

Even without the strikeout record, Ryan found himself in select company after his second no-hitter. He had become one of only six pitchers to have two no-hitters in a season.

Clearly he was not satisfied. Four days later, while bidding to match Johnny Vandermeer's feat of two successive no-hitter's, Ryan sought to become the first pitcher in baseball history to record three no-hitters in a season. But for Mark Belanger's bloop single leading off the eighth, the Texan fireballer held the Baltimore Orioles hitless through nine innings, before losing in the tenth 3–1.

"I was lucky to hit it," confessed Belanger afterward. "He had unbelievable stuff. The pitch was up and in; he jammed the hell out of me. . . . I just managed to push it over the infield."

Thwarted in his quest for three no-hitters and a single-game strikeout record, Ryan contented himself for the rest of the season with rolling up enough strikeouts to move within range of Sandy Koufax's major league record of 382 for a season. The record-breaker came not only in Ryan's final appearance of the year but on his final pitch as well.

The Twins and Angels had finished nine innings on September 27 tied 4–4. Ryan had struck out 15 batters in eight innings, tying Koufax's record, but Ryan began the tenth less than confident he could notch the record-breaker. In the ninth a severe leg cramp had badly hampered him. Even with between-innings massages from the trainer, Ryan found himself unable to deliver his fastball at top speed. And for a moment at least, it appeared that his teammates had not lost their penchant for sabotaging his strikeout quests. Facing Rich Reese with two outs in the eleventh and Rod Carew on first, Ryan delivered two strikes, on the second of which Carew took off for second. Catcher Jeff Torborg was hardly eager to end the inning by throwing out Carew, yet instinctively, he pegged to second anyway. "I was hoping he would be safe," Torberg confessed later. "I was just hoping to make a good throw." He covered himself admirably. The throw was accurate, but Carew just beat it.

Unwilling to give Torborg and Carew a chance for more mischief, Ryan hummed the next pitch past Reese for the final out of the inning and the record three hundred eighty-third strikeout of the year. Then the Angels considerately pushed across a run in the bottom of the eleventh, and Ryan had his twenty-first victory of the year as well as the strikeout mark.

As the baseball world showered praise on the young Texan, at least one of his fans remained not fully satisfied with Ryan's feats and the tributes they evoked. From Alvan, Texas, came the perfectionist's critique. "I think it's wonderful what Nolan has accomplished," said his mother, "but the thing I'm waiting for is a perfect game."

April 8, 1974

# Hank Aaron: Touches the Untouchable

Atlanta

|  |  | AB | R | H |
|---|---|---|---|---|
| Garr, | rf-lf | 3 | 0 | 0 |
| Lum, | 1b | 5 | 0 | 0 |
| Evans, | 3b | 4 | 1 | 0 |
| Aaron, | lf | 3 | 2 | 1 |
| Office, | cf | 0 | 0 | 0 |
| Baker, | cf-rf | 2 | 1 | 1 |
| Johnson, | 2b | 3 | 1 | 1 |
| Foster, | 2b | 0 | 0 | 0 |
| Correll, | c | 4 | 1 | 0 |
| Robinson, | ss | 0 | 0 | 0 |
| Tepedino, | ph | 0 | 0 | 0 |
| Perez, | ss | 2 | 1 | 1 |
| Reed, | p | 2 | 0 | 0 |
| Oates, | ph | 1 | 0 | 0 |
| Capra, | p | 0 | 0 | 0 |
| | Total | 29 | 7 | 4 |

Los Angeles

|  |  | AB | R | H |
|---|---|---|---|---|
| Lopes, | 2b | 2 | 1 | 0 |
| Lacy, | ph-2b | 1 | 0 | 0 |
| Buckner, | lf | 3 | 0 | 1 |
| Wynn, | cf | 4 | 0 | 1 |
| Ferguson, | c | 4 | 0 | 0 |
| Crawford, | rf | 4 | 1 | 1 |
| Cey, | 3b | 4 | 0 | 1 |
| Garvey, | 1b | 4 | 1 | 1 |
| Russell, | ss | 4 | 0 | 1 |
| Downing, | p | 1 | 1 | 1 |
| Marshall, | p | 1 | 0 | 0 |
| Joshua, | ph | 1 | 0 | 0 |
| Hough, | p | 0 | 0 | 0 |
| Mota, | ph | 1 | 0 | 0 |
| | Total | 34 | 4 | 7 |

Los Angeles
0 0 3 0 0 1 0 0 0—4
Atlanta
0 1 0 4 0 2 0 0 x—7

Errors—Buckner, Cey, Russell 2, Lopes, Ferguson. Left on base—Los Angeles 5, Atlanta 7. Stolen bases—Baker, Russell, Wynn. Home runs—Aaron 2. Sacrifice hit—Garr. Sacrifice fly—Garr. Bases on balls—Downing 4, Marshall 1, Hough 2, Reed 1, Capra 1. Struck out—Downing 2, Marshall 1, Hough 1, Reed 4, Capra 6. Hits off—Downing, 2 in 3 (pitched to four batters in fourth); Marshall, 2 in 3; Hough, 0 in 2; Reed, 7 in 6; Capra, 0 in 3. Wild pitch—Reed. Passed ball—Ferguson. Winner—Reed. Loser—Downing. Time—2:27. Attendance—53,775.

For some 40 years, the record of records was Babe Ruth's lifetime home run total of 714. Who could ever approach that mark? Sportswriters called it the most untouchable of records. They also doubted that anyone could equal Joe DiMaggio's 56-game hitting streak. And no one has. They said the odds against anyone amassing 4,191 hits as Ty Cobb has were out of sight. Up to now, they have been right. (Pete Rose may possibly disprove that.)

But Ruth's record? That one was absolutely beyond reach for a number of reasons. To begin with, to even approach Ruth's record, a man would have to average 35 homers a year for 20 years. How many players last 20 years in the major leagues, let alone hit 35 home runs in each of those years? The sportswriters were correct. It was impossible! It could never happen!

But it did happen. For more than 15 years, Hank Aaron had been lacing singles, doubles, triples, home runs, driving in runs, winning batting championships, and making the All-Star team year after year, but few regarded him as a challenger to Ruth. No one denied he was a superstar. But to put him in the same category as the Babe? Why, he had never even hit 50 home runs in a season, let alone 60.

For most of his career, Aaron languished in the shadows of other baseball greats. He lacked the flair of Willie Mays and the off-field outspokenness of Roberto Clemente. He didn't have the muscles of Mickey Mantle or the uniquely distinctive batting stance of Stan Musial. Nevertheless, he was one of the most

A jubilant Hank Aaron is hugged by his mother, as he clutches the ball that went over the fence for his record-breaking 715th home run off Los Angeles Dodgers' pitcher Al Downing.

remarkable athletes of the twentieth century.

Only when Aaron reached the plateaus of 500 career homers and 3,000 base hits, late in the 1960s, did the writers begin to notice him. They recognized him for what he was—a truly superlative all around performer, perhaps the best hitter of his day. But Ruth's record, the untouchable one, was still a couple of hundred homers away. And at 35, how many more seasons could he play?

The next five years provided the answer. Observe these numbers and marvel. 44...38...47...34...40. Long before Aaron had gotten close to Ruth's mark he had made believers out of skeptics. They had long ago begun to use the word "when" as opposed to "whether" when writing about Hank's chances of overtaking Ruth.

Henry Aaron finished the 1972 season with 34 home runs, placing him within striking distance of the Babe. The next year a 39-year-old Aaron hit 40 home runs, putting him exactly within one swing of the bat away from Ruth and one swing was all it took. The very first time the bat left Aaron's shoulder in the 1974 season he reached the 714 mark. After watching four pitches go by, Hank homered off the Red's Jack Billingham on April 4, 1974, in Cincinnati. The record breaker came four days later.

The 1974 season started in controversy. The Braves, wanting to see Aaron break the record in front of the hometown fans, had decided to keep him out of the first three games, all on the road. This was ruled out by Commissioner Kuhn. Hank would be in the opening day lineup. He did sit out the second game, went hitless in the third, then returned to Atlanta for the home opener. This time he was facing lefty Al Downing of the Dodgers.

Hank came up in the second inning. He watched Downing throw five pitches, didn't swing at any, and trotted to first on a base on balls. The capacity crowd booed. Then came the fourth inning. There was a man on base. Downing's first pitch was a ball. The next pitch was over the plate. Hank swung and the ball skyrocketed toward left field. The fans exploded as it cleared the fence. Home run number 715.

Aaron, normally lacking emotion, allowed a smile to light up his face. He waved to the fans as he circled the bases. He had done it at last.

"Thank God it's over," he sighed happily.

*At an after-game news conference, Hank Aaron, with joy and relief, describes his 715th record-shattering home run.*

October 22, 1975

# The Finest World Series Game Ever Played

### Cincinnati (NL)

| | AB | R | H |
|---|---|---|---|
| Rose, 3b | 5 | 1 | 2 |
| Griffey, rf | 5 | 2 | 2 |
| Morgan, 2b | 6 | 1 | 1 |
| Bench, c | 6 | 0 | 1 |
| T. Perez, 1b | 6 | 0 | 2 |
| G. Foster, lf | 6 | 0 | 2 |
| Concepcion, ss | 6 | 0 | 1 |
| Geronimo, cf | 6 | 1 | 2 |
| Nolan, p | 0 | 0 | 0 |
| Chaney, ph | 1 | 0 | 0 |
| Norman, p | 0 | 0 | 0 |
| Billingham, p | 0 | 0 | 0 |
| Armbrister, ph | 0 | 1 | 0 |
| C. Carroll, p | 0 | 0 | 0 |
| Crowley, ph | 1 | 0 | 1 |
| Borbon, p | 1 | 0 | 0 |
| Eastwick, p | 0 | 0 | 0 |
| McEnaney, p | 0 | 0 | 0 |
| Driessen, ph | 1 | 0 | 0 |
| Darcy, p | 0 | 0 | 0 |
| Total | 50 | 6 | 14 |

### Boston (AL)

| | AB | R | H |
|---|---|---|---|
| Cooper, 1b | 5 | 0 | 0 |
| Drago, p | 0 | 0 | 0 |
| R. Miller, ph | 1 | 0 | 0 |
| Wise, p | 0 | 0 | 0 |
| Doyle, 2b | 5 | 0 | 1 |
| Yastrzemski, lf | 6 | 1 | 3 |
| Fisk, c | 4 | 2 | 2 |
| Lynn, cf | 4 | 2 | 2 |
| Petrocelli, 3b | 4 | 1 | 0 |
| Evans, rf | 5 | 0 | 1 |
| Burleson, ss | 3 | 0 | 0 |
| Tiant, p | 2 | 0 | 0 |
| Moret, p | 0 | 0 | 0 |
| Carbo, lf | 2 | 1 | 1 |
| Total | 41 | 7 | 10 |

```
Cincinnati   0 0 0 3 0 2 1 0 0 0 0—6
Boston       3 0 0 0 0 0 0 3 0 0 0 1—7
```

Errors — Burleson. Double plays — Cincinnati 1, Boston 1. Left on base — Cincinnati 11, Boston 9. Two-base hits — Doyle, Evans, G. Foster. Three-base hit — Griffey. Home runs — Lynn (1), Geronimo (2), Carbo (2), Fisk (2). Stolen base — Concepcion. Hit by pitch — Drago (Rose). Sacrifice — Tiant. Bases on balls — Norman 2, Billingham 1, Borbon 2, Eastwick 1, McEnaney 1, Tiant 2. Struck out — Nolan 2, Billingham 1, Borbon 1, Eastwick 2, Darcy 1, Tiant 5, Drago 1, Wise 1. Hits off — Nolan 3 in 2, Norman 1 in 2/3, Billingham 1 in 1 1/3, C. Carroll 1 in 1, Borbon 1 in 2, Eastwick 2 in 1 1/3, McEnaney 0 in 2/3, Darcy 1 in 2 (None out when winning run was scored), Tiant 11 in 7, Moret 0 in 1, Drago 1 in 3, Wise 2 in 1. Winner — Wise. Loser — Darcy. Time — 4:01. Attendance — 35,205.

The 1975 World Series between the Cincinnati Reds and the Boston Red Sox was an incredible advertisement for the game of baseball. The fact that Cincinnati won the Series by a single run is an indication of what the Series was like.

It is the sixth game that has been hailed as the greatest game ever played in World Series history. It lasted four hours, and when it ended at 12:34 in the morning, the 35,205 emotionally drained spectators left Fenway Park convinced that they had just witnessed one of baseball's all-time great spine tinglers.

Those fans had lived through 12 innings of pure excitement and drama with everything imaginable happening. They saw each team overcome a three-run deficit. They saw the winning run choked off at the plate in the ninth. They saw a miraculous game-saving catch in the eleventh. And, finally, in the bottom of the twelfth, they saw Carlton Fisk face Pat Darcy, Cincinnati's eighth pitcher of the game. The Red Sox catcher measured a sinker, "down and in," and blasted it toward the wall in left field. The fans peered into the New England darkness, searching for the target area.

A few steps away from the plate, Fisk stopped and did a slight jig, and with body movement and hand signals tried to keep the ball from straying into foul territory. When the ball at last caromed off the foul pole for a home run, Fisk leaped convulsively and began romping around the bases.

People poured from the stands, ignoring

attendants and security personnel so that they could display their own special appreciation to the man of the moment. When Fisk stepped jubilantly on home plate, greeted by hysterical teammates, he was ending one of baseball's most pulsating dramas, a 12-inning, 7–6 Red Sox victory.

Fisk's home run, dramatic and climactic, was just one of many show-stoppers that occurred during the game. In the first inning Fred Lynn rapped a three-run homer. The Reds tied the score 3–3 in the sixth, Ken Griffey's triple being the key blow. Cincinnati gained the lead for the first time in the seventh when, with two out, George Foster doubled to score Griffey and Joe Morgan, who had singled. Cesar Geronimo made it 6–3 in the eighth with a home run.

There were two on and two out in the bottom of the eighth when Bernie Carbo,

Carlton Fisk's twelfth-inning home run ended one of baseball's most dramatic contests — a 7–6 victory over Cincinnati.

batting for pitcher Moret, homered to center. It appeared that the Red Sox would win the game in the ninth when Denny Doyle walked and took third on Carl Yastrzemski's single. Will McEnaney, replacing Rawly Eastwick, walked Fisk intentionally and got Lynn to foul to Foster in shallow left field. Doyle tried to score and was cut down on Foster's throw to the plate.

In the eleventh, with Griffey on first, Morgan smashed a drive toward the fence in right field. It looked like a certain double or triple, maybe a home run. Dwight Evans made a spectacular leaping catch and threw to first for a double play. Singles by Tony Perez and Foster had the Red Sox fans jittery in the top of the twelfth, but Rick Wise struck out Geronimo and turned center stage over to Fisk. The Red Sox catcher looked at one pitch from Darcy and then swung his way into baseball history.

August 21, 1977

# Tom Seaver's First Game Against the Mets

**Cincinnati**

| | AB | R | H |
|---|---|---|---|
| Rose, 3b | 4 | 2 | 2 |
| Morgan, 2b | 4 | 1 | 1 |
| Griffey, rf | 4 | 0 | 1 |
| G. Foster, lf | 4 | 1 | 1 |
| Bench, c | 3 | 0 | 1 |
| Concepcion, ss | 4 | 0 | 1 |
| Driessen, 1b | 3 | 0 | 1 |
| Armbrister, lf | 2 | 0 | 0 |
| Geronimo, cf | 1 | 0 | 0 |
| Seaver, p | 4 | 2 | 1 |
| Total | 33 | 5 | 8 |

**New York Mets**

| | AB | R | H |
|---|---|---|---|
| Randle, 3b | 4 | 0 | 1 |
| Harrelson, ss | 3 | 1 | 1 |
| Stearns, ph | 1 | 0 | 0 |
| Apodaca, p | 0 | 0 | 0 |
| Henderson, lf | 4 | 0 | 2 |
| Kranepool, rf | 3 | 0 | 2 |
| Milner, 1b | 4 | 0 | 0 |
| Hodges, c | 4 | 0 | 0 |
| Mazzilli, cf | 3 | 0 | 1 |
| Flynn, ss | 2 | 0 | 0 |
| Koosman, p | 2 | 0 | 0 |
| Lockwood, p | 0 | 0 | 0 |
| Boisclair, ph | 0 | 0 | 0 |
| L. Foster, 2b | 0 | 0 | 0 |
| Total | 30 | 1 | 6 |

```
Cincinnati      1 0 0 0 1 0 0 3 0—5
New York Mets   0 0 0 0 1 0 0 0—1
```

Errors—Harrelson, Flynn. Double plays—Cincinnati 1, Mets 2. Left on base — Cincinnati 4, Mets 5. Two-base hits — Rose, Seaver, Bench. Sacrifice fly — Kranepool. Bases on balls — Seaver 2, Koosman 2, Apodaca 1. Struck out — Seaver 11, Koosman 7, Apodaca 1. Hits off—Seaver 6 in 9, Koosman 7 in 7 1/3, Lockwood 0 in 2/3, Apodaca 1 in 1. Winner—Seaver. Loser—Koosman. Time —2:21. Attendance—46,265.

It did not win the pennant, it was not a record-breaking performance, it will not go down in baseball history as one of the greatest games ever pitched. But it is doubtful that Tom Seaver will ever forget it. The game, which writers dubbed "the Shootout at Shea," marked Tom Seaver's first homecoming since that memorable night when the Mets shocked the baseball world by trading the pitcher they called "the Franchise" to the Cincinnati Reds for four unheralded players.

Sunday, August 21, started out in bright sunshine and ended under gray skies. From the moment Seaver arrived at Shea Stadium, he was surrounded by photographers, reporters, and television cameras. He answered questions routinely. He was putting on a visitor's uniform in the Mets' park for the first time in 11 years. He had won 182 games in a New York uniform and had led the Mets to two pennants and a World Championship. Now he was about to pitch his first game against his old friends.

The instant he stepped out of the dugout, the cheering started. "SEA-VER! SEA-VER!" Right behind the bench were girls wearing red T-shirts with "Tom Terrific" in white letters. Taking batting practice, his every swing brought a burst of cheering.

Next time he made an appearance there were 46,265 present in the park, the Mets' largest crowd of the season except for a "Jacket Day" promotion. There were cheers when the public address announcer reached Seaver's name in the batting or-

der, but it was nothing like the ovation when Seaver took the mound for the bottom of the first inning.

Suddenly the multitude was on its feet, yelling, whistling, clapping. The ovation was unabated through all of Seaver's warm-up pitches, approximately two minutes. "Hello Dolly," the stadium organ played: "We're glad to see you back where you belong."

If Seaver was nervous, he managed to repress his feelings. He pitched as he had for the last ten years. He retired the first 11 Mets, striking out four of the first six. Then Steve Henderson, one of the quartet obtained for Seaver, sneaked a single up the middle with two out in the fourth, and Ed Kranepool lined one over Seaver's head into center. The rally ended on the next pitch when John Milner popped foul to first.

In the meantime, the Reds had gotten to Jerry Koosman, the Mets' starter, early. Koosman had skipped a day of rest to pitch against Seaver. He had volunteered to face his pal and former teammate. Pete Rose greeted him with a double and later scored the Reds' first run in the fifth when Seaver doubled and slid across the plate with what proved to be the winning run on a single by Rose.

The Mets got their lone run in the sixth. Bud Harrelson, who had roomed with Seaver for eight years and was his closest friend, scored the run. Tom had struck him out twice, but in the sixth, Bud reached out and tapped an off-speed pitch through the middle for a base hit. Henderson followed him with a ground single, sending Harrelson to third. Kranepool, after nearly hitting a three-run homer with a long drive that was foul by several yards, scored Harrelson with a sacrifice fly.

The Reds broke the game open in the eighth. With one out, back-to-back errors by Harrelson and Doug Flynn opened the door for a three-run inning, putting the game out of reach. Seaver continued to sail along smoothly. He struck out Henderson to start the ninth, gave up a single to Kranepool, got Milner to ground out, then fired his last fastball past Ron Hodges for his eleventh strikeout.

As Seaver trudged off the mound, the crowd of almost 47,000, nearly all of them Mets' rooters, stood up and wildly cheered the pitcher who had just annihilated their favorites. But for this day, they forgot about

*Tom Seaver fires a pitch to former team-mate and opposing pitcher Jerry Koosman.*

their allegiance, and in a demonstration rarely witnessed on a playing field, showered the former Mets' pitching mainstay with their love and loyalty. The organ played "Goodnight, Sweetheart."

"I'm glad it's over, very glad," Seaver told reporters. "I'm exhausted physically and emotionally."

He had beaten the Mets, and he had walked two and struck out 11, his high for the season, and he had given up six hits. He was happy about the victory, but far from jubilant. "It was no fun out there at all," he said.

Maybe he was thinking of Jerry Koosman and the ten years they pitched together. In 1969 the Tom and Jerry show had pitched the Mets to their first and only World Championship.

There were tears in Koosman's eyes as he spoke of this poignant meeting with his friend.

"It's tough to pitch against a superstar," he said. "You know you're up against a guy who will give up one or two runs at the most. You know you've got to be at your best. I felt it would be a one-nothing or a two-to-one game. I was kind of disappointed when it got out of hand. But let's face it. Tom Seaver is the best pitcher in baseball."

# The Dodgers Accomplish the Impossible

**Los Angeles**

| | AB | R | H |
|---|---|---|---|
| Lopes, 2b | 5 | 1 | 1 |
| Russell, ss | 5 | 0 | 2 |
| Smith, rf | 5 | 0 | 0 |
| Cey, 3b | 4 | 1 | 1 |
| Garvey, 1b | 4 | 1 | 1 |
| Baker, lf | 4 | 1 | 2 |
| Monday, cf | 3 | 0 | 1 |
| Grote, c | 0 | 0 | 0 |
| Yeager, c | 2 | 0 | 1 |
| Davalillo, ph | 1 | 1 | 1 |
| Burke, cf | 0 | 0 | 0 |
| Hooton, p | 1 | 0 | 1 |
| Rhoden, p | 1 | 0 | 0 |
| Goodson, ph | 1 | 0 | 0 |
| Rau, p | 0 | 0 | 0 |
| Sosa, p | 0 | 0 | 0 |
| Rautzhan, p | 0 | 0 | 0 |
| Mota, ph | 1 | 1 | 1 |
| Garman, p | 0 | 0 | 0 |
| Total | 37 | 6 | 12 |

**Philadelphia**

| | AB | R | H |
|---|---|---|---|
| McBride, rf | 4 | 0 | 0 |
| Bowa, ss | 4 | 0 | 0 |
| Schmidt, 3b | 4 | 0 | 0 |
| Luzinski, lf | 3 | 0 | 1 |
| Martin, pr | 0 | 0 | 0 |
| Hebner, 1b | 5 | 2 | 1 |
| Maddox, cf | 4 | 1 | 1 |
| Boone, c | 4 | 1 | 2 |
| Sizemore, 2b | 3 | 1 | 1 |
| Christenson, p | 0 | 0 | 0 |
| Brusstar, p | 0 | 0 | 0 |
| Hutton, ph | 1 | 0 | 0 |
| Reed, p | 0 | 0 | 0 |
| McCarver, ph | 1 | 0 | 0 |
| Garber, p | 0 | 0 | 0 |
| Total | 33 | 5 | 6 |

| | | |
|---|---|---|
| **Los Angeles** | 0 2 0 1 0 0 0 0 3 | 6 |
| **Philadelphia** | 0 3 0 0 0 0 0 2 0 | 5 |

Errors — Schmidt, Cey, Sizemore, Garber, Smith. Double play — Philadelphia 1. Left on base — Los Angeles 6, Philadelphia 9. Two-base hits — Baker, Hooton, Cey, Russell, Mota. Sacrifice — Garber. Bases on balls — Hooton 4, Rhoden 2, Brusstar 1, Reed 1. Struck out — Hooton 1, Rau 1, Christenson 2, Reed 2. Hits off — Hooton 2 in 1 2/3, Rhoden 2 in 4 1/3, Rau 0 in 1, Sosa 2 in 2/3, Rautzhan 0 in 1/3, Garman 0 in 1, Christenson 7 in 3 1/3, Brusstar 0 in 2/3, Reed 1 in 2, Garber 4 in 3. Winner — Rautzhan. Loser — Garber. Save — Garman. Time — 2:59. Attendance — 63,719.

It wasn't a dream. It really happened. The Los Angeles Dodgers, one out away from defeat, rallied for three runs to defeat the Philadelphia Phillies 6–5 to take a two-games-to-one lead in the best-of-five National League championship series.

The unbelievable come-from-behind triumph did not give the Dodgers the championship. They still had to win another game. But it seemed clear that it was all over. It is likely that the Phillies knew it, too. They appeared listless the next day when the Dodgers officially wrapped it up. The long season struggle really ended on Friday, October 7, 1977, when, in full view of 63,719, the Dodgers slipped their heads out of the noose and all but moved into the World Series.

It had been a close game for seven innings. The Phillies snapped a 3–3 deadlock that had prevailed since the fourth inning, assaulting reliever Elias Sosa for two runs in the eighth. Rich Hebner's double, a single by Garry Maddox, and two throwing errors by the Dodgers had thrust the Phillies into the lead and lifted the second largest crowd in Veterans Stadium history from frenzy to euphoria.

Gene Garber, coming off two innings of perfect relief, took the crowd even higher. He started the ninth by retiring Dusty Baker and Rick Monday. The cheers rose to a crescendo. Seldom had one team's grip on another team's windpipe seemed more secure.

Tom Lasorda, the Dodgers eternally optimistic manager, called on the first of his two 38-year-old pinch hitting specialists, Vic Davalillo. Garber shot over two quick strikes. With the count against him, Little Vic caught the Phillies' defense flat-footed, beating out a perfect drag bunt past the mound by an eyelash.

Now, Lasorda called upon the second of his ancient emergency batters, Manny Mota, to hit for relief pitcher Lance Rautzhan. There was still no cause for alarm. It would take a home run to tie the score, and Mota, although a valuable pinch hitter, had managed to hit only one home run in the last five years of regular season play.

After a called first strike, Mota took his big swing — and missed. Now it was 0–2. The Phillies were a single tantalizing strike away from victory, a strike they never got. Mota swung at the next pitch and lined the ball hard to left. Greg Luzinski raced back and managed to deflect the ball just before it touched the fence. He trapped it, but could not catch it. It was a double, and the play wasn't over yet. Luzinski wheeled and threw to second base. The throw was on line, but it escaped second baseman Ted Sizemore for an error. Davalillo scored and Mota reached third.

Nothing would bounce right for the Phillies now. Dave Lopes smashed a vicious grounder to third. The ball bounced off the seam of the Astroturf, struck third baseman Mike Schmidt, and ricocheted to shortstop Larry Bowa, who fired to first base. Both runner and baseball appeared to arrive at the same time. Umpire Bruce Froemming called the fleet-footed Lopes safe. Mota crossed the plate with the tying

run. The Phillies, supported by their staunch fans, disagreed with Froemming, but the decision stood. The score was tied, and the worst was yet to come.

Garber attempted a pickoff, but the ball eluded first baseman Hebner and Lopes raced to second. The stage was set for Bill Russell, whose two errors had played prominently in the Phillies' victory in the first game. Russell wasted little time. He smashed a single up the middle, and the swift Lopes scored easily with the lead run. All that remained was for right-hander Mike Garman to set down the Phils in the ninth to complete one of the most dramatic finishes in league championship history. The Phillies' dreams of the first championship since 1950 were washed away the next day when they succumbed 4–1 to the Dodgers in the rain before a record crowd of 64,924. For the Dodgers it was the culmination of a remarkable comeback. After losing the opening game of the best-of-five series in their own stadium, they rallied to win three straight, the last two in Philadelphia's backyard.

Opposite: *National League play-off game number 3 proved especially painful to Phillies' second baseman Ted Sizemore.*

Left: *Dodgers' Dusty Baker slams a two-run homer off Phillies' pitcher Steve Carlton in play-off game number 4.* Above: *First-year Dodger manager Tom Lasorta bathes in champagne following his National League pennant victory over Philadelphia.*

October 18, 1977

# Reggie Jackson: Three Swings in a Row

Above: *Dodger pitcher Elias Sosa delivers the pitch that Reggie Jackson knocks into the stands for his second homer of the game. Opposite; Chris Chambliss (left) and Thurman Munson congratulate Reggie Jackson on his fourth-inning home run in game 6.*

When Reggie Jackson signed a five-year contract with the New York Yankees for three million dollars, he became the highest paid player in baseball history. Differences of opinion with his teammates, some of them precipitated by jealousy; public encounters with his manager, Billy Martin; and altercations with fans, combined to bring about what Jackson proclaimed his most frustrating year in baseball. More than once he talked of chucking the whole thing and retiring from the game.

No one could have predicted that this controversial athlete, who had suffered the ignominy of a benching in the final play-off game against Kansas City for the American League championship, would make World Series history. He had been at the pinnacle before, as in 1973 when he'd been named the World Series Most Valuable Player with Oakland against the New York Mets. And he had a track record for excelling time and time again when the pressure and attention were at their greatest. But as those cross-country rivals, the New York Yankees and Los Angeles Dodgers, paired off to decide the 1977 World Series, there were no hints of the drama to come.

Jackson had been held to two hits in 15 times at bat during the five-game play-off series with Kansas City. The future looked no more promising as the Yankees and Dodgers went into the third game of the World Series tied atone victory apiece. In those first two games, Jackson had only one single in six official at bats. After three games, he still had only two singles to show for nine trips to the plate.

Game number 4 was a harbinger of things to come. Reggie began to strut after hitting a double off left-hander Doug Rau and an opposite-field home run off right-hander Rick Rhoden. The 31-year-old southpaw swinger clouted another homer in his final time at bat in the fifth game.

The Dodgers, down three games to two, jumped ahead 2–0 in the top of the first inning of the sixth game. Burt Hooton, the Los Angeles pitcher, had defeated the Yankees in game 2 in which Jackson had gone 0 for 4 with two strikeouts. So when he led off the bottom of the second with a walk, it presaged nothing special. The Dodgers were still ahead 3–2 when Jackson came up in the fourth following a single by Thurman Munson. One swing and Jackson hit Hooton's fastball on a line into the right field stands. The fact that Jackson had homered on his last two swings — in the eighth inning of game 5 and here in game 6 — was little more than a curiosity.

In the fifth inning Mickey Rivers singled off reliever Elias Sosa. There were two out

when Reggie came to bat. BOOM! On his third swing in two games, Jackson lined his third homer into the right field stands to balloon the Yankees' lead to 7–3. Now everyone believed that this truly great slugger was on the threshold of baseball immortality.

Mike Torrez, the Yankees' strong-armed right-hander, maintained the Yankees' lead through the eighth, and when Jackson stepped up to the plate for the fourth time in the game, the capacity crowd at Yankee Stadium rose to its feet, screaming itself hoarse.

"REG-GIE! REG-GIE! REG-GIE!"

Pandemonium was gaining momentum as baseball's most contradictory, enigmatic, and explosive spirit faced Charlie Hough, the Dodgers' relief ace.

At precisely 10:51, on the very first pitch by Hough, Jackson delivered the coup de grace. With one mighty swing he caught hold of a knuckleball and smote it to the far reaches of center field, halfway up the bleacher seats some 450 feet away, adding his own gem to the jeweled tiara of World Series legends. Four home runs on four swings in two games. Most homers: five. Most runs: ten. Most total bases: 25.

The incredibly happy Yankee clean-up hitter pranced around the bases. It was an unbelievable finish to an unbelievable season for the always charismatic and sometimes tormented outfield.

"The greatest single performance I've ever seen," said an admiring loser, Dodger manager Tom Lasorda.

247

June 14– August 31, 1978

# Pete Rose: 44-Game Hitting Streak

Above: *Cincinnati slugger Pete Rose begins his swing into his 44th consecutive-game hit.* Opposite: *"If my record had to be broken," said Tommy Holmes, "I'm glad it was broken by a player like Rose."*

On Wednesday, June 14, Pete Rose broke out of a 5-for-44 batting slump with two hits against the Chicago Cubs. No one in the crowd of 34,658 at Cincinnati's Riverfront Stadium imagined that one of baseball's greatest stories was beginning.

For six and a half weeks after that, in game after game, Pete Rose was unstoppable as he relentlessly chased and caught up with one consecutive-game hitting mark after another. The entire baseball world, ignoring the pennant race for the time being, stopped to look and wonder at this continuing drama. And Rose kept on hitting, getting them in the top of the first, the bottom of the ninth, or in between, with line drive singles, deft bunts, and Charlie Hustle doubles, en route to the second longest hitting streak in the history of professional baseball.

In the maddening process that had everyone on edge except the unperturbable principal character, Pete proceeded to pound pitchers of eight teams for a rousing .387 average, and he raised his average from .267 to .315. Along the way he said hello and good-bye to notable streakers from every baseball generation.

The 37-year-old Rose caught up with the modern Reds' record holders, Edd Roush (1920 and 1924) and Vada Pinson (1954) in game 28, with switch-hitting leader Red Schoendienst (1954) in game 28, with the pre-1900 Reds' record holder Elmer Smith (1898) in game 30, and with Tommy Holmes's modern National League mark (1945) in game 37. In ensuing days, he drew abreast of Ty Cobb's 40-game string of 1911, George Sisler's 41 of 1922, and Bill Dahlen's 42 of 1894.

Finally, the only person who stood between Rose and Joe DiMaggio's "unbreakable" Major League standard of 56 consecutive hitting games was Willie Keeler. Wee Willie had established the all-time National League record in 1897 by "hitting them where they ain't" in 44 straight games.

Rose's streak provided plenty of drama even before Wee Willie and Joltin' Joe came into view. And he kept it going without any assistance from kindly official scorers and bonus turns at bat in extra-inning games. Six times he saved himself with hits in his last at bat; four times his only hit was a bunt.

On July 23, against Montreal, Pete produced a single and a double to extend his hitting streak to 36 games, one shy of the National League record set by Tommy Holmes in 1945. Only six other players — Joe DiMaggio, Willie Keeler, Bill Dahlen, George Sisler, Ty Cobb, and Holmes — had compiled longer hitting streaks than the one Rose took into the series opener with the Mets in New York on Monday night, July 24. DiMaggio was 26 when he reeled off his 56-game hitting streak; Keeler was 25 when he hit in 44 straight games in 1897; Dahlen was 24 when he hit in 42 straight in 1894; Sisler was 29 when he hit in 41 straight in 1922; Cobb was 25 when he connected in 40 straight in 1911; and Holmes was 28 when he got his 37 straight. So Rose's 37 years made this streak even more amazing.

For a while, it appeared that Rose might not catch Holmes. In his first three appearances in game 37 on July 24 against the Mets' Pat Zachry, he flied out twice and hit into a fielder's choice. For once, it seemed as if Rose was pressing too hard. When Pete came up again in the seventh, many in the crowd of 40,065 stood up in nervous anticipation. Rose bunted the first pitch foul and then took a ball high and outside. Zachry's third delivery was a change-up. Rose jumped at it, lining the pitch to left field to tie Holmes's record. The following night Rose, with Holmes looking on, cracked three hits off Craig Swan to break the 33-year-old record. "If my record had to be broken," said Holmes, "I'm glad it was broken by a player like Rose."

Having reached his first goal, Rose set out after the five men who remained ahead of him, particularly Keeler. "I wanna be first in my League," he said. "Second isn't anything. I know Keeler played before nineteen hundred. But what's the difference? He was in the National League, wasn't he?"

Rose extended his streak to 39 games on July 26 with a double in the fifth inning off the Mets' Nino Espinosa. After a day of rest, the Reds traveled to Philadelphia for a doubleheader. Pete kept the streak alive with a double in the third inning of the opener but went hitless in his first two trips to the plate in the nightcap against Steve Carlton, against whom he was now 0 for 13 in the season. In the sixth inning Pete laid a bunt down the third base line and beat it out to stretch the streak to 41. A crowd of 51,779 was on hand to witness the historic event. The following afternoon, on July 29, he singled in each of his first three trips to the plate to extend his streak to 42 games.

Another large Philly crowd of 44,092 was on hand on July 30 to see Rose extend his streak. Spectacular plays by right fielder Jerry Martin and second baseman Davy Johnson robbed Rose of hits in his first two times up. But in the fifth, Pete whistled a hot smash past third baseman Mike Schmidt into left field. Now he was only one behind Keeler.

A crowd of 45,007, the largest of the season in Atlanta Stadium, came out on July 31, and openly rooted for Rose to get a hit off the Braves' pitching ace, Phil Niekro, to tie Keeler's 81-year record. Pete obliged with a ground single to right to open the sixth inning.

The National League record was tied. There was still another goal ahead, an even bigger one, Joe DiMaggio's legendary 56. Rose set out after it the next day, August 31. With another banner Atlanta crowd of 31,159 looking on, and a rookie left-hander, Larry McWilliams, on the mound, Rose walked in the first inning, then whacked a vicious low liner that appeared headed out for center field. McWilliams, almost in self-defense, stuck out his glove and speared it. Twice more Pete hit the ball hard only to line out to the shortstop in the fifth and the third baseman in the seventh. His last chance came in the ninth. By this time, Gene Garber, the Braves' right-handed relief ace, was doing the pitching for Atlanta. The count was one ball and two strikes when Garber threw a change-up. Rose, expecting a fast ball, took a half-hearted swing at the pitch and missed. The streak was over, but of all the accomplishments of Rose's lustrous career, none brought quite the acclaim that was generated by the streak. He has won the Rookie of the Year and MVP, he has played in 11 All-Star Games and four World Series. He has led the League in hitting three times, and on May 5, 1978, he got his three-thousandth hit. But all those achievements were just a prelude to the streak, which, said teammate Tom Seaver, "is a reaffirmation" of who Pete Rose really is.

October 17, 1979

# Pops Did It!

*Pirates' hero Willie Stargell being hugged by teammates in celebration of their seventh-game victory over the Baltimore Orioles to take the World Series.*

For one moment, with one swing, the great man was the center of their universe. If the Pittsburgh Pirates were a family, then Willie "Pops" Stargell was their baseball father — the moral center of a team that had to face the harsh reality of winning three straight World Series games.

The 1979 World Series, in fact, the entire 1979 Pittsburgh Pirates season, was wrapped up in that one moment. For in that one stirring, stimulating moment, the 38-year-old patriarch of the Pirate "family" did it for the Bucs as he had done it all year — as he had done it for 18 years. He did it with the big clutch hit in the big moment. That clutch blow brought Stargell and his teammates from behind, gave them one more comeback in a year of comebacks, and led them to a 4—1 victory over the Baltimore

Orioles. That hit typified this stubborn, never-say-die team that eventually became the champions of baseball for the fifth time in their history—the first time since 1971.

It was a remarkable comeback by the Pirates. Down three-games-to-one, they became only the fourth team in World Series history to come from that far behind and win a seven-game series. And it was Willie Stargell, the heart and soul, the strength and spirit of the Bucs, who did it. He had driven in the tying run in the sixth inning of game five to start the comeback. He had driven in an insurance run in game six as the Pirates prolonged the series and made the showdown seventh game possible. And he was the big man in game seven.

In the sixth inning of the final game, before 50,000 partisan, yelling, Oriole fans in Baltimore's Memorial Stadium, Willie Stargell was swinging his big, brown bat in the on-deck circle when Bill Robinson bounced a single off Kiko Garcia's glove into center field. Now the leader of the Pirates, the father of "the family," moved up toward the batter's box. Behind him in the Pirates' dugout voices were yelling, "C'mon, Pops, hit one for us." And Scott McGregor's first pitch, a slider, a good slider, down and away but not far enough away, was attacked by Willie Stargell's big, brown bat. The ball soared out to right field over the head of the Baltimore Orioles' right fielder Ken Singleton, and over the fence into the right field

*Pittsburgh Pirates' Willie Stargell follows through on his two-run homer in the sixth inning of the final game of the World Series against the Baltimore Orioles.*

bullpen—the Pirate dugout was in a frenzy. The Pirates were ahead now, 2—1, and there was no stopping them.

The final score, 4—1, was almost anti-climactic. Somehow the Pirates, from manager Chuck Tanner on down, sensed that the World Series was virtually over and their godfather, Willie "Pops" Stargell, had ended it in their favor. Nothing could turn it around after that hit. Not the bases-loaded try in the eighth by the Baltimores. Nothing.

It surprised no one when Stargell was unanimously voted by a nine-man panel as the World Series' Most Valuable Player. The line on him was a .400 batting average that included a record seven extra-base hits, three home runs, and four doubles. He had a total of one dozen hits and tied Reggie Jackson's Series record for total bases with 25. Besides his homer, he also hit two doubles and a single in the final game.

But the real line on Stargell showed in the voices of his Pirate teammates when they spoke about him and in the eyes of his manager when he tried to shape words to explain what Willie Stargell meant to the Pittsburgh franchise.

"It was only right that Pops should win it for us," said Dave Parker, the man who will try to succeed Stargell as the team leader one day. "The man is a legend. Right now, to me, he's like a god."

"What can you say about a guy who's so great that he's going to be in the Hall of Fame some day," said Tanner. "When we were down one-to-nothing, the guys on the bench said to him, 'C'mon, Pops, hit one for us,' and Pops did. Don't you see? Stargell had to win the series for us. No one else but Willie Stargell."

*Members of the Pittsburgh Pirates mob relief pitcher Kent Tekulve after he saved Pirates' victory to clinch the World Series against Baltimore. Stargell rushes to join the gang.*

253

October 12, 1980

# A 30-Year Wait

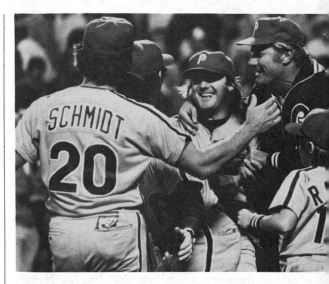

*Philadelphia pitcher Tug McGraw being hugged by coach Dallas Green and teammates after coming in on relief to beat the Kansas City Royals 4–3 in the fifth game of the World Series.*

There may never be another play-off like it —five games, all cliff-hangers, and four consecutive extra-inning struggles. Fifty heart-stopping innings before a tired Philadelphia team finally outlasted a crippled and equally weary Houston club to win the Phillies' first National League pennant in 30 years.

In the recorded history of baseball, there may never have been another to match the fourth game of that National League championship series. Perhaps it was significant that the game was played in the Astrodome, initially referred to as "the eighth wonder of the world." The contest overflowed with bizarre plays, flawed by mental as well as physical misplays, and controversy.

One episode involved players, umpires, and even the league president and lasted nearly 20 minutes before a decision was reached. The episode occurred in the fourth inning, an inning that started normally enough with singles by Bake McBride and

Manny Trillo off Vern Ruhle. After that, things got crazy, Garry Maddox stroked a soft liner back to the box, Ruhle fielded the ball and, disregarding the other bases, tossed to first for an apparent putout.

Plate umpire Doug Harvey's initial reaction was no catch and, he signaled with his hands, fair ball in play. Then the Houston manager dashed from the dugout claiming that Ruhle had caught the ball on the fly and Trillo, who had taken off for second, should be declared out. Harvey, later claiming his vision had been obstructed by the batter breaking from the plate, asked for help. Third base arbiter Bob Engel, and Ed Vargo at first, agreed that Ruhle had caught the ball. The Phillies protested that Ruhle had trapped the ball. While the umpires huddled around the mound, first baseman Art Howe noticed that McBride had left second and run to the next bag, claiming a triple play. Confusion reigned while the umpires struggled to reach a verdict. Finally, Harvey made his way to the first base boxes where Chub Feeney, the league president, sat nervously chewing his cigar.

*Astros' Jose Cruz scores on a seventh inning wild pitch as Phillies' pitcher Larry Christenson grabs at the ball in final play-off game.*

255

*Astros' Joe Morgan and Phils' Pete Rose sprawl over second base after Rose was caught stealing in third inning of the fifth and final play-off game.*

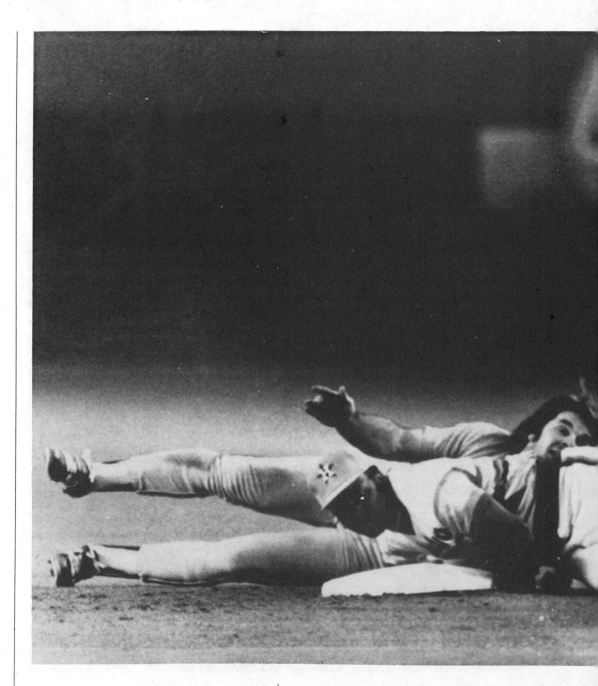

At last, Harvey returned from the conference and decreed that Ruhle had indeed caught the ball and his throw to first had doubled Trillo at first base. The umpire disallowed the putout at second, explaining that time had been called prior to the play made there. The ruling evoked protests from both clubs that were eventually retracted as the inning ended without a score and Philadelphia won the game.

The rhubarb, consuming 20 minutes of the 3-hour 55-minute game, overshadowed but scarcely minimized the day's other whacky events. In the sixth inning, with the Astros leading, 2–0, at the expense of Steve Carlton and enjoying a bases-loaded, one-out situation, Luis Pujols lifted a fly to McBride in right field and Gary Woods tagged up and scored on the sacrifice fly. The Phillies, claiming that Woods left third base too soon, made the play at third as Engel concurred and nullified the run. In the eighth, an ill-advised throw to third by Astros' right fielder Jeff Leonard allowed Pete Rose to take an extra base, resulting in a run that gave the Phillies a 3–2 lead. The Astros tied the score in the ninth on a walk, sacrifice, and single by Terry Puhl but the Phillies rallied for two runs in the 10th on a single by Pete Rose and two-out doubles by Greg Luzinski and Trillo.

Incredible as game four was, it was merely a prologue for the final-game showdown that produced a long-awaited pennant for the Phils after play-off defeats in 1976, 1977, and 1978. Manager Dallas Green entrusted the starting assignment to rookie Marty Bystrom, activated as an eligible only five days earlier. The opposing pitcher was Houston fireballer Nolan Ryan. Bystrom

lasted until the sixth inning when Alan Ashby's pinch single drove in Walling with the run that tied the score, 2–2.

In the seventh, with Larry Christenson on the mound, the Astros erupted for three runs, capped by Art Howe's triple, to take what appeared to be a comfortable 5–2 lead. Ryan lost his touch, however, and left in the eighth after giving up three singles and a bases-loaded walk to Pete Rose that made the score 5–3. A force play and Del Unser's pinch single off Ken Forsch tied the score. Trillo, the Most Valuable Player of the series, then tripled and the Phils led, 7–5.

Now it was Houston's turn to retaliate against Tug McGraw—appearing in a record fifth play-off game. With Craig Reynolds and Puhl on base as the result of singles and two outs, Rafael Landestoy and Jose Cruz singled and the score was tied again, 7–7. The score was still tied in the 10th when doubles by Unser and Maddox produced the run that sent the Phillies into

their first World Series since 1950.

McGraw redeemed himself in the World Series. He appeared in four of the six games, saving the first and sixth and gaining credit for the fifth-game victory against Kansas City. The veteran left-hander, one of the true heroes in the Phillies' first and only World Series triumphs in their long National League history, gave the Phils more relief than they ever dreamed he could deliver. After coming off the disabled list on July 17, McGraw worked 52 innings in 33 games, allowing just three earned runs. From September 2 until the regular season's end, he was in 15 games, allowed just one earned run, had five saves and five victories. He appeared in all but 2 of the 11 post-season games and was superb in all but two. He saved his best for games five and six of the World Series, striking out Amos Otis with the bases full in the ninth inning of game five and Willie Wilson, again with the bases loaded in the ninth, in game six.

September 26, 1981

# Nolan Ryan's Record Fifth

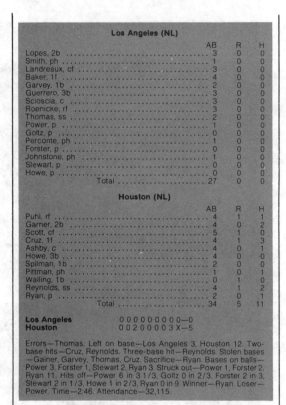

**Los Angeles (NL)**

| | AB | R | H |
|---|---|---|---|
| Lopes, 2b | 3 | 0 | 0 |
| Smith, ph | 1 | 0 | 0 |
| Landreaux, cf | 3 | 0 | 0 |
| Baker, lf | 4 | 0 | 0 |
| Garvey, 1b | 2 | 0 | 0 |
| Guerrero, 3b | 3 | 0 | 0 |
| Scioscia, c | 3 | 0 | 0 |
| Roenicke, rf | 3 | 0 | 0 |
| Thomas, ss | 2 | 0 | 0 |
| Power, p | 1 | 0 | 0 |
| Goltz, p | 0 | 0 | 0 |
| Perconte, ph | 1 | 0 | 0 |
| Forster, p | 0 | 0 | 0 |
| Johnstone, ph | 1 | 0 | 0 |
| Stewart, p | 0 | 0 | 0 |
| Howe, p | 0 | 0 | 0 |
| Total | 27 | 0 | 0 |

**Houston (NL)**

| | AB | R | H |
|---|---|---|---|
| Puhl, rf | 4 | 1 | 1 |
| Garner, 2b | 4 | 0 | 2 |
| Scott, cf | 5 | 1 | 0 |
| Cruz, lf | 4 | 1 | 3 |
| Ashby, c | 4 | 0 | 1 |
| Howe, 3b | 4 | 0 | 0 |
| Spilman, 1b | 2 | 0 | 0 |
| Pittman, ph | 1 | 0 | 1 |
| Walling, 1b | 0 | 1 | 0 |
| Reynolds, ss | 4 | 1 | 2 |
| Ryan, p | 2 | 0 | 1 |
| Total | 34 | 5 | 11 |

| | | |
|---|---|---|
| **Los Angeles** | 0 0 0 0 0 0 0 0 0 | —0 |
| **Houston** | 0 0 2 0 0 0 0 3 X | —5 |

Errors—Thomas. Left on base—Los Angeles 3, Houston 12. Two-base hits—Cruz, Reynolds. Three-base hit—Reynolds. Stolen bases —Gainer, Garvey, Thomas, Cruz. Sacrifice—Ryan. Bases on balls—Power 3, Forster 1, Stewart 2, Ryan 3. Struck out—Power 1, Forster 2, Ryan 11. Hits off—Power 6 in 3 1/3, Goltz 0 in 2/3, Forster 2 in 3, Stewart 2 in 1/3, Howe 1 in 2/3, Ryan 0 in 9. Winner—Ryan. Loser—Power. Time—2:46. Attendance—32,115.

September 26, 1981, Nolan Ryan had the stamina, the heart, and the marvelous talent to shackle a Dodger offense rated best in the National League. For nine innings, he walked 3, struck out 11, and needed one out-of-the-ordinary defensive play from his Astro teammates to be the first major league pitcher to achieve a fifth no-hitter.

In the Houston Astrodome, 32,115 onlookers were cheering Ryan with each succeeding out, sensing they might be part of baseball history in the making. Only one Astro player was unflappable before and after the last out, securing the record-breaking fifth.

"I don't get emotional about these things anymore," Nolan Ryan explained. "This is something I've wanted for a long time, but I've been too close too many times in the late innings. To tell you the truth, I'd about given up on ever getting another. I've had a few no-hitters going into the seventh and lost them. I was beginning to think I'd lost the stamina for a fifth."

In historical fact, it was in the seventh inning that Terry Puhl made a running catch near the right-center-field wall to gather in Mike Scioscia's long drive and save Nolan's no-hitter. Final score: Houston 5, Los Angeles 0.

Ryan began his string of no-hitters early in the 1970s, notching four in a three-year span. It took another six years to get the one that became the new record, putting him one game ahead of Sandy Koufax, with whom he had shared the record of four. (It might be noted in passing that Ryan also has pitched seven one-hit ball games.)

Pitching this fifth no-hitter offered Ryan other satisfactions. His victims were the Dodgers, who had lost to him only one time in nine previous decisions. In two Astro seasons, he had not had one win over Los Angeles. This day, the game was being nationally televised and his wife, Ruth, and his mother were in the stands.

Ryan also was able to relish the win as a native of Texas who had come home in the winter of 1979, signing on with the Astros as a free agent. When he signed, it was for the richest sum in baseball history—a four-year pact at $1.125 million per season. Sceptics quickly pointed to his .500 won-and-lost record and wondered whether he was worth the money. True, Ryan owned all kinds of strikeout records, but his career won-and-lost record was 188-174. He also held the unenviable record as baseball's wildest pitcher, with 1,809 bases on balls.

In his first year with the Astros in 1980, Ryan struggled to an 11-10 record and a 3.35 earned run average. In 1981, however, he had one of his best seasons. He recorded 11 wins against 5 losses and a league-leading 1.69 ERA. When he fanned 11 Dodgers on September 26, it was the one-hundred-and-thirty-fifth game in which he had struck out 10 or more.

"I know the National League batters better now," Ryan explained. "I know

*With this ninth-inning pitch, Ryan exhibits the style that enabled him to retire the last 19 batters he faced and claim 1981 as one of his best seasons.*

which pitch to throw to which hitters and where to throw. It means I'm more relaxed out on the mound and more confident."

At 34, Ryan had just about given up hope of ever achieving another no-hitter. "I never envisioned one that day, that's for sure," he recalled. "My back was hurting and I didn't have any rhythm in the early innings."

Nolan issued all three walks in the first three innings, as he struggled with his control. He also uncorked a wild pitch and was continually behind on the count. In the fourth, pitching coach Mel Wright came to the mound to suggest that he might be overstriding. Whatever the reason, Ryan found the groove and not another Dodger reached base. He retired the last 19 batters.

"I let up a little in the late innings," Ryan said. "I didn't get so many strikeouts (ten in the first six innings, only one in the final three) but I had better control."

He certainly didn't let up in the ninth. He threw three straight strikes past leadoff pinch-hitter Reggie Smith. The last was a 97-mile-an-hour fastball. He induced Ken Landreaux to bounce out to the first baseman Denny Wallins for the second out. Dusty Baker, a .322 hitter and a clutch performer, represented the last challenge. Ryan's first two pitches were out of the strike zone. The next was a curve. Baker bounced it feebly to Art Howe at third base, whose toss to first for the final out touched off a mob scene on the mound.

## RYAN NO-HITTERS

| Date | Opponent | Score |
|---|---|---|
| May 15, 1973 | Kansas City (AL) | 3-0 |
| July 15, 1973 | Detroit (AL) | 6-0 |
| September 28, 1974 | Minnesota (AL) | 4-0 |
| June 1, 1975 | Baltimore (AL) | 1-0 |
| September 26, 1981 | Los Angeles (NL) | 5-0 |

With a wave of a glove, Nolan Ryan acknowledges the crowd's excited appreciation of his record-breaking fifth no-hit pitching performance. Ryan, at 34, became the first pitcher ever to achieve this feat in the Astros' 5-0 win over the Los Angeles Dodgers.

October 19, 1981

# Dodgers Win in Final Inning of Final Game

**Los Angeles (NL)**

|  | AB | R | H |
|---|---|---|---|
| Lopes, 2b | 4 | 0 | 1 |
| Russell, ss | 4 | 0 | 2 |
| Baker, lf | 4 | 0 | 0 |
| Garvey, 1b | 4 | 0 | 0 |
| Cey, 3b | 3 | 0 | 0 |
| Monday, rf | 4 | 2 | 2 |
| Landreaux, cf | 0 | 0 | 0 |
| Guerrero, cf | 4 | 0 | 1 |
| Scioscia, c | 3 | 0 | 0 |
| Valenzuela, p | 3 | 0 | 0 |
| Welch, p | 0 | 0 | 0 |
| Total | 33 | 2 | 6 |

**Montreal (NL)**

|  | AB | R | H |
|---|---|---|---|
| Raines, lf | 4 | 1 | 1 |
| Scott, 2b | 3 | 0 | 0 |
| Dawson, cf | 4 | 0 | 0 |
| Carter, c | 3 | 0 | 1 |
| Manuel, pr | 0 | 0 | 0 |
| Parrish, 3b | 3 | 0 | 1 |
| White, rf | 3 | 0 | 0 |
| Cromartie, 1b | 3 | 0 | 0 |
| Speier, ss | 3 | 0 | 0 |
| Burris, p | 2 | 0 | 0 |
| Wallach, ph | 1 | 0 | 0 |
| Rogers, p | 0 | 0 | 0 |
| Total | 29 | 1 | 3 |

| Los Angeles | 0 0 0 0 1 0 0 0 1—2 |
|---|---|
| Montreal | 1 0 0 0 0 0 0 0 0—1 |

Errors—Speier. Double play—Los Angeles 1, Montreal 1. Left on base —Los Angeles 5, Montreal 5. Two-base hits—Raines, Parrish. Three-base hit—Russell. Home run—Monday (1). Stolen base—Lopes. Sacrifice—Scott. Bases on balls—Valenzuela 3, Burris 1. Struck out— Valenzuela 6, Burris 1, Rogers 1. Hits off—Valenzuela 3 in 8 2/3, Welch 0 in 1/3, Burris 5 in 8, Rogers 1 in 1. Winner—Valenzuela. Loser—Rogers. Time—2:41. Attendance—36,491.

The 1981 National League pennant race was not decided until the final inning of the final game. The end came in the afternoon on Monday, October 19, the latest date in baseball history in which a pennant winner was crowned. There were two out in the ninth inning and a three-one count on Rick Monday when the Dodger outfielder slammed a Steve Rogers pitch for a home run, the Dodgers defeating the Expos 2-1 in the fifth game of the best-of-five play-off for the National League championship.

It was a dramatic finish to a dramatic set of play-offs in which the Dodgers twice came within one defeat of elimination. After winning the first half of the split season in the National League's Western Division, the Dodgers suffered two defeats and then came bck to win three

*Emotional manager Tom Lasorda embraces winning-pitcher Fernando Valenzuela after the Dodgers grabbed the National League championship from out of the mouths of the Montreal Expos, 2-1.*

*Taking aim on a hitter is 20-year-old pitching sensation and Cy Young award-winner Fernando Valenzuela.*

straight from Houston in the five-game divisional championship season. Then they rallied to win the last two of five games in the pennant play-off with Montreal.

It was a bitter loss for the Expos and their fans, much more difficult to accept than the final-day eliminations in 1979 and 1980. They held a 1-0 lead over Dodgers' mound ace, rookie-sensation Fernando Valenzuela until the fifth inning and were prepared to go to bat in the last of the ninth with no worse than a 1-1 tie. Rick Monday dashed those hopes by connecting with a Rogers "hanging" sinker, lashing it over the center-field wall to put the Expos behind for the first time.

It was ironic that the winning hit came off the delivery of the pitcher who had hurled four straight clutch victories, two against Steve Carlton of the Philadelphia Phillies. In his last 36 innings, Steve Rogers had allowed just two runs. He had won his game three days earlier and had volunteered to go to the bullpen to be ready if needed. Manager Jim Fanning had summoned him in relief of starter Ray Burris at the start of the fateful ninth.

In his last 37 innings, Steve Rogers had allowed just two runs. Unfortunately, Rick Monday stepped up to the plate and smashed a run that killed the Expos' dreams of the 1981 World Series.

It was truly a game decided in storybook fashion, with the victory credited to Valenzuela, the 20-year-old Mexican hurler who had captured the hearts of all *Angelinos* with his brilliant pitching throughout the strike-plagued season—and who won the Cy Young award in November 1981. Fernando won 13 games and equalled the major league rookie record by pitching 8 shutouts, although more than 50 games had been canceled during the players' strike. He led the National League in victories, shutouts, complete games (11), innings pitched (192), and strikeouts (180). In this all-important deciding game, he pitched eight and two-thirds innings of three-hit ball to keep pace with Burris, who had beaten him in their previous play-off encounter.

The Expos were first to score, taking a 1-0 lead in the first inning; Valenzuela was lucky it wasn't more. Tim Raines led off with a double. Rodney Scott bunted near the mound and Raines beat Valenzuela's throw to third with a headlong slide. The Dodgers added to the danger by failing to run down Scott after picking him off first. But Valenzuela survived at the cost of only one run, which scored when Andre Dawson hit into a double play. The inning ended as Gary Carter flied out. The Expos had a 1-0 lead, but had missed a great chance to break open the game.

Burris protected the lead until the fifth, when Monday led off with a single to center and raced to third on a single by Pedro Guerrero to right center. Mike Scioscia lined out to Scott at second, but Monday scored when Valenzuela grounded out to the same player.

The score remained unchanged through the eighth, both pitchers stingy with hits and walks. Burris had allowed five hits, Valenzuela only three. Then came Fanning's fateful choice. He called for Rogers to replace Burris. Rogers retired Steve Garvey on an infield popup and Ron Cey on a fly to deep left. Monday then teed off on a sinker that didn't dip.

"It was a hanging sinker," the disconsolate Rogers said later. "I wanted it to break down and away....I just didn't throw the pitch properly. It was right down the middle."

Monday said that, after he hit the ball, he had no idea where it went. "I saw the infielders turn their backs and look over the wall, and I knew it was out of the park. Then I almost fell down between second and third."

A one-run lead in hand, Valenzuela looked like a sure winner when he retired Scott and Dawson to open the ninth. Then he walked Carter and Larry Parrish, and Tommy Lasorda called to his bullpen for Bob Welch. The batter was Jerry White, whose home run had won the third game for Rogers. Welch threw one pitch and White bounced it to Davy Lopes at second for the final out.

There was nothing more ahead for the come-back Dodgers except a little item like the World Series, where they would fall behind 2-0 and come on to win the next four—1981's champions of the baseball world.

May 6, 1982

# Gaylord Perry's Three-Hundredth

### Seattle

| | AB | R | H |
|---|---|---|---|
| J. Cruz, 2b | 3 | 1 | 0 |
| Castillo, 3b | 4 | 2 | 2 |
| Bochte, lf | 4 | 0 | 2 |
| Zisk, dh | 4 | 0 | 1 |
| T. Cruz, ss | 4 | 1 | 2 |
| Cowens, rf | 4 | 0 | 1 |
| Simpson, cf | 4 | 0 | 0 |
| Maler, 1b | 3 | 1 | 1 |
| Bulling, c | 3 | 2 | 2 |
| Total | 33 | 7 | 11 |

### New York Yankees

| | AB | R | H |
|---|---|---|---|
| Randolf, 2b | 5 | 1 | 1 |
| Griffey, rf | 4 | 2 | 3 |
| Mumphrey, cf | 4 | 0 | 2 |
| Mayberry, 1b | 4 | 0 | 0 |
| Winfield, lf | 4 | 0 | 1 |
| Gamble, dh | 4 | 0 | 1 |
| Smalley, 3b | 3 | 0 | 1 |
| Cerone, c | 4 | 0 | 0 |
| Dent, ss | 2 | 0 | 0 |
| Murcer, ph | 1 | 0 | 0 |
| Milbourne, ss | 1 | 0 | 0 |
| Total | 36 | 3 | 9 |

| | | | | | | | | | |
|---|---|---|---|---|---|---|---|---|---|
| **Seattle** | 0 | 0 | 5 | 0 | 0 | 0 | 2 | 0 | X—7 |
| **New York Yankees** | 0 | 0 | 0 | 0 | 1 | 0 | 2 | 0—3 |

Errors—Castillo, Cerone. Double play—New York 1, Seattle 1. Left on base—New York 7, Seattle 3. Two-base hits—Bochte, Zisk, Bulling, Castillo. Three-base hits—Mumphrey, Maler, Cowens. Home run—Griffey (1). Stole home—J. Cruz. Bases on balls—Perry 1. Struck out—Alexander 2, May 2, Perry 4. Hits off—Alexander, 6 in 3; May 5 in 5; Perry, 9 in 9. Wild pitch—May. Winner—Perry. Loser—Alexander. Time—2:29. Attendance—27, 369.

It was on October 5, 1981, that the Atlanta Braves handed Gaylord Perry his unconditional release. With an 8–9 record and a 3.93 ERA, he was a mediocre pitcher with a mediocre team. Much more incriminating, he was 43—an age when pitchers were more closely related to hay and horseshoes.

The 1982 season was approaching and Gaylord Perry was still unemployed. He offered his services free, requesting only a modest salary based on performance. But there were no takers. With a majority of the clubs bent on a "youth movement," there was no room for an aging arm, particularly one belonging to a man long suspected of resorting to a "spitter."

Even his wife, Blanche, wanted him out. "You've had a great career," she said. "You don't have to beg. Where's your pride?"

Perry's pride was in his arm, which was still strong, and his will, which was even stronger. He had pitched 20 seasons in the major leagues and in 13 of those, he had won 15 games or more. His career total of victories was 297, and he didn't get to the summit of the Three Hundred Mountain to quit. It mattered everything in the world to Gaylord Jackson Perry to become one of just 15 pitchers in the 107-year history of major league baseball to get 300 wins. He also had his eye on another peak—with 3,368 strikeouts he was only 140 behind Walter Johnson's record.

To best appreciate the grandeur of the Three Hundred Mountain, one must consider who has not climbed it along with those who have. Sandy Koufax did not

267

make it. Neither did Bob Feller, Robin Roberts, Whitey Ford, Bob Lemon, Dazzy Vance, Red Ruffing, Carl Hubbell, Dizzy Dean, Rube Waddell and Mordecai Brown—all Hall of Famers.

Perry was already a legend in his own right. At age 40, he had won 21 games for the San Diego Padres. He lost only six games for a team that could do no better than fourth place in its division, barely winning more games than it lost. For that he was voted the National League's Cy Young Award, becoming the oldest pitcher ever to receive the coveted honor.

That was in 1978, Perry's 17th season as a big league pitcher. He had enjoyed his greatest season six years previously when, as a member of the Cleveland Indians, he won 24 games and was nearly a unanimous winner of the Cy Young Award as the best pitcher in the American League. No other pitcher has ever won the award in both leagues. For that matter, only a handful had ever won 20 games in both leagues.

But now he had to sell himself to get a chance to pitch. One of the calls Perry made, in early February of 1982, was to Dan O'Brien, President and General Manager of the Seattle Mariners. O'Brien agreed to give Gaylord an opportunity to make the club but not before he had obtained the unenthusiastic approval of owner George Argyros and field manager Rene Lachemann.

Perry made the team despite a nightmarish spring debut—he walked six in three innings in a 12–3 loss to the Cubs—

268

and pitched well in his first two regular-season starts. He went the route in both games although he lost 5–3 to Oakland and 3–2 to California. Victory no. 298 and no. 1 as a Mariner came on April 20, when he fanned a club record 13 in a 6–4 defeat of the Angels. After a no-decision in his next start, Perry posted no. 299 with a 6–3 triumph over the New York Yankees.

Thursday, May 6, 1982, was not just another day in the life of 43-year-old Gaylord Perry. Richard Nixon called the clubhouse with good wishes before the game. President Reagan had offered his good wishes the day before. A mere 27,369 fans were in the 59,418-seat Kingdome to witness Perry's historic outing, the Yankees once more the antagonists. They were even easier to handle this time. The Mariners got Perry five runs in the third and two more in the seventh. Gaylord was in real trouble only in the eighth when the Yankees loaded the bases with one out. Perry fanned cleanup hitter John Mayberry on three pitches and after two infield singles scored a pair of runs, Roy Smalley flied out to end the threat.

Gaylord breezed through the ninth. Rick Cerone lined softly back to the mound. Larry Milbourne popped out to second base. Willie Randolph grounded to second and Perry had scaled the mountain, becoming the first pitcher since Early Wynn on July 13, 1963, to reach 300, and only Perry, Wynn and Warren Spahn had won 300 in the last 40 years.

Perry went on to win seven more games before the season's end to give him a career total of 307 victories, ranking him 11th among the all-time winners. He struck out 116 to raise his total to 3,452, only 56 strikeouts behind Walter Johnson's record. At 44, Perry may have run out of pitching miracles. But don't bet on it. Not as long as he can lift his resilient right arm.

*Gaylord Perry takes aim at his 300th win, as the Mariners host the New York Yankees, May 6, 1982.*

# Darrell Porter's Greatest Battle

### St. Louis

| | AB | R | H |
|---|---|---|---|
| L. Smith, lf | 5 | 2 | 3 |
| Oberkfell, 3b | 3 | 0 | 0 |
| Tenace, ph | 0 | 0 | 0 |
| Ramsey, 3b | 1 | 1 | 0 |
| Hernandez, 1b | 3 | 1 | 2 |
| Hendrick, rf | 5 | 0 | 2 |
| Porter, c | 5 | 0 | 1 |
| Lorg, dh | 3 | 0 | 2 |
| Green, ph | 0 | 0 | 0 |
| Braun, dh | 2 | 0 | 1 |
| McGee, cf | 5 | 1 | 1 |
| Herr, 2b | 3 | 0 | 1 |
| O. Smith, ss | 4 | 1 | 2 |
| Total | 39 | 6 | 15 |

### Milwaukee

| | AB | R | H |
|---|---|---|---|
| Molitor, 3b | 4 | 1 | 2 |
| Yount, ss | 4 | 0 | 1 |
| Cooper, 1b | 3 | 0 | 1 |
| Simmons, c | 4 | 0 | 0 |
| Oglivie, lf | 4 | 1 | 1 |
| Thomas, cf | 4 | 0 | 0 |
| Howell, dh | 3 | 0 | 0 |
| Moore, rf | 3 | 0 | 1 |
| Gantner, 2b | 3 | 1 | 1 |
| Total | 32 | 3 | 7 |

| | | | | | | | | | | |
|---|---|---|---|---|---|---|---|---|---|---|
| **St. Louis** | 0 | 0 | 0 | 1 | 0 | 3 | 0 | 2 | X—6 | |
| **Milwaukee** | 0 | 0 | 0 | 0 | 1 | 2 | 0 | 0 | 0—3 | |

Errors—Andujar. Left on base—Milwaukee 3, St. Louis 13. Two-base hits—Gantner, L. Smith 2. Home run—Oglivie 1. Runs batted in—Cooper 1, Oglivie 1, L. Smith 1, Hernandez 2, Hendrick 1, Porter 1, Braun 1. Sacrifice fly—Cooper. Bases on balls-Vuckovich 2, McClure 1, Haas 1. Struck out—Vuckovich 3, Haas 1, Andujar 1, Sutter 2. Hits off—Vuckovich, 10 in 5 1/3; McClure, 2 in 1/3; Haas, 1 in 2; Caldwell, 2 in 1/3; Andujar, 7 in 7; Sutter, 0 in 2. Winner—Andujar. Loser—McClure. Time—2:50. Attendance—53,723.

It doesn't happen in real life. Only in fiction—or the movies. But it did happen. It happened to Darrell Porter.

"It's a dream," exclaimed the strapping catcher of the newly acclaimed World Champion St. Louis Cardinals as he accepted congratulations for being voted the Most Valuable Player of the 1982 World Series. Porter batted .286 during the Series and won praise for the way he handled the Cardinal pitchers. "It's a beautiful dream," Porter exclaimed again and again.

Porter's "beautiful dream" began as a nightmare, however, a painful, agonizing nightmare that lasted years while he struggled to overcome drug addiction, alcohol dependency, and a suicide attempt.

Porter broke into major league baseball as a 19-year-old catcher with the Milwaukee Brewers in 1971. He admits, "I began using alcohol, uppers and downers, and cocaine to ease the pressure, and I smoked marijuana. After a while being high became reality." Porter's marriage broke up, his drinking increased, and he was traded to Kansas City. There, under Whitey Herzog's managerial direction, he became an excellent receiver and hitter for the Western Division champion Royals in 1978 and 1979.

By then, Porter's addiction threatened his baseball playing career. "I lost my desire to train for baseball. I bottomed out." Joe Burke, the Royals' General Manager, told him: "You don't play for us until you get straightened out." Porter was enough in control to realize drugs were destroying him. He had reached a point where he felt, "I could end it all. But I was too chicken to do it. I don't think I could have done it, but you never know. I was going downhill fast."

Porter spent six weeks at the Meadows, a sanatorium in Arizona. Released, he learned there would be no miracle comeback for him. That year he had a mediocre season. Happily the Royals won the World Series pennant, but Porter batted only .143.

That winter the Royals, not willing to sign him to a long-term, high-pay contract, allowed Porter to become a free agent. The Cardinals, with Herzog as manager, decided Porter was worth the gamble. Whitey thought he knew something of Porter's mettle and determination from their three years together with the Royals. The Cardinals signed Porter to a five-year contract in 1981, a signing that enabled Herzog to ship 11-year Redbird hero Ted Simmons to the Brewers as part of a seven-player trade. Herzog's confidence wasn't shared by most of the Cardinal fans, however. Resentful of the trade that robbed them of Simmons, their longtime favorite, St. Louisians refused to accept his replacement and booed Darrell from day one.

Porter's first season as a Redbird was not a happy one. He batted only .224 in the strike-shortened season, hitting six home runs and driving in 31 runs. His second season was not much better. He missed 42 games in the regular season because of a hand injury. He battled slumps and had to contend with a hostile home crowd. His .231 batting average was 20 points off his average and another 30 points short of what was expected of him. His 12 homers and 48 RBIs were half what the Cards had hoped for in return for an approximate $700,000 annual salary.

If Herzog was disappointed in Porter's regular-season performance, he gave no indication. "All I know," he said, "is that he's a good money player; that he can handle pitchers real well; and that the teams he has played for in each of the last six seasons have had the best records in their division."

Porter made a prophet of his manager, rising to unprecedented heights in the post–1982-season games. The Cards laid waste to the Braves in the three-game sweep in the National League Championship Series and Porter supplied the most devastating punch to walk away with Most Valuable Player honors. He reached base 10 times in 14 appearances at bat—5 hits, including 3 doubles, 5 walks, 3 runs, and an important RBI. He threw out two runners attempting to steal, both times nipping a possible rally.

Porter stayed hot in the World Series. He collected eight hits in the seven-game triumph over Milwaukee, rapped a home run and two doubles, and drove in five runs. He propelled the Cards to an equalizing 5–4 victory in the second game, doubling home a pair of runs in the sixth inning off Don Sutton to tie the score and contributing a single during the winning rally in the eighth. Darrell hammered his homer in the sixth game and also rapped

*Determination and strength rewarded, Darrell Porter cracks a double during the sixth inning of the final 1982 World Series game. Porter's hit scored teammate George Hendrick and tied the game.*

*Darrell Porter (left) slides across the plate after a sixth-inning sacrifice fly by pitcher Bob Forsch. St. Louis took NL play-off game 1 from the Atlanta Braves, 7–0.*

an RBI-single in the seventh game as the Cardinals came from behind to win their first world championship in 15 years.

At the World Series–MVP celebration in the Waldorf-Astoria, Darrell Porter toasted his success with grape juice. Since 1980, he's been clean; he's not even tasted a beer. Porter admits that winning the MVP award is the greatest high he's ever had. "In fact, I didn't believe it when they told me I was named MVP. I guess every time

I got a hit, a few of 'em stopped booing. I knew during the season there were some people who kept cheering me. I knew they were there, but it was hard to hear through the boos."

Porter fought his battle and won, earning the respect, support, and admiration of Cardinal fans and baseball fans everywhere. He ranks among the heroes of the past, in a day when heroes are hard to find.

July 25, 1983-August 18, 1983

# Pine Tar Episode

### Kansas Ciy

| | | AB | R | H |
|---|---|---|---|---|
| Wilson, | cf | 3 | 0 | 0 |
| Sheridan, | ph-cf | 2 | 0 | 0 |
| Washington, | ss | 5 | 1 | 1 |
| Brett, | 3b | 5 | 1 | 3 |
| Pryor, | 3b | 0 | 0 | 0 |
| McRae, | dh | 4 | 0 | 0 |
| Otis, | rf | 4 | 0 | 1 |
| Wathan, | 1b-lf | 3 | 2 | 1 |
| Roberts, | lf | 3 | 0 | 2 |
| Aikens, | ph-1b | 1 | 0 | 0 |
| Simpson, | lf | 0 | 0 | 0 |
| White, | 2b | 4 | 1 | 2 |
| Slaught, | c | 4 | 0 | 3 |
| | Total | 38 | 5 | 13 |

### New York Yankees

| | | AB | R | H |
|---|---|---|---|---|
| Campaneris, | 2b | 4 | 1 | 2 |
| Griffey, | 1b | 0 | 0 | 0 |
| Nettles, | 3b | 3 | 0 | 0 |
| Piniella, | rf | 4 | 1 | 1 |
| Mumphrey, | cf | 0 | 0 | 0 |
| Wynegar, | c | 0 | 0 | 0 |
| Baylor, | dh | 4 | 1 | 1 |
| Winfield, | cf-lf | 4 | 1 | 3 |
| Kemp, | lf-rf | 4 | 0 | 0 |
| Balboni, | 1b | 2 | 0 | 0 |
| Mattingly, | 1b-2b | 2 | 0 | 0 |
| Smalley, | ss | 4 | 0 | 1 |
| Cerone, | c | 2 | 0 | 0 |
| Guidry, | cf | 0 | 0 | 0 |
| Gamble, | ph | 1 | 0 | 0 |
| | Total | 34 | 4 | 8 |

Kansas City
0 1 0 1 0 1 0 0 2—5
New York Yankees 0 1 0 0 0 3 0 0 0—4

Errors—None. Runs batted in—Brett 2, White 2, Slaught 2, Baylor 2, Winfield 2. Double play—New York 1. Left on base—Kansas City 8, New York 5. Three-base hits—White, Slaught, Baylor. Home runs—Winfield, Brett. Bases on balls—Armstrong 2, Rawley 2. Struck out—Black 2, Rawley 2, Murray 2, Frazier 1. Hits off—Black, 7 in 6; Armstrong, 1 in 2; Quisenberry, 0 in 1; Rawley, 10 in 5⅓; Murray 2 in 3⅓; Gossage, 1 in 0 (pitched to one batter in ninth); Frazier, 0 in ⅓. Winner—Armstrong. Loser—Gossage. Time—2:52. Attendance—33,944.

Mark down July 25, 1983 on your calendar as Pine Tar Day. But don't invite Billy Martin, George Steinbrenner, and Goose Gossage, who will forever recognize the anniversary of a day of infamy.

It didn't appear that way at first. The Kansas City Royals had lost a game they thought they had won, 5-4, because George Brett had used an excessively tar-tainted bat to hit a ninth-inning home run. The Yankees had won a game they thought they had lost because the umpiring crew had allowed their claim regarding the infraction. Although stunned beyond words, Kansas City manager, Dick Howser, had the presence of mind to raise an official protest to American League President Lee MacPhail.

In any event, the Yankees' apparent 4-3 victory was that rare moment in baseball when a game ended on a home run by the losing team.

In the Yankee locker room, there was a slick Billy Martin, smug and smiling. Down the hall, there was the fuming George Brett, frustrated and furious. Only minutes earlier, Brett and the Royals had been deprived of winning a game because of a rule few knew existed and none had ever obeyed. The circus started when Rich Gossage was summoned to the mound to face Brett with two out in the top of the ninth and a runner on first, recalling for anyone who was there that fateful Friday night in October 1980, when Brett lashed a three-run homer off the Goose at Yankee Stadium to insure the Royals' first and only pennant. By golly, if Brett didn't do it again, driving Gossage's second pitch deep into the right-field stands.

Immediately, pandemonium broke loose, but unlike that of three years ago. No sooner had Brett circled the bases when Martin bounded from the Yankee dugout contending that Brett's bat had pine tar above the legal limit of 18 inches from the handle. The bat was examined by home plate umpire Tim McClelland, then by crew chief Joe Brinkman. They measured it against the width of the 17-

George Brett is collared by umpire Joe Brinkman as he flails at onrushers.

inch home plate and found that Brett's bat had tar well over the 18-inch limit. McClelland called Brett out and the game had incredibly ended on a home run from the visiting team. That's when all hell broke loose, and Brett had to be physically restrained from assaulting McClelland, Brinkman, and any other umpire who got in his way.

Rule 1:10B reads: "The bat handle for more than 18 inches from the end shall not be covered with or treated with any material to improve the grip. Any such material, including pine tar, which extends past the 18-inch limitation, in the umpire's judgment, shall cause the bat to be removed from the game." Another rule states that anyone using an "illegal" bat be declared out. Exactly when and why this rule was imposed no one seems to know, although Calvin Griffith, a member of the Rules Committee, believes the rule was adopted in 1955 for sanitary purposes to keep baseballs unmarked. One suspects also because too many balls, smudged by impact with the pine tar, had to be thrown out.

Certainly there is no advantage to the batter in hitting with such a bat. Pine tar does not provide additional distance. But as Martin said with a thin smile, "Look, the guy was using an illegal bat. It may be a lousy rule, but it's in the books and a rule is a rule."

Brinkman conceded the rule didn't make a whole lot of sense, but added he had no choice but to apply it once the Yankees appealed.

Then came the shocker. League President Lee MacPhail, after four days of agonizing deliberation, overturned the decision of his own umpires, ruling that Brett's homer would count and the game would be resumed at that point, with the Royals leading, 5-4. The decision stunned Martin and Steinbrenner. It not only cost the Yankees a victory, but dropped them from a first-place tie with Baltimore in the American League East.

"If they don't honor the umpires' decision," growled Martin, "then everything in the rule book means nothing."

Steinbrenner labeled MacPhail's decision "ridiculous." "I don't question his [MacPhail's] integrity," George said, "I just think it was a dumb ridiculous decision. He's opened up a Pandora's box where no rule means anything any more."

Conceding that the Yankees and the umpires' impression of the "Pine Tar Rule" was technically defensable, MacPhail stated nevertheless that "it is not in accord with the intent or spirit of the rules and does not provide that a hitter be called out for excess use of pine tar."

The final four outs were played on August 18, some 600 hours after the "Pine Tar Home Run" and after the issue had been dragged through the courts with a judge of the Appelate Division of the Supreme Court overruling a judge of the state supreme court, who had ruled to enjoin the Yankees and Royals from completing the suspended game of July 25.

The finish was anticlimatic. It lasted 9 minutes and 41 seconds. Four batters—one Royal and three Yankees—batted and made outs. Twenty-five days, one upheld protest, and two court decisions later, the Royals finally defeated the Yankees, 5-4, on a "Pine Tar Home Run" in a game that had grabbed the attention of the baseball world throughout the country.

September 23, 1983

# Steve Carlton Strikes Again

## Philadelphia

| | | AB | R | H |
|---|---|---|---|---|
| Morgan, | 2b | 4 | 1 | 1 |
| Garcia, | 2b | 1 | 0 | 1 |
| Matuszek, | 1b | 5 | 0 | 2 |
| Schmidt, | 3b | 5 | 2 | 3 |
| Lefebvre, | rf | 5 | 1 | 2 |
| Matthews, | lf | 5 | 2 | 3 |
| Holland, | p | 0 | 0 | 0 |
| G. Gr's, | cf-lf | 3 | 0 | 2 |
| Diaz, | c | 4 | 0 | 1 |
| DeJesus, | ss | 4 | 0 | 1 |
| Carlton, | p | 4 | 0 | 1 |
| Dernier, | cf | 0 | 0 | 0 |
| | Total | 40 | 6 | 17 |

## St. Louis

| | | AB | R | H |
|---|---|---|---|---|
| L. Smith, | lf | 4 | 0 | 0 |
| O. Smith, | ss | 3 | 0 | 1 |
| McGee, | cf | 4 | 0 | 1 |
| Hendrick, | 1b | 4 | 1 | 1 |
| Green, | rf | 4 | 1 | 2 |
| Sexton, | 3b | 4 | 0 | 0 |
| Lyons, | 2b | 4 | 0 | 0 |
| Brummer, | c | 4 | 0 | 3 |
| Andujar, | p | 1 | 0 | 0 |
| Lahti, | p | 0 | 0 | 0 |
| Rayford, | ph | 1 | 0 | 0 |
| Von Ohlen, | p | 0 | 0 | 0 |
| Oberkfell, | ph | 1 | 0 | 0 |
| | Total | 34 | 2 | 8 |

Philadelphia
0 1 1 0 3 1 0 0 0—6
St. Louis
0 0 0 2 0 0 0 0 0—2

Errors—None. Runs batted in—Schmidt 1, Matthews 1, G. Gr's 1, Diaz 2, Carlton 1, Green 2. Double plays—St. Louis 4. Left on base—Philadelphia 8, St. Louis 4. Two-base hits—Matthews, Morgan, Schmidt. Home-run—Green. Stolen bases—Schmidt, Lefebvre. Sacrifice hit—Andujar. Passed ball—Brummer. Struck out—Carlton 12, Holland 2, Andujar 3, Lahti 1. Hits off—Carlton, 7 in 8, Holland, 1 in 1; Andujar, 11 in 4⅓; Lahti, 4 in 2⅔; Von Ohlen, 2 in 2. Winner—Carlton. Loser—Andujar. Time—2:31. Attendance—27,266.

Steven Norman Carlton is a man on the march to the Hall of Fame in Cooperstown, New York. Currently the greatest strikeout pitcher in the history of baseball, the strong, silent southpaw has set another goal for himself—he wants to win 400 big league games, which would establish him as the best left-hander baseball has ever produced.

Warren Spahn, who pitched from 1942 to 1965, retired with 363 victories and 245 defeats, and no left-hander has won more times. Carlton goes into the 1984 season, his twentieth in the big leagues, with an even 300 victories against 199 defeats. If it takes extreme durability to reach the magic 400 victory circle, a feat achieved only by two pitchers—right-handers Cy Young and Walter Johnson—then Carlton already ranks high among modern ballplayers. He is a 6-foot-5-inch 220-pounder and a fervent student of the martial arts. He is dedicated to physical culture and may be the strongest player in the game today. In 1983, at age 38, Carlton worked 284 innings, the most in the major leagues.

Carlton became the sixteenth pitcher to win 300 games, achieving that feat on September 23, 1983, with a 6-2 triumph

*Phillies' pitcher Steve Carlton gracefully pow-
ered his way through the Cardinals' lineup to
get his 300th big league win.*

over the St. Louis Cardinals. It was a strong performance that was threatened only once, when David Green clipped him for a two-run homer in the fourth inning. That tied the score, 2-2, but the Phillies promptly scored three runs in the top of the fifth against Juaquin Andujar, and Carlton coasted. Steve struck out 12 in eight innings and finished the season with 275 strikeouts, the most in the majors.

Baseball's number-one strikeout pitcher finished the 1983 season with 3,712 strikeouts. He struck out his first batter in the big leagues in 1965 as a rookie with the Cardinals. Seven years later, he became embroiled in a salary dispute with August A. Busch, Jr., the club's owner. Carlton wanted his $30,000 salary doubled, and Busch, angered by the demand, traded him to the Phillies for another pitcher, Rick Wise.

As a Phillie, Carlton quickly developed into one of the game's greatest pitching stars. In his first season in Philadelphia, he posted a remarkable 27-10 won and lost record for a last-place Phillie team that was able to win only 59 games. In 12 seasons, he won 237 games, an average of just under 20 victories a season. He was a 20-game winner six times and is the only pitcher ever to win four Cy Young Awards as the top pitcher in his league. Among his other achievements are 6 one-hitters, 55 shutouts, and 18 seasons of 100 or more strikeouts. He was the first to register 19 strikeouts in a nine-inning game, a record still unsurpassed. He holds the record of 463 consecutive starting assignments without relief appearances. The last time he pitched in relief was in 1971, when he worked one hitless inning against the Montreal Expos.

Carlton's fast ball doesn't have the velocity it once had, but he more than makes up for it with his assortment of pitches, which includes the most wicked slider in baseball. If he has a secret for his longevity, Carlton won't tell. He hasn't talked to the press since the time he believes he was victimized by a reporter five years ago. On the night he won his three hundredth, the Phillies closed their locker room for 25 minutes for a champagne toast in private. When they opened the door, Carlton had disappeared into the trainer's room, keeping his silence even on this memorable occasion.

September 12, 1984

# Dwight Gooden: A Record-Breaking Rookie

### New York Mets

| | AB | R | H |
|---|---|---|---|
| Wilson, cf | 4 | 0 | 1 |
| Chapman, 2b | 4 | 0 | 1 |
| Hernandez, 1b | 4 | 1 | 1 |
| Foster, lf | 4 | 0 | 0 |
| Brooks, ss | 3 | 1 | 1 |
| Strawberry, rf | 3 | 0 | 0 |
| Knight, 3b | 3 | 0 | 1 |
| Fitzgerald, c | 3 | 0 | 2 |
| Gooden, p | 3 | 0 | 2 |
| Total | 31 | 2 | 9 |

### Pittsburgh

| | AB | R | H |
|---|---|---|---|
| Wynne, cf | 4 | 0 | 0 |
| Lacy, lf | 4 | 0 | 1 |
| Ray, 2b | 4 | 0 | 1 |
| Thompson, 1b | 4 | 0 | 1 |
| Pena, c | 4 | 0 | 0 |
| Morrison, 3b | 3 | 0 | 0 |
| Frobel, rf | 3 | 0 | 0 |
| Gonzolez, ss | 3 | 0 | 0 |
| Tudor, p | 2 | 0 | 1 |
| Orsulak, ph | 1 | 0 | 1 |
| Scurry, p | 0 | 0 | 0 |
| Total | 32 | 0 | 5 |

| | | | | | | | | | | |
|---|---|---|---|---|---|---|---|---|---|---|
| New York Mets | 0 | 0 | 0 | 2 | 0 | 0 | 0 | 0 | X | — 2 |
| Pittsburgh | 0 | 0 | 0 | 0 | 0 | 0 | 0 | 0 | 0 | — 0 |

Left on base — Pittsburgh 5, Mets 5. Two-base hit — Lacy. Home run — Brooks. Stolen base — Orsulak. Struck out — Tudor 7, Scurry 1, Gooden 16. Hits off — Tudor 9, Scurry 0, Gooden 5. Bases on balls — Tudor 0, Scurry 0, Gooden 0. Winner — Gooden. Loser — Tudor. Time — 2:11. Attendance — 12,876.

Dwight Gooden, 19-year-old flame-throwing right-hander of the New York Mets, did not win 20 games in his rookie season in the major leagues. He did not strike out 300 batters. But it is doubtful if any pitcher ever had a greater freshman season than Gooden experienced in 1984. Certainly his mound heroics and his spectacular strikeout feats caught the imagination of the entire baseball world.

Only three years out of a Tampa, Florida, high school, the gifted teenager led the major leagues with 276 strikeouts in 218 innings and established a big league record for first-year pitchers, eclipsing previous strikeout records set by Grover Cleveland Alexander and Herb Score. Gooden won 17 games against only 9 losses and finished second to Rick Sutcliffe of the Chicago Cubs in the voting for the National League's Cy Young Award for 1984.

Gooden pitched a one-hitter and struck out 10 or more batters in 15 of his 31 starts, including 2 straight 16-strikeout games in September. His 2.60 ERA was bettered only by Alejandro Pena of the Dodgers, who led the league with 2.48.

What Gooden accomplished in 1984 would be impressive enough if he were a seasoned veteran with a half dozen big league years under his belt. To have done all this at 19, in his third professional season (his first in the majors), is mind-boggling. He finished the season with a strikeout-per-9-inning ratio of 11.39, well ahead of Sam McDowell's old 1965 mark of 10.71.

It was on the night of Wednesday, September 12, 1984, that Gooden became the greatest strikeout pitcher in a 2−0, 5-hit, 16-strikeout jewel against the Pittsburgh Pirates. Dwight entered the game with 235 strikeouts, 10 shy of the major league record of 245, set by Herb Score of the Cleveland Indians in 1955. Gooden already had nine strikeouts by the fifth inning, and he had just struck out the last four batters he had faced. Pirate starter John Tudor became Dwight's tenth strikeout victim to start the sixth. That tied Score's record, and by now the meager Shea Stadium gathering of 12,876 was on its feet as Marvell Wynne came to the plate. He ran the count to 2−2 before going down, swinging at a vicious fastball to make Gooden the major leagues' all-time rookie strikeout pitcher.

"I thought about the record," said Gooden, whose personal high of 16 strikeouts in his second straight shutout brought his league-leading strikeout total to 251. "But at that moment, I didn't know how many strikeouts I had."

He was the only one at Shea Stadium who didn't.

Gooden didn't walk a batter. Of his 120 pitches, 92 were strikes and 28 were balls. Behind a fastball that stayed between 87 and 94 miles per hour and a devastating curve that fell off the table, not once did he go to a three-ball count on a batter.

The victory was Gooden's seventh straight. He received all the offense he needed from Hubie Brooks' two-run fourth-inning homer.

"I had the same stuff as I did the last time," said the youngster. "The last time" was a one-hit shutout of the Chicago Cubs on September 7.

In his next start, on September 17, Gooden again struck out 16 batters but lost 2−1 to the Philadelphia Phillies when he balked home opposing pitcher Shane Rawley with the winning run in the eighth inning. Gooden's 32 strikeouts in 2 consecutive games broke one of Sandy Koufax's league records and tied Nolan Ryan's major league record. The three-game National League record of 41 that was held by Koufax also was shattered. The Dodger great set that mark in 1959, but Gooden's total for three games was 43.

No wonder, then, that a new tradition has been born in Shea Stadium.

A white *K* on a big black card is flipped down in place over the upper right-field balustrade every time "Dr. K" strikes again.

*Nineteen-year-old Dwight Gooden prepares to unleash the pitch that sets a new all-time major league strikeout record for a rookie.*

*Gooden and his catcher, Mike Fitzgerald, share a jubilant moment after a setting record against the Pirates.*

## Gooden's 1984 highlights

Here's a list of Dwight Gooden's major accomplishments during 1984:

Set major league record for rookies with 276 strikeouts. Previous major league mark was 245 set by Herb Score, Cleveland, in 1955. National League record was 227 set by Grover Cleveland Alexander, Philadelphia, in 1911.

●

Set Mets' rookie strikeout record. Previous mark was 178 by Jerry Koosman, in 1968. Set single game Mets' rookie record with 16 strikeouts in one game.

●

Established major league record with an average of 11.39 strikeouts per nine innings. Previous mark of 10.71 was set by Sam McDowell, Cleveland, in 1965.

●

Became first teen-aged rookie to lead major leagues in strikeouts.

●

Shared 1984 major league high of 16-strikeouts in one game with Mike Witt, California. Gooden had two 16 strikeout games, coming in consecutive starts against Pittsburgh September 12 and Philadelphia, September 17.

●

Tied major league record with 32 strikeouts in consecutive games. Record set by Nolan Ryan, California, in 1974.

●

Set major league record with 43 strikeouts in three consecutive nine-inning games. Old record was 41 in American League by Nolan Ryan, California, in 1974 and 33 in National League by Dazzy Vance, Brooklyn, in 1925.

●

Set club record with 15 games, 10 or more strikeouts one season. Old record was 13 by Tom Seaver in 1971.

●

Set club record with five consecutive games, 10 or more strikeouts. Old record was three by Tom Seaver, 1970 and 1971.

●

Became youngest player to be selected to All-Star team—struck out the side in the first inning he worked.

●

Was near-unanimous pick for National League Rookie-of-the-Year.

October 14, 1984

# Sparky Anderson: A Winner In Both Leagues

## Detroit

|  | AB | R | H |
|---|---|---|---|
| Whitaker, 2b | 3 | 1 | 1 |
| Trammell, ss | 4 | 1 | 0 |
| Gibson, rf | 4 | 3 | 3 |
| Parrish, c | 5 | 2 | 2 |
| Herndon, lf | 4 | 0 | 1 |
| Lemon, cf | 3 | 0 | 0 |
| Garbey, dh | 1 | 0 | 0 |
| Grubb, ph | 0 | 0 | 0 |
| Kuntz, ph | 0 | 0 | 0 |
| Johnson, ph | 1 | 0 | 0 |
| Evans, 1b | 4 | 0 | 0 |
| Bergman, 2b | 0 | 0 | 0 |
| Castillo, 3b | 3 | 1 | 2 |
| Total | 32 | 8 | 11 |

## San Diego

|  | AB | R | H |
|---|---|---|---|
| Wiggins, 2b | 5 | 0 | 2 |
| Gwynn, rf | 5 | 0 | 0 |
| Garvey, 1b | 4 | 0 | 1 |
| Nettles, 3b | 3 | 0 | 1 |
| Kennedy, c | 4 | 0 | 0 |
| Bevacqua, dh | 3 | 2 | 1 |
| Martinez, lf | 4 | 0 | 2 |
| Salazar, cf | 0 | 0 | 0 |
| Templeton, ss | 4 | 1 | 1 |
| Brown, cf | 2 | 1 | 1 |
| Bochy, ph | 1 | 0 | 1 |
| Roenick, pr | 0 | 0 | 0 |
| Total | 35 | 4 | 10 |

**Detroit**  3 0 0 0 1 0 1 3 X—8
**San Diego**  0 0 1 2 0 0 0 1 0—4

Errors — Parrish, Wiggins. Double play — San Diego 1. Left on base — San Diego 7, Detroit 9. Two-base hit — Templeton. Home runs — Gibson 2, Parrish, Bevacqua. Stolen base — Wiggins, Parrish, Lemon. Sacrifice — Whitaker, Trammell. Sacrifice fly — Brown, Kuntz. Bases on balls — Hawkins 3, Lefferts 1, Gossage 1, Petry 2. Struck out — Hawkins 1, Lefferts 2, Gossage 2, Petry 2, Lopez 4. Hits off — Thurmond, 5 in ⅓; Hawkins, 2 in 4; Lefferts, 1 in 2; Gossage, 3 in 1⅔; Petry, 6 in 3⅔; Scherrer, 1 in 1; Lopez, 0 in 2⅓; Hernandez, 3 in 2. Hit by pitch — by Hawkins (Grubb). Wild pitch — Hawkins. Winner — Lopez. Loser — Hawkins. Time — 2:55. Attendance — 51,901.

The dream came true. On the night of October 14, 1984, George, better known as "Sparky" Anderson, became the first manager to win a World Series in both the National and American leagues. Not even Casey Stengel or Joe McCarthy or Leo Durocher or John McGraw could do that.

"In five years, I will bring a pennant to Detroit," Anderson promised on the day he was named to manage the Detroit Tigers. That was on June 14, 1979. Detroit was in fifth place. Five years later the Tigers reeled off 104 regular season victories to win their division by 15 games, swept the Kansas City Royals in three straight to capture the American League pennant, and climaxed a fantastic year by overwhelming the San Diego Padres in five games to give Detroit its first World Championship since 1968.

Anderson accomplished this with a team that finished the season without a single player driving in or scoring 100 runs. No Tiger played in 150 games or had 600 at-bats. The pitching staff registered just 19 complete games. But the Tigers won 104 games, more than any American League team since Earl Weaver's Baltimore Orioles won 108 games in 1970. The pennant race was over almost before it began. They won their first nine games, 17 of their first 18, 35 of 40 — and never let up. When Toronto crept 3½ games behind Detroit the first week in June, the Tigers turned back the challengers by defeating Toronto in three straight games. That was the last threat by any of the opposition.

Everybody got into the act. The Tigers

Left to right:
Doug Bair, Bill Scherrer, Marty Castillo, Darrell
Evans, Willie Hernandez, and Lance Parrish
(with arms in the air) celebrate their team
victory over the Padres in the final game
of the World Series.

had 8 players drive in 50 or more runs. They got 20 or more home runs from 7 positions. And the pinch hitters contributed, hitting .312 with 6 homers and 42 RBIs. The three-man starting staff of Jack Morris, Dan Petry, and Milt Wilcox finished the season with a combined 54–27 record. Then there was the one-two bull-pen punch of Willie Hernandez (32 saves in 33 chances), a 9–3 record and 1.92 ERA in 80 appearances, and Aurelio Lopez, 10–1 with a 2.94 ERA and 14 saves in 71 games. The team's greatest strength, aside from the bull pen, was up the middle, from catcher Lance Parrish through shortstop Alan Trammell and second baseman Lew Whitaker to center fielder Chet Lemon.

Another Tiger who contributed greatly was outfielder Kirk Gibson. Most Valuable Player in the American League play-offs, Gibson hit two home runs and drove in five runs to lead the Tigers in the World Series clincher. Gibson's second homer came in the eighth inning with two runners aboard after San Diego manager Dick Williams considered walking him but was convinced by Padre ace reliever Goose Gossage to pitch to Gibson. Gibson hit the ball into the upper deck in right field.

But it was Anderson, more than anyone else, who provided the spark that ignited the team. It was Sparky, also known as Captain Hook, who manipulated the pitching staff; platooned the men (at first, third, and left field); cajoled, praised, and flattered his players; and drove them without a letup. A nonstop talker, he was always in the middle of things, talking a blue streak and sounding like a cross between Tom Lasorda and Casey Stengel. Anderson is 50 going on 10. No individual enjoys the game more. No one is easier to approach. No one sells the game more.

"This is a kid's game," he repeats. "When you lose the kid in you, you lose it all."

For all his talking, Anderson's managerial skills are taken for granted. In his 15 years of managing, he has won 1,342 games and lost 970. He has won six division titles, five pennants, and four World Series. He has won more than 90 games in a season 9 times. In 1984, he became the first to win 100 games in a season in both leagues.

It was Charley Dressen, his manager at Toronto, who first told Anderson he had the potential to be a manager. After a brief stay as an infielder with the Philadelphia Phillies, Sparky went to Toronto in the International League, where he played for four years. He began managing in 1964.

Anderson began his playing career in the Dodger organization in 1953 as a second baseman. At the time, the Dodgers had a second baseman named Jackie Robinson. Unneeded at second, Anderson moved up through the chain to Montreal in 1958; then he was sent to Philadelphia in a deal for Rip

*Sparky Anderson (left) and Tigers' president Jim Campbell are doused with champagne as Campbell tries to hear a congratulatory phone call from President Reagan.*

Repulski. He hit .216 in one Phillie season, went back to the minors in 1960, began managing at Toronto four years later, coached for the Padres in 1969, was named Angels' coach that October—and 24 hours later was hired by Bob Howsam to manage the Cincinnati Reds.

The Reds won the pennant in Anderson's first year at the helm and repeated in 1973. They were beaten by the Mets in the play-offs in 1973 but came back to win back-to-back pennants and the world championship in 1975 and 1976. It marked the first time a National League manager had won the World Series in two successive years since John McGraw had won with the New York Giants in 1921 and 1922.

Dick Wagner, who succeeded Howsam as Cincinnati president, fired Anderson after two straight second-place finishes. After a brief turn as a broadcaster, Anderson was approached by Detroit general manager Jim Campbell to manage the Tigers. He agreed.

"I really didn't want to manage anymore," Anderson said. "But Campbell persuaded me."

"He was the best man I could find," said Campbell, "and I wouldn't quit until I had him."

August 4, 1985. September 11, 1985. October 6, 1985.

# They Climbed Mt. Everest

Perhaps once every 25 years a baseball season comes along like the one that enthralled the nation's sports fans in 1985. It was baseball at its best. Not even a strike and a scandal could blemish it. You know a baseball season is beautiful when it leaves you craving more.

The 1985 season had it all—record crowds, suspenseful pennant races, thrilling playoffs, and a controversial and surprising World Series. The season was also blessed with great individual performances. Dwight Gooden, Wade Boggs, Vince Coleman, Don Mattingly, John Tudor, George Brett, Pedro Guerrero, and Willie McGee put some incredible statistics on the board, but all were thrust into the shadows by the remarkable achievements of a quartet of senior citizens—with an average age of 42 plus.

The four—Pete Rose, Tom Seaver, Rod Carew, and Phil Niekro—reached milestones dreamed of by many but accomplished by few. Rose, in particular, surpassed a long-standing record that until recently appeared inviolate—Ty Cobb's remarkable total of 4,191 career hits. Carew became only the sixteenth player to reach 3,000 hits, Seaver and Niekro only the seventeenth and eighteenth pitchers to record 300 victories.

Of the four, Seaver's was the most dramatic, Carew's the most predictable, Niekro's the most heartwarming, Rose's the most historic. It was in the first inning of the game between the Reds and Padres in Cincinnati on the night of September 11, 1985, that Rose lined a single to left center off right-hander Eric Show for career hit number

*"Knucksie" Niekro squeezes out the magic 300th win on the final day of the '85 season.*

289

*The spotlight is on Pete Rose as he connects for hit number 4,192 and a new baseball career hit record.*

4,192. That hit climaxed Rose's season-long assault on Ty Cobb's all-time hit record and brought the crowd of 47,237 to its feet. They gave Pete a rousing seven-minute standing ovation that brought tears to the eyes of this 44-year-old warrior of 23 big-league seasons. Consider that it took 57 years for Cobb's record to be broken, and you get an idea of the enormity of Pete Rose's achievement.

But Pete wasn't finished. He added a triple in the seventh inning and scored, giving him both runs in Cincinnati's 2–0 triumph. Rose still refused to call it quits. He continued to put himself in the lineup whenever the opposition started a right-hander and finished the season with 4,204 career hits, a mark for some future great to challenge.

Perhaps. But don't bet on it.

Tom Seaver's quest for his 300th victory came under even more dramatic circumstances. August 4, 1985, was the day Seaver climbed his Mt. Everest. The scene was Yankee Stadium, not Shea, home of the Mets that twice discarded him, but it was New York, and the emotion and significance of the moment was lost on no one in attendance. The capacity crowd of 54,032 broke out in cheers upon Seaver's every appearance. Yes, Tom Seaver had come home to carve another niche in his storied career.

The man who had made the Mets, who was called "The Franchise," finally had come face-to-face with a long-sought goal. He was 40, in his nineteenth season, and he stood on the threshold of becoming only the seventeenth pitcher to win 300 games. Somehow, few in the crowd doubted that he would succeed—even when his Chicago White Sox trailed 1–0 in the early innings. A four-run sixth, climaxed by Brian Little's two-run single, gave Tom the lead he was determined to preserve. The decisive moment came in the eighth when Dave Winfield, the Yankees' big gun, presented what would be the last major roadblock for Seaver. Tom had retired ten straight batters before Bobby

*Tom Seaver fires away at the Yankee lineup in anticipation of his long-sought 300th win.*

Meacham got New York's fourth hit to start the eighth. Ken Griffey forced Meacham, and Don Mattingly singled, bringing on Winfield. Seaver ran the count to 3–2, then served up a tantalizing change-up knee high. Winfield swung and missed to end the inning.

As Seaver walked to the mound in the ninth, the crowds applauded. Each pitch car-ried with it the kind of tension and emotion normally reserved for pennant races. Dan Pasqua led off with a single. Then Ron Hassey became Seaver's seventh strikeout victim, and Willie Randolph flied to Harold

*Rod Carew wills a good one to put him in the 3,000-Hit Club.*

Baines, who made a leaping catch in right field. Mike Pagliarulo walked, but Don Baylor, representing the tying run, hit the first pitch to left for the final out.

The score was 4–1, matching Tom Seaver's uniform number, 41.

While Seaver reached the magic 300 number in his first attempt, it took Phil Niekro five tries to scale the crest...and he did it with a flourish, shutting out the division-leading Toronto Blue Jays on the final day of the 1985 season. It was the sixteenth victory of the year for the 46-year-old knuckleball artist, who became the oldest pitcher to win that many games in a season. Niekro, who spent 20 years with the Braves in Milwaukee and Atlanta before coming to the Yankees as a free agent in 1984, will be 47 when the 1986 season rolls around, and he plans to continue pitching. Why not? Knucksie has always refused to act his age and has been scoffing at the calendar for years.

Except for Ty Cobb, Rod Carew has won more batting titles than any American Leaguer, 7, so it is merely poetic justice that Sir Rodney join the elite 3,000-hit corps. The sweet Angel, California style, rapped his all-important hit on August 4, the same day that marked Seaver's coronation. The single off Minnesota's Frank Viola in the third inning enabled the 40-year-old Carew to become the first player since Carl Yastrzemski in 1979, and the sixteenth in history, to reach 3,000 career hits.

## 3,000 Hit Club

| | |
|---|---|
| Pete Rose | 4,204 |
| Ty Cobb | 4,191 |
| Henry Aaron | 3,771 |
| Stan Musial | 3,630 |
| Tris Speaker | 3,515 |
| Honus Wagner | 3,430 |
| Carl Yastrzemski | 3,419 |
| Eddie Collins | 3,309 |
| Willie Mays | 3,283 |
| Napoleon Lajoie | 3,252 |
| Paul Waner | 3,152 |
| Adrian Anson | 3,081 |
| Rod Carew | 3,053 |
| Lou Brock | 3,023 |
| Al Kaline | 3,007 |
| Roberto Clemente | 3,000 |

## 300 Victory Club

| | |
|---|---|
| Cy Young | 511 |
| Walter Johnson | 416 |
| Christy Mathewson | 373 |
| Grover Alexander | 373 |
| Warren Spahn | 363 |
| Kid Nichols | 361 |
| Jim Galvin | 361 |
| Tim Keefe | 342 |
| John Clarkson | 327 |
| Eddie Plank | 327 |
| Gaylord Perry | 314 |
| Steve Carlton | 314 |
| Hoss Radbourn | 308 |
| Mickey Welch | 307 |
| Tom Seaver | 304 |
| Phil Niekro | 300 |
| Lefty Grove | 300 |
| Early Wynn | 300 |

October 30, 1985

# Backs to the Wall

It couldn't have been any better: last game of the World Series; the best left-hander in the National League, John Tudor, against the best right-hander in the American League, Bret Saberhagen.

The fact that the seventh game was a Kansas City romp, 11–0, did not detract in the least from the drama and excitement of the 1985 World Series, which nearly all the experts prophesied would be a boring, sleep-inducing postseason meeting between two unevenly matched ball clubs. Some even predicted a four-game sweep by the National League champion St. Louis Cardinals.

Instead, it turned out to be a hard-fought, seven-game Series waged between two scrappy, pitching-dominated ball clubs that was a joy to watch and a second-guesser's delight. A controversial call in the ninth inning of the sixth game proved pivotal to the final outcome and added spice to make the '85 Series most memorable.

The '85 Series was one in which a grim, gutsy gang of Kansas City Royals, doomed by odds-makers to a quick exit, won through sheer determination, clutch performances, and a stubborn refusal to accept defeat. Just as they had in the American League championship series against the Toronto Blue Jays, the Royals scraped and scrambled back into contention. After losing the first two games of the Series to St. Louis, the Royals went on a winning spree and pulled even. The decisive seventh game was almost anticlimactic.

Although St. Louis' pitching fell apart in the final game, it was the Cardinals' futility at the plate, particularly throughout the final three games, that lost them the Series. The Redbirds set a record for ineptness in a seven-game Series with a .185 team batting average. They scored only 13 runs, and their vaunted running game was limited to just 2 stolen bases.

Still, the '85 Series will be long remembered—more for the Royals' indomitable fighting spirit. They had their backs to the wall, but refused to fold. No team in World Series history had lost the first two games at home and come back to win the championship. Only four teams ever had rallied to win after being down three games to one. But it was old hat to those rally-bent Royals.

The Series was actually decided in the bottom of the ninth inning of the sixth game, won by the Royals 2–1, largely due to a controversial call by first-base umpire Den Denkinger. Kansas City was trailing 1–0. Pinch hitter Jorge Orta hit a chopper wide of first. Jack Clark came off the bag to field the ball, and Todd Worrell, the pitcher, broke off the mound for the tag. The ball and the pitcher appeared to arrive ahead of the runner, but Denkinger gave the safe sign. An infuriated manager Whitey Herzog charged to the mound to argue but got nowhere. Steve Balboni got a life when Clark misjudged his pop foul outside of first for a single. Jim Sundberg's bunt resulted in a force play at third base, but catcher Darrell Porter muffed a pitch. The runners advanced a base on the passed ball. With first base open, pinch hitter Hal McRae was walked inten-

*After shutting out the Cards 11–0, Bret Saberhagen gets a jubilant hug from George Brett.*

tionally. Manager Dick Howser called upon a third pinch hitter, Dane Iorg, and Iorg dropped a single to right that scored the tying and winning runs.

So frustrated were the Cardinals by the Series' turns of events that two of them—manager Herzog and pitcher Joaquin Andujar—were ejected from the game in the fifth inning the next day. Even seventh-game pitcher Tudor punched an electric fan in the St. Louis dugout after being kayoed in the third—suffering a gash in the index finger—and had to be taken to a local hospital for stitches.

Kansas City had its share of heroes. George Brett, the team leader, performed consistently, finishing with four hits in the finale. Willie Wilson batted .367 and his 11 hits led all the players. Darryl Motley ignited the winning outburst in the seventh game with a two-run homer, and, of course, there was Dane Iorg. But in the final analysis, it was the Royals' pitching that excelled. The arms of Danny Jackson, Bud Black, Charlie Liebrandt, and Bret Saberhagen shut down the Cardinals' hitting, cut off their power, and held down their running game. Jackson's 5-hit, 6–1 triumph in game 5 started the Royals on the comeback road, and Leibrandt's four-hit pitching in game 6 kept the Royals alive. The pièce de résistance was fashioned by the 21-year-old Saberhagen, who won both his starts, allowing only 1 run in 18 innings, walking only 1 while striking out 10. Being named the Series MVP and 1985's American League Cy Young award winner was just icing on the cake for the skinny right-hander.

So it was that, in their seventeenth year of existence, the Kansas City Royals reached baseball's pinnacle for the first time—a time no one will ever forget.

| Kansas City | AB | R | H |
|---|---|---|---|
| L. Smith, lf | 3 | 1 | 2 |
| L. Jones, lf | 1 | 0 | 0 |
| Wilson, cf | 5 | 1 | 2 |
| Brett, 3b | 5 | 2 | 4 |
| White, 2b | 4 | 1 | 1 |
| Sundberg, c | 3 | 1 | 1 |
| Balboni, 1b | 4 | 2 | 2 |
| Motley, rf | 4 | 1 | 3 |
| Biancalana, ss | 3 | 0 | 0 |
| Saberhagen, p | 4 | 2 | 0 |
| Total. . . . | 36 | 11 | 14 |

| St. Louis | AB | R | H |
|---|---|---|---|
| O. Smith, ss | 4 | 0 | 1 |
| McGee, cf | 4 | 0 | 0 |
| Herr, 2b | 4 | 0 | 0 |
| Clark, 1b | 4 | 0 | 1 |
| Van Slyke, rf | 4 | 0 | 1 |
| Pendleton, 3b | 3 | 0 | 1 |
| Landrum, lf | 2 | 0 | 1 |
| Andujar, p | 0 | 0 | 0 |
| Forsch, p | 0 | 0 | 0 |
| Braun, ph | 1 | 0 | 0 |
| Dayley, p | 0 | 0 | 0 |
| Porter, c | 3 | 0 | 0 |
| Tudor, p | 1 | 0 | 0 |
| Campbell, p | 0 | 0 | 0 |
| Lahti, p | 0 | 0 | 0 |
| Horton, p | 0 | 0 | 0 |
| Jorgensen, lf | 2 | 0 | 0 |
| Total. . . . | 32 | 0 | 5 |

| | | | | |
|---|---|---|---|---|
| Kansas City | 023 | 060 | 00X— | 11 |
| St. Louis | 000 | 000 | 000— | 0 |

Errors—None. Double play—St. Louis 2, Kansas City 0. Left on base—St. Louis 5, Kansas City 7. Two-base hit—L. Smith. Home run—Motley. Stolen base—L. Smith, Brett, Wilson. Bases on balls—Tudor 4, Campbell 1, Andujar 1. Struck out—Tudor 1, Campbell 1, Lahti 1, Frosch 1, Saberhagen 2. Hits off—Tudor 3 in 2⅓, Campbell 4 in 1⅔, Lahti 4 in ⅔, Horton 1 in 0, Andujar 1 in 0, Frosch 1 in 1⅓, Saberhagen 5 in 9. Wild pitch—Forsch. Winner—Saberhagen. Loser—Tudor. Time—2:46. Attendance—41,658.